Online Counselor Education

To my mentors: Larry Loesch, Harry Daniels, Tom Clawson, Joe Wittmer, Nick Hanna, Joe Maola, Pete Sherrard, and the many others who shaped my journey through counselor education. I strive to pass on to students all that you have given to me.

Carl J. Sheperis

To my students—past, present, and future—in the hope that it will help them as they learn, train, and prepare to help others.

R. J. Davis

Online Counselor Education

A Guide for Students

Edited By

Carl J. Sheperis
Lamar University

R. J. Davis
Lamar University

Los Angeles | London | New Delhi
Singapore | Washington DC

Los Angeles | London | New Delhi
Singapore | Washington DC

FOR INFORMATION:

SAGE Publications, Inc.
2455 Teller Road
Thousand Oaks, California 91320
E-mail: order@sagepub.com

SAGE Publications Ltd.
1 Oliver's Yard
55 City Road
London, EC1Y 1SP
United Kingdom

SAGE Publications India Pvt. Ltd.
B 1/I 1 Mohan Cooperative Industrial Area
Mathura Road, New Delhi 110 044
India

SAGE Publications Asia-Pacific Pte. Ltd.
3 Church Street
#10–04 Samsung Hub
Singapore 049483

Acquisitions Editor: Kassie Graves
Editorial Assistant: Carrie Montoya
Production Editor: Bennie Clark Allen
Copy Editor: Lana Todorovic-Arndt
Typesetter: Hurix Systems Pvt. Ltd.
Proofreader: Sue Schon
Indexer: Robie Grant
Cover Designer: Michael Dubowe
Marketing Manager: Shari Countryman
eLearning Editor: Lucy Berbeo

Printed in the United States of America

Library of Congress Cataloging-in-Publication Data

Names: Sheperis, Carl, author. | Davis, R. J., author.

Title: Online counselor education: a guide for students / Carl J. Sheperis, R.J. Davis.

Description: Los Angeles: SAGE, [2016] | Includes bibliographical references and index.

Identifiers: LCCN 2015029685 | ISBN 9781483359434 (pbk.: alk. paper)

Subjects: LCSH: Counseling—Study and teaching (Graduate)—Handbooks, manuals, etc. | Web-based instruction—Handbooks, manuals, etc. | Internet in education—Handbooks, manuals, etc.

Classification: LCC BF636.65 .S54 2016 | DDC 158.3078/5—dc23 LC record available at http://lccn .loc.gov/2015029685

This book is printed on acid-free paper.

15 16 17 18 19 10 9 8 7 6 5 4 3 2 1

Brief Contents

Detailed Contents

PART I. GETTING STARTED 37

Chapter 3 Managing Family, Work, and School

Melissa Wheeler and Laura Shannonhouse **39**

Chapter 4 Understanding the Quality of Your Online Program

Amy L. McLeod **61**

Chapter 7 Interacting Productively With Faculty and Peers

Preface

As students entering the world of online counselor education, you might be somewhat nervous about the journey ahead. Trust that learning is a developmental process and that you aren't supposed to know everything the day you begin. In my first class of my master's degree, I was sitting and staring at a quote on the blackboard. While I can't remember the quote, I can remember that it was attributed to LB. I sat there dejected because I had no idea who LB was and instantly knew that I didn't belong in graduate school. I was a failure 5 minutes into my journey! We had a class break and shuffled out into the hallway to get drinks and snacks. As I was standing in the hall, I heard my classmates asking each other, "Who is LB?" Redemption! I once again had a chance to be successful after such a quick downslide to dropping out of school. I later discovered that the quote was by Leo Buscaglia (whom I have still never read) and realized that he was a favorite author of that professor. The quote had little to do with my graduate education, and yet the lack of knowing it created a sense of dread.

As you begin this process, give yourself permission to be a willing learner and to explore the things that you don't know. You are not only entering graduate school, but also taking a step into the online platform for learning. In many ways, you have more resources available to you than you would in a traditional classroom with LB written on the blackboard. In the online world, you would simply copy and paste the quote into the browser and immediately discover the source. There wouldn't be a sense of dread . . . just a sense of discovery. Embrace that feeling and take each new learning opportunity head on. You will truly benefit from the process and will find that you are getting the maximum benefit from your graduate education.

As you read through the chapters of this book, I hope it becomes clear that online learning and counselor training are integrally intertwined in today's world and that you have made an excellent decision to take this route toward becoming a professional counselor. The goals for this text are to help you build your confidence in the online learning process, to help you understand the different aspects of online counselor training, and to prepare you to move toward becoming a professional counselor. Through this text, you will be exposed to various aspects of online training and you will have to examine them in light of your particular program. The chapter authors will guide you through the process of becoming a counselor and will help you to have a little more confidence than I experienced on my first day in graduate school.

Carl J. Sheperis, PhD, NCC, CCMHC, MAC, ACS, LPC
Austin, Texas

Acknowledgments

Editing a book for new online learners in counselor education requires a broad range of perspectives. It could not be completed without the knowledgeable voices of each contributing author in this book. We thank the authors for helping to shape the next generation of professional counselors. Bringing the book to publication requires the support and dedication of a large number of individuals. First and foremost, we would like to thank our editor, Kassie Graves, for guiding us through the project and helping to bring it to life. We would also like to thank the rest of the support team at SAGE Publications for their work on editing and production. A special thanks goes to Carrie Montoya for all of her follow-up and attention to detail.

We also want to thank our personal editors, Bridget Badovick and Ellis Starkey, for their skills in track changes, grammar, flow, voice, tone, prompting for responses, cutting extraneous material, and bringing everything within page limits. They both have an excellent future in the editing and publishing business.

Carl J. Sheperis and R. J. Davis

SAGE was founded in 1965 by Sara Miller McCune to support the dissemination of usable knowledge by publishing innovative and high-quality research and teaching content. Today, we publish more than 850 journals, including those of more than 300 learned societies, more than 800 new books per year, and a growing range of library products including archives, data, case studies, reports, and video. SAGE remains majority-owned by our founder, and after Sara's lifetime will become owned by a charitable trust that secures our continued independence.

Los Angeles | London | New Delhi | Singapore | Washington DC

About the Editors

Carl J. Sheperis, PhD, NCC, CCMHC, MAC, ACS, LPC, is chair of the Department of Counseling and Special Populations at Lamar University. Carl Sheperis' professional life has spanned more than 20 years. He is an author of the following books: *Research in Counseling: Quantitative, Qualitative, and Mixed Methods* (Pearson); *Foundations of Clinical Mental Health Counseling* (Pearson); *Assessment for Counselors and Helping Professionals* (Pearson); *DSM Disorders in Children and Adolescents* (Wiley); and *The Peace Train* (Educational Media). In addition to textbook authorship, Dr. Sheperis is a member of the NBCC Board of Directors, past president of the Association for Assessment and Research in Counseling (2012–2013), associate editor for the *Journal of Counseling and Development*, past chair of the American Counseling Association Research & Knowledge Committee, and he has served as the Editor of the *Journal of Counseling Research and Practice.* He has chaired the Public Policy and Legislation Committee of the Association for Assessment in Counseling and Education and was a co-chair of the association's national conference. Dr. Sheperis has contributed articles and entries to the *Journal of Counseling & Development; The Family Journal; The Journal of Mental Health Counseling; The Clinical Supervisor; The Journal of Professional Counseling, Practice, Theory, and Research; The Professional School Counselor's Handbook; Assessment for Counselors;* the *ACA Encyclopedia;* and elsewhere. A frequent speaker and presenter at professional conferences and workshops, as well, Carl Sheperis has appeared at such recent events as the American Counseling Association World Conference, the Association for Counselor Education and Supervision Conference, the National Assessment Conference for the Association for Assessment in Counseling and Education, and the National Head Start Conference.

R. J. Davis, PhD, NCC, LPC-intern, is an assistant professor and coordinator of the Clinical Mental Health Counseling program at Lamar University. R. J. Davis' teaching career began in secondary education with a decade of experience working with and teaching multiple subjects to diverse populations. Davis' experience as a counselor comes from his service as a university career counselor and later as a director of a counseling and training clinic. Davis is active in service to the profession in his current role as president of Texas Counselors for Social Justice and past president of Texas Career Development Association. Davis is also an active member of state and national counseling associations and has presented at state, national, and international conferences including the Texas Counseling Association, Texas School Counseling Association, Texas College Counseling Association, the American Counseling Association, Association for Counselor Education and Supervision, the Association for Assessment and Research in Counseling, and the Online Learning Consortium. In addition, R. J. Davis is a contributing author to *Foundations of Clinical Mental Health Counseling* (Pearson).

1

Introduction to Online Training for Professional Counselors

Carl J. Sheperis

Chapter Overview

This chapter will provide you with a basic introduction to the world of online counseling training programs. We start by providing a comparison of learning outcomes between counseling graduate students in online settings and on-campus settings. Once we help to build confidence in your decision, we will then explore some of the keys to maximizing your learning experience. Finally, this chapter will help you prepare for ultimate licensure and certification from the start of your program.

Learning Outcomes

After reading this chapter, you will be able to

1. Describe the quality and accreditation status of your online program

2. Understand the difference in performance of online students vs. traditional students

3. Describe methods for maximizing the benefits of your online learning experience

4. Analyze and apply different approaches toward mental preparation for graduate school

5. Understand the elements of physical space preparation for online learning

6. Examine methods for preparing for certification and licensure from the onset of graduate school

7. Recognize methods to make the graduate school experience enjoyable

Introduction to Online Training for Counselors

Welcome to your online graduate program in professional counseling. You probably weighed your options before enrolling and reviewed the costs and benefits of pursuing a degree online, and even though you may have explored different options, you may still be somewhat skeptical about the online learning process. By the end of this book, you will be confident in your choice and be ready to reap the full benefits of an online graduate program in professional counseling. In order to help you get to this level of confidence, we will provide you with the key information that will help you to successfully navigate the online learning experience and be able to apply it to the world of counseling practice.

Our goal is to ensure that you are prepared to get the full benefit of an online counselor preparation program and to help clear any potential obstacles so that you may enjoy your journey toward becoming a professional counselor or advancing your graduate education in professional counseling.

Performance of Online Students Versus Traditional Students

As you made the decision to enter an online graduate program in counseling, you probably wondered if you would receive the same level of training that you would from an on-campus program (note: these are often referred to as brick-and-mortar programs by faculty members in the online world). People decide to pursue online graduate education for various reasons, but two of the primary reasons are flexibility and convenience. What most students don't know is that online programs can have a much more rigorous and in-depth training experience than a traditional classroom. In an online environment, students are required to demonstrate their understanding of concepts and skills in a variety of ways (e.g., discussion board entries, written assignments, quizzes, projects, video recordings, and others). Of course, many of the assessment methods used by faculty members in an online environment are the same as those that occur in a campus environment.

A primary difference between campus and online training is the use of an online discussion board versus in-class interaction. Have you ever been in a classroom where a small number of students are eager to answer every question a professor asks? How about a classroom where some students remain silent throughout the entire class? In an online environment, every student has a voice and faculty members often require students to use the discussion board to demonstrate their understanding of concepts and to engage in scholarly discourse. Of course, programs differ, and you may be required to answer just one discussion board question, multiple discussion board questions, or to complete responses with peers and faculty members. Regardless of the requirement for your specific program, you will have to participate and demonstrate that you have read the material, understand it, and know how to cite it. You will also have to read the discussion board posts of your peers and engage in communication with them about the course materials. This process ensures that you have the opportunity to reinforce your learning throughout each week of a course. In contrast, traditional counseling graduate courses often meet once per week and students might have little to no contact between scheduled class times.

Hopefully, you can already see the logical advantage of online learning versus traditional classrooms. However logic isn't enough to create confidence in your choice to pursue online learning in professional counseling. In a recent study, Dr. R. J. Davis and I examined the differences in learning outcomes between traditional students and online students. For our experiment, we examined differences in students' scores on written assignments, major projects, and GPAs. We were able to determine that a statistically significant difference existed between the two groups and that online students outperformed campus students in a consistent and meaningful way. After determining our statistical significance, we conducted a qualitative analysis related to online student experiences to gain a better perspective of the reasons driving better performance. The general factor that consistently emerged in our research was "time in class." Because online students participate throughout each course week and have multiple interactions with peers and professors, they had a distinct learning advantage over traditional classroom students. As we examined classroom discussion boards across online counseling classes, we found that each online classroom discussion board produced over 100 interactions per week among classes of 20 to 25 students. While other factors also played a role in the success of online students, the level of interaction online is so dramatically different from a traditional classroom that students have to make a considerable effort to avoid a positive learning experience. As you begin your journey, we strongly suggest that you take full advantage of your discussion board interactions. Take the time to read the posts of your peers and relate their posts to what you learned from your books, articles, and other course materials. Take time to engage in a scholarly discussion with your peers throughout each week and maximize the learning experience that is available to you.

In addition to ongoing interaction, the amount of time engaged in the classroom was also a primary component of online student success. In contrast to a traditional graduate class that occurs once per week for 3 hours, students in online graduate counseling programs often visit the classroom daily and review course materials multiple times. In any given week, we found that online students are logged into their classrooms for at least 5 hours and that many students are logged in for up to 10 hours. While logged in students view videos, review assignment directions, post in their discussion boards, send e-mail messages to their professor or peers and review other course resources. Our research provided a clear indication that online students are fully engaged in the learning process throughout their courses and that they spend more than double the time of traditional brick and mortar students in the classroom environment. As you prepare to begin your online program, it is important to recognize these success factors and to fully engage in the learning process right from the start.

Maximizing the Benefits of Your Experience

Although we have already given you some clues to a successful online experience (e.g., interaction and classroom time), there are many more ways to take advantage of the resources in an online environment. If you have been

Table 1.1   A Guide to Success

Step	Task	Self-Check	Action
Step 1	Read the chapter and make notes as you find points to remember.	Review your notes to see if they are detailed enough for you to recall later.	Create a digital folder for your graduate degree program and place the notes in a folder labeled "Guide to Success."
Step 2	Make a list of the things you need to do in order to maximize your learning experience.	Review the chapter to ensure that you captured the essential information.	Prioritize the list and give yourself some deadlines for completing tasks.
Step 3	Do an Internet search for the licensure and/ or certification requirements for counseling in your state.	Review the requirements and compare them with your graduate degree program.	Create a digital folder for your licensure/ certification and place the file with your state requirements inside.
Step 4	Take a few minutes to identify the top five things you want to achieve through your graduate education program.	Review the list to determine if it is a true reflection of your goals. Make any corrections necessary.	Place the list in your "Guide to Success" folder.
Step 5	Think about at least five things that bring you joy.	Review the list and determine how each of the things can be incorporated into your pursuit of a professional counseling degree.	Place the list in your "Guide to Success" folder.

in an online classroom before, the experience in your graduate program will likely be quite different, and you may have to open yourself to a different set of operating principles. If you are completely new to an online environment, then you will have to recognize that there is a learning curve to every system and that you will have to dedicate time to your preparation for success. In order to help both the novice and the experienced online learner, we will review some methods for preparing mentally for the experience, preparing physical space to be online learning friendly, preparing for the end of your program from the onset, and preparing to embrace the excitement of your overall experience.

Mental Preparation

In Chapter 3, we will review methods for managing family, work, and school. One of the biggest factors in your successful balancing act will be mental preparation. We find that many students enter graduate school without a clear understanding of the demands that surround a professional degree and lack the mental preparation necessary. For example, it will be important for you to be mentally ready for the time commitment involved in an online program. In a focus group study, we examined the typical day for an online graduate student. We determined that many students worked full time, had families, and added graduate school to an already full plate. A typical day for these students included waking up around 6 in the morning and getting their kids ready to go to school while getting themselves ready for work. The students then spent a full day at work and picked the kids up after work to transport them to various activities. The students would either prepare dinner or eat out after the activities ended. Around 7 in the evening, the students would help their children to do homework and then get them ready for bed. Around 9, the students would either log in to their online classrooms or complete reading assignments. They would continue working until around 11:30 or later (depending on due dates for assignments). After midnight, the students would go to bed and begin the day again at 6. As you can see, this is quite a full day, and one that would require a great deal of perseverance to tackle for 2 to 3 years of graduate school. The important point is that students do tackle life tasks and graduate school every day. Furthermore, students manage all of these things with a high degree of success. Those students who succeed recognize the challenges and evaluate their life commitments realistically. They prepare for the challenges ahead and make a commitment to tackle them head on.

Motivation and personal responsibility for learning. One of the first things you should do as you read this book is to consider your level of motivation. Of course, it is exciting to begin a new chapter in your life. Many of you will be pursuing the highest level of education attained by anyone in your families, and walking across the stage for graduation may be one of the proudest moments of your life. Stop for a moment and imagine yourself dressed in your graduation robe and getting ready to walk. Feel the sense of pride that is emanating from within. Now see yourself sitting in a counseling office with the degree on your wall. Imagine a client thanking you for helping them to overcome some major life issues. Concentrate on the feeling you get from helping someone to grow and be successful. These thoughts can and will become reality if you can persevere.

For some, just the idea of an advanced degree and helping others might be motivating enough, but we want to make sure you sustain that motivation throughout graduate school. In order to do that you will need to take a realistic appraisal of the road ahead. For example, a graduate school course requires at least 20 hours of dedicated time per week. Are you mentally prepared to dedicate that time to your studies consistently? What challenges might pop up that could threaten that motivation? How will you manage those challenges and stay on track to graduate?

Remember that you are ultimately responsible to learn the material that is presented throughout your graduate degree. This means that the time you dedicate to learning should be clear of distraction and should have high priority. It is easy to procrastinate and to put other responsibilities ahead of school. Once you begin to make those types of choices, it becomes easier and easier to let school slip to the background. Do you recall the number of discussion board entries in a week during a course? An online environment is fast paced and information rich. Once you get behind, it is difficult to catch up without skipping some of the learning process.

As a counselor-in-training, the learning process has serious implications beyond your career goals. Once you get to the world of counseling practice, you will have to apply all of the material that you learn in your degree program. Applying the knowledge correctly can literally mean life or death in some cases. Imagine that you are conducting a counseling session with a woman who is experiencing interpersonal violence. Being able to recall the information you learned about crisis intervention and then being able to apply it correctly can have an impact on what happens in the life of this client. An example like this is not meant to scare you, but is rather intended to raise consciousness that your learning will have a significant impact on the lives of others. Hopefully, being conscious of the impact you will have on others will help increase your hunger for knowledge and encourage you to embrace every aspect of the learning process. Your program will provide you with all of the information necessary to become an excellent counselor, but it is your responsibility to Read, Engage, Apply, and Demonstrate (READ).

Taking pride in becoming a professional counselor. In addition to the motivation you can derive from your personal goals and the ability to help others, you might also consider the fact that you will be joining a profession that has over 500,000 practicing counselors throughout the United States. Counseling is a well-respected profession and is recognized in legislation, policy, and by the general public. Now that you have started the journey toward a degree, pay attention to the news and listen for words like: counselor, counseling, mental health, guidance, and school counseling. You will start to notice how often these are used in the media and how important your professional choice is to the public. Visit some professional organization websites like nbcc.org or counseling.org and read some of the news articles about counselor accomplishments. You will be amazed at some of the things that professional counselors accomplish. Consider Trish Barton who is a Licensed Mental Health Counselor (LMHC) in Florida. She is working at the Five STAR Veterans Center in collaboration with the University of North Florida's Clinical Mental Health Counseling program. Her work is dedicated to providing mental health assessments and intervention for veterans who are experiencing the effects of post-traumatic stress disorder and symptoms related to traumatic brain injury. The Five STAR program received a large grant to provide these services to veterans and the program is receiving national recognition for its efforts. Also consider Dwight Hollier, an LPC in North Carolina and a National Certified Counselor (NCC). Dwight is a member of the Board of Directors for the National Board for Certified Counselors (NBCC) Foundation. In his professional work, Dwight serves as the Director of Clinical and Transition Services for the National Football League. As just one more example, consider Jodi Vermaas, a graduate of Walden University who used her education in mental health counseling to develop a nonprofit organization (Priority One Worldwide) that provides support for women and children in India. The examples of counselors doing outstanding work are endless. Gathering information like this will fuel your motivation and get you started on the right path. Being proud of your choice for a professional career will carry you a long way through the difficult nights studying and the sacrifices you will have to make to be successful.

As you might guess, we believe in what we do as professional counselors and want you to have the same sense of pride. Every author in this book is proud to be a professional counselor and most of us have served the profession in various leadership roles in counseling-related organizations. We have also spent time talking with legislators about counseling-related issues, presenting information to local community organizations, and advocating for our clients in various ways. In a short time, you will be practicing in the field and someone will ask you to come and speak to their group about school violence, parenting, depression, wellness, or some other topic. You will be the expert that guides the public in understanding the need for professional counselors, and your online program will prepare you for that role.

Physical Preparation

Although mental preparation is a critical component in graduate school success, it is difficult to tackle the demands of an online graduate program without having adequate physical space and materials preparation. We will walk you through the various aspects of physical preparation that we believe are necessary for getting off to a good start and maximizing the impact of your efforts. Some of the things you will have to consider are learning space, computer standards, and Internet requirements.

Learning space. In traditional brick-and-mortar schools, students travel to campus and sit in a classroom to hear lectures, participate in group discussions, and complete course activities. In your case, all of your graduate school activities will be completed at a distance, and it will be important to have your own personal classroom space where it will occur. We have had students establish personal classrooms for their online learning experiences in a variety of ways. In some cases, students who work full time have used their office desk or office space as their classroom. While this allows for existing dedicated workspace, the obvious complication is the overlap with work and the potential for a negative impact on employee/employer relations. Even when students have transitioned their office space to a classroom solely after hours, there have been a number of issues. In these instances, students often have solely relied on work resources rather than obtaining computers or Internet access for their home environments. While this arrangement establishes a specific time for pursuit of your graduate education, it removes the flexibility for course access that is often a benefit of online learning. It also places all of your online graduate degree time (aside from reading) in a single location. Most of our students use a variety of technology (computers, tablets, smartphones, and other resources) to access course materials from almost any location. Thus, they can be more efficient in completing course requirements. We recognize that some of you will use existing work resources for financial reasons and that there may be an inability to initially invest in your own computer or Internet resources. If that is the case, then we suggest adding other free resources such as the public library as one of your graduate school classroom locations. However, you should be aware that the use of public access computers and Internet may be much slower than a personal computer or may result in access errors (e.g., timeouts or access problems). It also important to note that public access computers may have restrictions on access time as well as security restrictions that prevent access to your course materials.

While we recognize the sizable cost of personal computers and Internet access, we recommend that you have these to maximize your potential for success. Of course many of you will have already had these resources before you even decided to pursue a career as a professional counselor. If you have these resources or are purchasing these resources, then we believe that you have to also spend time deciding where you will complete your coursework within your home environment. While a dedicated desk or office space might be ideal, that is not the reality for most of our students. In most cases, students must have the space within their home for multiple purposes. In other words, the living room couch often becomes the study lounge after 9 p.m. or the kitchen table becomes a desk after dinner is over. In these cases, being organized will be critical. Taking time to establish a permanent place for books, notebooks, computers, and other resources will help to reduce your clutter and the time it will take to prepare to engage in your coursework (e.g., taking everything out of its permanent space and setting up the classroom) and to transition your classroom back to its regular function (e.g., putting everything back in its permanent storage location).

As you decide upon your online education classroom area, you should account for distractions that may impact your ability to concentrate. For example, many of our students have children. While they may use the kitchen table for their classroom area, they wait until after the children have gone to bed to begin class. Remember that the majority of your online education will be asynchronous (i.e., not real time interaction) and you can decide when to log on, and although you may be tired after a long day, the best time to avoid distraction might be later in the evening. Conversely, some of our students find that early morning is the best time for them to commit full attention to their coursework. You will have to determine the best time for your classwork to begin.

Computer standards. In today's world of graduate education, it is not only important to have access to a computer, but to have access to one that has a large capacity for operating memory and processing speed. In the online world, these components are essential. Because online counselor education is delivered through Learning Management Systems (LMS) such as Blackboard, Moodle, Edmodo, and Skillsoft, computers must be able to handle the task demands of the LMS components. A typical online course within an LMS has a number of modules with discussion boards, videos, journal articles, and various resources. Resources such as online video can have a major impact on computer performance. As such, we suggest that you have a computer with at least a 2 GHz processor. Of course, most computers, regardless of price, have adequate processing speeds today. However, you may need to learn a variety of ways to optimize your computer performance (e.g., closing applications running in the background, defragmenting a hard drive, or upgrading memory).

The majority of entry-level computers come with 4GB of Random Access Memory (RAM) or better. RAM allows data to be read and written almost simultaneously, regardless of the order in which bytes of data are accessed. While 4GB of RAM may be enough to operate in an online environment, your online educational experience may be enhanced with more operating memory. By adding more ability to your physical memory, your computer system can be much more responsive.

In addition to computer memory, it will be important for you to make a conscious decision about the size monitor you will use. With desktop computers, the monitor sizes are almost limitless. As professors, many of us use two monitors so that we may have multiple documents open on the screens at one time. Having two monitors allows a more efficient process for our workflow. However, even with two monitors size remains important. Because you will spend countless hours learning about counseling theories, techniques, and various roles of professional counselors, it will be important to consider the level of strain a small monitor may have on your eyes. As a counselor educator and administrator, I use two 27-inch monitors for my office desktop iMac. Because I spend most of each day on the computer, having large screen sizes allows me more concentrated work time without breaks.

Although a desktop computer and multiple monitors can be a great asset, many online counseling students use laptop computers to complete their coursework. In some cases, students use laptop computer docking stations or connection cables (e.g., HDMI or VGA) to access single or multiple monitors. If you decide to use a laptop and connect to a monitor, then you can have the benefits of both a laptop and a desktop. If using a laptop without a monitor, then the screen size will be an important decision. Like separate monitors, laptop screen sizes can vary with the largest sizes being approximately 17 inches. As you make this decision, be aware that computer monitors are relatively low cost, while adding larger size screens to laptops can increase the cost of a laptop dramatically.

In addition to selecting a monitor or screen size, it will be important to select a video card that produces 1024x768 or greater resolution. Imagine that you have a course assignment to watch a video of a counseling session and to reflect on the counselor's skills. You are specifically required to comment on the counselor's use of facial expressions and microbehaviors like eye contact. It would be extremely difficult to complete your assignment if you did not have adequate screen resolution. Like other resources, there are numerous options for screen resolution. You will have to select the one that fits best for your financial resources and the tasks you have ahead in graduate school.

We also suggest that our students purchase speakers/headphones, a microphone (if not built into your system), a web camera capable of video web conferencing, and a DVD/CD-ROM drive to install software necessary for certain courses. Each counselor education program has different requirements for computer resources. It will be important for you to review the specific requirements for your program to ensure that you are adequately prepared to meet the demands for your online courses. However, we suggest that you attempt to exceed the minimum requirements that programs post. The quality of your online experience may depend heavily on the computer and related equipment you use.

Internet requirements. Many counselor education programs recommend that you have a high-speed Internet connection with a minimum connection speed of 1.5 megabits (Mb or Mbps) to participate in online courses. Internet speed can range from 0 to 500+ Mbps, depending on the type of service you have. Most counselor education programs suggest that you use a cable Internet service provider to ensure that your online course materials work correctly. However, we recognize that cable Internet service is not available in all locations. We have had students who have been successful in their graduate program using satellite Internet and even using their smart phones as a hot spot for Internet. For the most part, either satellite service or cellular service is strong enough to manage most online course functions. However, you should recognize that the use of satellite and cellular connections could result in slowness or errors (timeouts, access problems) when accessing the classroom and course materials. Students also have consistently encountered issues with satellite and cellular services when attempting to view video online or when attempting to connect to interactive web conferences.

Contingency plans. Because satellite and cellular service often produce timeouts and slow performance, students using these options should develop contingency plans for course access. We suggest that students using satellite or cellular service become familiar with other community resources that they can access when connecting to the online classroom becomes a problem. Remember that even community services may limit types of access, prohibit the use of webcams, block certain sites, or also have limited bandwidth.

Prepare for Certification and Licensure From the Onset

Now that we have discussed mental and physical preparation for success in an online counselor education program, we shift our attention to planning for the end of your program from the onset. Although you are likely reading this book as you start your graduate school journey, it is important to be keenly aware that you will have to demonstrate your comprehensive knowledge of professional counseling at the end of your program. From the first time you log into a course, you should begin to organize information that you will need to review and build upon as you move toward professional practice. Many online counseling programs require students to complete a comprehensive exam before graduation. The Counselor Preparation Comprehensive Exam (CPCE) is a standardized exam that is developed by the Center for Credentialing in Education (CCE) and many programs use the CPCE for a final measure of your overall knowledge of counseling. The CPCE is quite similar in structure to the National Counselor Exam (NCE), which is used to become Board

Certified in General Counseling through NBCC and is also used as the licensure exam for professional counseling in most states. Regardless of whether your program uses the CPCE or if you plan to pursue professional licensure, you will likely have to complete some type of credentialing exam. We suggest that you explore the types of exams you may have to take to practice in your specialization area and begin to prepare from the onset of graduate school. We also suggest that you review the various advanced certifications available through NBCC. You may want to add to the minimum entry credentials that you obtain from your initial exams and become Board Certified in a number of areas. Most Board Certified credentials require an exam, and it is in your best interest to prepare for them along the way to graduation.

After reviewing the types of exams you will have to take for your degree and/or specialization area, you should then develop a method for organizing information from your courses so that you can access it in a meaningful way while studying for the exams. Many students use cloud storage for their course materials. Cloud storage is no different from a filing cabinet in an office setting. The information is only readily accessible in a filing cabinet if care was taken to enter the information in an organized and logical fashion. The same goes for cloud storage. We suggest creating storage files according to the elements of your credentialing exams. For example, the NCE is based on the eight CACREP core areas for preparation (e.g., professional orientation and ethical practice; social and cultural diversity; human growth and development; career development; helping relationships; group work; assessment; and research and program evaluation). It is likely that you will have courses in these specific areas but that you will also have information related to these topics in multiple courses. Prepare for success by having the exam areas already established in your filing system and commit to adding the material to those files as you progress through each course.

Enjoy Your Journey

Now that we have reviewed all of the elements of preparation for success in an online graduate program in professional counseling, we want to shift gears and remind you that you decided to pursue this degree for a reason. Most of you have a passion for helping others and want to facilitate change in people's lives. By enrolling in your program and reading this book, you are already on the way to your career goal. Any graduate program will require sacrifices and will be a challenge. However, you can allow yourself to enjoy the process while taking your studies seriously. Unlike an undergraduate degree where you complete a wide range of courses in multiple disciplines, every course in your graduate degree is related to professional counseling. We suggest spending some time during each course reflecting on your learning and setting your mind toward being grateful for your experience. Creating a regular focus on the positive aspects of your graduate school adventure will be an incredible aid during the times when life is pulling you in multiple directions. If you are able to stay focused on your goals and the positive aspects of striving toward them, you will more likely be able to persevere during the most difficult times. We often tell our students that the key to success in graduate school is perseverance. So, plan to enjoy your experience and all the benefits it will provide for you and your family. Recognize that being able to pursue an online graduate degree in counseling is a relatively new phenomenon that allows flexibility in education that was not available to others who came before you. You have a truly unique opportunity ahead. Enjoy the journey.

Summary

Deciding to become a professional counselor is a lifelong goal for many counseling students. Following through with that decision comes with enormous personal and professional sacrifices but is ultimately so worth it! We hope this chapter serves as a foundation for the rest of this book that will be a guide to help you in your journey. While many decisions lay ahead, and there are numerous variables that will impact those decisions, we hope that any questions you may have can begin to be answered within the pages of this text.

2

Getting Comfortable With Technology

Kylie P. Dotson-Blake and J. Scott Glass

Chapter Overview

The chapter begins with an exploration of the primary hub of online learning in Counselor Education, the Learning Management System (LMS), and then proceeds into a discussion of the typical computer software used in online learning. Along with an examination of software, the discussion will present technology tools that are essential to successful engagement in online learning. You will be introduced to the process of learning and student engagement in order to help clarify expectations for you in online Counselor Education classes and to calm the anxieties of those for whom online learning is a new experience. The chapter will close with a sharing of tools for support including ancillary resources such as cloud-based storage and university technical support.

Learning Outcomes

After reading this chapter, you will

1. Be able to express the purpose of the LMS for an online course in Counselor Education from the perspective of both the student and the university

2. Analyze the differences between synchronous and asynchronous learning and describe how each of these might be used in an online Counselor Education course

3. Examine the purpose for utilizing video capture in an online course and articulate three tools you might use for video capture

4. Synthesize some of the prominent anxieties you express when enrolling in an online class for the first time and provide suggestions for ways to overcome these anxieties

Introduction: Getting Comfortable With Technology

Online education has opened opportunities for the pursuit of a counseling degree from all corners of the world. A full-time high school science teacher in a rural community far from any brick and mortar university can now decide to pursue a graduate degree in counseling without uprooting her life. A human resources manager for a mid-sized industry, with three children enrolled in two extracurricular activities each, can fit pursuing a degree in counseling into his busy schedule. Online learning makes degree pursuit possible for any number of individuals from every imaginable life circumstance (Poole, 2000). The broad array of online learning options and the accessibility of technology and Internet access, however, can mask the real and present difficulties with transitioning into online learning.

Yes, the opportunities are there, but students enter online learning with capabilities ranging from no previous engagement with online learning tools to having taught in K–20 classrooms using online learning tools (Palloff & Pratt, 2003). Students who enter a graduate program have much to become familiar with, and technology is only one part of that process. For many Counselor Education programs, the focus will naturally be on content, and those processes required to help you acclimate to the pace and requirements of graduate school. Given the focus, the learning curve of technology requirements is something that may too easily be overlooked. For example, professors and administrative assistants will spend time registering students for courses, only following up to see that they have paid tuition on time and helping them fill out required paper-work for admission. Therefore, newly admitted graduate students may be left to their own devices to learn what technology tools are needed and how to operate that software. Along with differences in skills and abilities, students also bring different levels of comfort with technology. The anxieties that one expects with entering a graduate program may be amplified by an individual's worries about the program's technology expectations (Muilenburg & Berge, 2005). This chapter is designed to ease some of those worries by sharing information with you about the technology products and tools that you might expect to encounter, the learning process in a typical online classroom, and ways to navigate resources for support and extra help.

Throughout the chapter, comparisons between the traditional, face-to-face graduate education experience and the online graduate experience will be drawn. By helping you to understand the intent of components of online learning and the mechanisms for achieving outcomes that are important for learning in all settings, we seek to calm the fears of students new to the online learning environment. Online learning is like going into a diner in 2015 to order a burger. You know it isn't going to look like a soda-shop of the 1950s, but you want your burger to be just as filling and your contentment to be comparably complete. Though the process and environment look different, you want the outcome to be equally posi-tive. This is the same for the Counselor Education classroom in an online setting instead of a traditional, campus-based setting; the outcomes, the student competencies, the student-student interactions and the learner engagement must be just as positive and just as present as one would find in a face-to-face course, but the environment and the mechanisms for achieving these results are going to be different. Overall, this chapter will increase your comfort with the technology used in online learning in Counselor Education.

Learning Management Systems

The LMS is the core of the online learning environment and is likely one of the first components of online learning with which you will be less familiar. Understanding the purpose of the LMS and how it will be used to facilitate online courses is the first step in becoming a well-informed online learner who is comfortable with technology (Coates, James, & Baldwin, 2005). Different universities and colleges use various systems to deliver online learning opportunities for you. The LMS is the hub that allows the institution to manage the organization and delivery of curriculum and evaluation of student learning outcomes. It is most comparable to the face-to-face classroom in traditional learning. It is the space where you will participate in lectures, group discussions, and where you will receive your grades and instructor feedback (Lonn & Teasley, 2009). You enter the LMS virtually, but in every other capacity, it takes the shape of the classroom. For the institution, the LMS occupies a more complex space. While it is the hub for delivering academic content, facilitating class discussions, and returning grades to you, it also interfaces with institutional student academic warnings, technology tools to enhance classroom curriculum delivery (like the technology cart of old), and the institution's system of tracking academic outcomes for certain accreditation benchmarks. In total, the LMS is a software product that includes functional capabilities for delivering and managing learning content, tracking your engagement with delivered content, tracking and analyzing student progress, and facilitating learner-learner and learner-faculty interactions (Coates et al., 2005).

There are a number of different LMS that are typically used by colleges and universities. The most widely recognized LMS currently include BlackBoard, WordPress LMS plug-ins, D2L (formerly Desire2Learn), eCollege, and the commercial version of Canvas. Technology companies are developing new LMS daily; however, there are a smaller number of highly visible, commercial LMS products. These are the ones that most institutions have adopted as their product of choice. Universities typically invest heavily in one of these larger, fee-based systems that allow for consistency in the online learning experience across diverse programs within the university, while also providing a greater sense of software security for you, faculty, and the institution.

In addition to the larger, commercial products, there are also open-source LMS products that allow for a high level of customization by institutions due to the free, open-source code of the product (Beatty & Ulasewicz, 2006). These products, including Moodle and Sakai, often include some optional for-fee elements provided by third parties that institutions add to supplement the curriculum engagement and course delivery experience. A benefit of an open-source LMS is the rapid evolution of additional elements in response to observed participant needs and institution needs. However, a perceived downside of these products for institutions is the lack of access to support staff and more limited security measures. The companies delivering these products have noted these drawbacks, and third parties are continually adding supplemental for-fee services and plug-ins, not to mention many of the open-source LMS have a robust community of users and staff who provide tech-support through forums and e-mail. On the whole, you will discover that larger institutions often prefer the larger, for-fee, commercial LMS for the consistency in course delivery components and design, enhanced security measures, and comprehensive technology support offered by the LMS to the institution's technology staff. Though, as one expects with rapidly evolving technology, popularity of LMS products will wax and wane.

The product chosen by your university or college will impact how the online classroom looks and how you move through online content and engage in course discussions. No matter what LMS an institution chooses, however, most online learners will discover that as they log into the LMS, they are stepping into the virtual classroom, and all of the opportunities they would expect to encounter in a traditional face-to-face classroom, including lectures, classroom discussions, small-group meetings, turning in assignments, taking tests, and receiving grades all occur directly within the LMS. When you log into the system, you are granted access to course content (including the syllabus, assignment descriptions, etc.), rosters of colleagues in the course, space for collaborative work sessions for small groups, and partner assignments and announcements from the course instructor. When you walk into a traditional, campus-based graduate classroom, you have opportunities to interact with other students, ask questions of the faculty instructor, and engage with course content. This is the same in the LMS. Though you may not be occupying the same physical space at the same time, opportunities for all of the same sorts of interactions are provided in the LMS environment.

Asynchronous Learning

The dimensions of space and time are the two most significant differences in online learning in Counselor Education and the typical, face-to-face graduate course (Dunderstadt, 2001). Prior to enrolling in their first online course, many Counselor Education students have never heard the word *asynchronous*. Asynchronous learning can be defined as learning opportunities that do not require students to interact with each other at a common/shared time. It has allowed online learning to become a tool for integrating the pursuit of education so seamlessly into the lives of modern students (Hrastinski, 2008). Students who are familiar with asynchronous learning may expect more of a correspondence course style of learning, but they will be in for a surprise. In the earliest form of distance education, the correspondence course, an instructor would mail curriculum materials to you through the postal service, and you would then complete assignments and return them to the instructor via the mail. As distance education expanded to include online learning, many of the early online courses worked in much the same fashion as these early correspondence courses, with content being posted by the faculty, reviewed by students and assignments submitted to the instructor for grading. There was very limited student-student engagement in these courses, and they did not include opportunities for synchronous full-class discussions (Slagter van Tyron & Bishop, 2009). The asynchronous learning in these courses happened at the student's own pace and schedule, but each experience was completely isolated from the experiences of other students in the class. Fortunately, technology tools and innovations in education have allowed asynchronous learning to become cleverly threaded throughout comprehensive, experiential education experiences in Counselor Education.

Contemporary asynchronous learning allows education to happen in a unique environment, an environment that fosters interactions between you and interactivity of curriculum on a schedule that can be adapted to fit within the daily lives of students from diverse life circumstances (Palloff & Pratt, 2005). You are able to engage with the content, share reflections, participate in discussions, and complete class activities at a time defined by each individual. Synchronous learning, in contrast, requires that you engage with each other in in-class discussions or activities at a defined time and within a group context. Asynchronous learning is intended to provide flexibility to learners while promoting self-direction and autonomy in the learning experience (Richardson & Swan, 2003).

In practical terms, learners in online Counselor Education classrooms can expect that asynchronous learning will include content delivery, course discussions, reflection opportunities, and some class activities (Darabi, Arrastia, Nelson, Cornille, & Liang, 2011). Content delivery for most classes will include recorded lectures, PowerPoint, or Prezi presentations, readings, videos, and other resources designed or identified by the faculty instructors as appropriate content elements. You will have span of time established for reviewing this content once posted.

In addition to content delivery, asynchronous learning will likely include discussion and reflection opportunities. You may post initial responses to discussion prompts or topics and then respond to the posts made by your colleagues. Some faculty instructors will have set expectations for the quantity or quality of discussion posts for each student, and there may be grading rubrics provided.

Asynchronous class discussions afford the faculty instructor an opportunity to gauge how well you are understanding content shared in the course (Swan, 2001) and how competently you are able to apply this content to your process of making-meaning as counselors. Journals and reflection responses are additional examples of asynchronous learning you will experience in online Counselor Education classes. Additionally, you will encounter class activities including partner activities, role-playing, and experiential activities. These activities may need to be scheduled at a shared time with a partner from the class or may be able to be completed with a volunteer partner from your life outside of class. However, these activities would still be considered asynchronous because you are responsible for scheduling time to complete the activity, rather than it being something that happens during a specific time for the entire class.

Opportunities for innovation and meaningful connection abound in the online classroom and counselor educators are increasingly making use of tools and strategies to help the incorporation of these opportunities for you. Consequently, when you enroll in an online Counselor Education class you should not expect to be a passive receiver of information. Asynchronous learning leads to increased opportunities for engaging with other students, not fewer. It requires that you be willing to work within a dynamic context and flexible enough to adjust to try new things, but the payoff is that you are able to incorporate learning experiences into your already busy life at a pace and schedule that you are able to manage.

Typical Computer Software

New technology tools are being introduced by developers every day, and it would be impossible to cover all of the tools that are used in every online Counselor Education course in one chapter. However, most of the tools will be used for a smaller number of defined purposes. In this section, we will share and discuss some of the most prevalent tools used in online Counselor Education courses and their related purposes. Additionally, we will try to introduce you to some tips and strategies that will help you to be successful in achieving the intended outcome no matter the tool used.

Asynchronous and synchronous learning will likely both be required of you, and for these contrasting learning opportunities, different technology tools may be utilized (Anderson, 2003). Therefore, it is important for you to be familiar with the tools needed in order to be able to engage effectively. Many students enrolling in online Counselor Education classes for the first time find themselves overwhelmed by the sheer volume of technology components used to promote classroom engagement. In an effort to reduce the tech-overload that some students experience, we will try to answer some of the typical questions posed by students in their initial forays into online courses.

Assignment Preparation Software: Documents, Spreadsheets, and Presentations

In all Counselor Education classes, and definitely in online courses, you are expected to be adept at the development and use of digital documents, spreadsheets, and presentations. Most students in online Counselor Education courses will have been using the Microsoft Office suite of products for years to prepare Word documents, Excel spreadsheets, and PowerPoint presentations. You should expect to prepare all papers, essays, journals, and responses to discussion prompts using document preparation software like Microsoft Word or GoogleDocs.

GoogleDocs, Zoho, and Microsoft Office Live are three tools that allow groups of people to revise and edit a document together in real-time online. These documents have transformed the group paper preparation from individuals sitting around a table writing together or e-mailing revised versions of the same document between group members to the synchronous development of a paper with space for comments, discussion, brainstorming, and writing, all while each team member sits in the comfort of his or her own home. Documents developed collaboratively online are dynamic, with changes showing up immediately, and each group member able to see who is making comments.

Spreadsheets are a staple of graduate coursework, and Excel is one of the most widely used spreadsheet software products in Counselor Education. Most statistical software packages used for research by graduate students will allow the export of datasets into an Excel spreadsheet, and there are a number of online tools to help individuals learn how to use Excel more adeptly for data analysis. EZAnalyze is one that is often used by school counselors and in school counseling programs (Poynton & Baker, 2007). EZAnalyze is an Excel add-in that will allow you to do many easy and interesting analytic procedures within Excel and to display results in easily formatted charts (Young & Kaffenberger, 2013).

Presentations are another type of assignment format that you are often required to complete. One of the more widely recognized presentation software products is Microsoft PowerPoint. This software allows the user to develop slide shows and movies created from a template with multiple slides already formatted for presentation. Using PowerPoint allows you to tell a story through slides using audio clips, text, clip art, video clips, transitions, animation, and other elements (Atkinson, 2011). There are many forums and resources on the Internet that can help you learn to use Microsoft PowerPoint effectively. However, for some people and some situations, PowerPoint may be a little too static. Prezi is an online, cloud-based presentation product that allows for a high level of customization within your presentation. It also allows you to store presentations and develop them collaboratively with other users (Perron & Stearns, 2011).

Cloud-based computing. Cloud-based computing is another technology term that will be new to you. For those most comfortable with having assignments on paper, the cloud can be somewhat disconcerting. The idea that your data and the assignments you create can be stored and accessed virtually on servers located far away can be scary. However, most of us would be surprised to learn how much of our information and data is already held in the cloud. Most mobile apps operate using the cloud; some operating systems have cloud-based components; insurance providers and other businesses store some customer information in the cloud; and when people upload photos to Facebook, those photos are being uploaded to the cloud (Goldman, 2014). Many of the assignments that you complete collaboratively with student teams or partners will include the use of cloud-based computing products, such as Google Drive or Dropbox. These products allow for storage and shared editing of documents, spreadsheets and presentations and are very useful for online students (Lee, 2014). Additionally, as movies and photo files can require a lot of space when stored on a computer's hard drive, cloud-based storage will free up space on the hard drive and allow it to run more efficiently and quickly.

Assignment Preparation Software: Video Capture

Documents, spreadsheets, and presentations are not the only types of assignments you will create. As previously mentioned, videos also play a prominent role in assignments in online courses. You may be surprised at how often you video yourself during an online Counselor Education class. You worry about how you sound, what is in the background of your video and how to prevent outside distractions, and, truthfully, these are very real challenges that you must consider. However, take hope! These issues can easily be overcome and you'll be on your way to successful video capture. The term *video capture* refers to the process of converting analog video from a video camera to digital video so that it may be produced and uploaded to the Internet so others may view it (Chandra, 2007). In short, video capture refers to making a video you then post on the Internet or share via e-mail or the LMS. There are numerous ways that persons may successfully navigate this process, and while this section will not be exhaustive, it will examine a couple of popular options that you may choose to use.

To begin, owning a webcam or other device that allows someone to record video and post directly to the Internet is a necessity for online course engagement. Webcams are essentially video cameras that input directly to a computer connected to the Internet so that videos and pictures generated by the device can be easily uploaded to the Internet. In online Counselor Education courses, these webcams are able to serve a variety of uses including recording videos, taking photographs and allowing for videoconferencing, which we will discuss later.

In online courses, discussion boards or online chats are often used as a method to carry on conversations between class members and instructors. These tools allow an instructor to post a discussion and/or reflection prompt that may require you to read materials or a case scenario and then respond. Instead of simply being asked to type a response professors choose to have you post a video response believing that having you verbally respond gives voice to your perspectives and allows for enhanced inflection and range of tone and emotion. This would mean that you would make a video recording of yourself responding to the material in the prompts and then posting that video in an environment where other class members can view it. This may include posting the videos on sites such as YouTube or directly into the class LMS or blog site, depending on the private nature of the material being discussed. Webcams offer you the opportunity to quickly record yourself so that the video can then be uploaded into the format required by the instructor.

It is important to note that other devices are able to perform the same function, so having a separate webcam might not be necessary as long as you possess another device that is able to complete the same functions. For example, smartphones have progressed so dramatically that many of them have cameras that record with equal or better quality than some webcams. However, it is important that you make sure your phone is compatible with your computer, or at least that the phone has the capability to post directly into the environment required by the professor. Digital cameras also typically have a video function, and this function may also be used to develop videos that can be transferred to your computer in the same manner you transfer digital pictures (Chandra, 2011).

Another aspect of video capture for you to consider is how available programs might facilitate the process more easily. Webcams often come with internal software that allow users to record video and post directly onto some Internet sites (i.e., YouTube). The same is often true when using the camera feature on smartphones. It is also possible to input a webcam into a computer but use software found on the computer to aid in the video capture process (Chandra, 2011). The software options available to users may depend on the operating system of the computer being used. For example, a popular choice for PC users may be Microsoft Movie Maker, while many Macintosh users prefer iMovie. It is important to note that both of these tools have been created to work on either system, although they only come standard on the operating system most native to the program (i.e., iMovie is standard on Apple laptops and desktops). Still, each can be downloaded for free.

These software options provide you with the ability to customize presentations that may include video clips and photographs, while also allowing for transitions between clips. Whereas this level of detail is not always demanded in class discussions, it does give you more control over the production of your videos and certainly provides a greater level of professionalism for projects and assignments. A typical question posed to faculty when using these movie production software products is, "Why won't my movie play for my classmates when they click it?" The answer is almost always that you have developed a "project" using the movie production software, but have not finalized the process of producing a movie. For most of these movie production products, when you begin working on making a movie, you are working in a project format.

To finalize this project and complete the process of transitioning the project into a movie viewable by others, you must choose a "share" option that will allow the project to be transitioned into a Quicktime movie file or a .mp4, .mov, or to upload the file to YouTube. This process, in part, compresses the movie file to a size suitable for uploading to the Internet and being viewed by others. With this final step, users may be asked to select either the intent of the use of the video (typically web-streaming, computer playback, etc.) or the size of the file (small, medium, or large). If the user selects web-streaming or medium or small, it will take a shorter time to share the movie and it will render more clearly on other computer screens if they have slower Internet access. There are many user discussion forums available on the Web with the answers to most any questions you could imagine regarding video capture and the use of popular software tools. Making and sharing creative videos can be one of the most enjoyable components of your online learning experience, but it will take a little time and practice to become adept with the software programs and process.

Video Conferencing

As discussed earlier, asynchronous learning opens the world of education to the flexibility of your schedule. Alternatively, synchronous learning provides powerful opportunities for students to be present with each other in the same space of time to engage in course discussions and activities. Synchronous learning refers to learning opportunities that require that you log into online conferencing system/program/products. Though students often report initial anxiety regarding video conferencing, research has demonstrated that students in classes using synchronous video conferencing report higher levels of satisfaction with the learning experience than those in courses using primarily asynchronous course delivery (Moridani, 2007).

While video capture refers to the recording and display of materials, the term *video conferencing* refers to the technology that allows persons in varying locations to engage in face-to-face meetings without having to be present in the same location. The benefits of such technology are numerous, and it allows instructors a variety of creative ways to engage with their virtual classrooms. This mode of communication provides you with the opportunity to pay attention to the nonverbal gestures and responses of your classmates, something that is lost in text-based conversations.

Given that the profession of counseling places such an emphasis on nonverbal communication, it is helpful for you to have the chance to witness these as you talk with others. It allows students who might not ever meet in the same physical space the chance to connect visually with one another, which instructors hope would help students create a stronger sense of comfort with one another, and therefore a stronger connection to the program.

An additional tangible benefit for the use of video conferencing is the removal of physical space reservation on-campus and time in transit for participants. Rather than being tasked with the responsibility of finding a room capable of housing a class, video conferencing allows students from a variety of settings to meet online. While deciding on a particular time to meet is still a necessity, travel and distance implications have been negated. It enables educational institutions to cast a wider net when recruiting students, and allows students to mitigate some expenses that might typically be involved in the pursuit of educational opportunities.

There are no shortages of tools that will allow people to communicate through video conferencing. It is important to note that there are free options, as well as those that require payment. Many of the fee-for-service video conferencing options may come with additional tools and options not found in free software. A few of the better-known pay services include programs such as Citrix WebEx, GoToMeeting, and Adobe Connect. These programs allow users to pay a fee to allow a number of people to join in on the conversations and meetings. In addition, there are other options embedded within these programs that also may be used to enhance the video conference experience, including letting someone take control of the meeting leader's cursor and desktop, as well as the ability to mute various members, and share collaborative workspace. The cost for these services will typically increase based on the number of users one would like to be able to engage the system during each video conference.

There are other video conferencing options that are free to use as well that may be used by students or faculty to connect members of the class. Skype is a popular service that is free for up to two users in a video conference, but the additional users require the fee-based service. With Skype, it is possible to communicate with one other person, such as a professor or a classmate for free, but group video conferencing is a fee-based service. Synchronous audio-conferencing without the video component is free, however, in Skype, and though it provides no opportunities for visual connections, it does allow students and faculty to meet in a real-time setting for a verbal discussion. Google Hangouts is another free alternative for video conferencing, which will allow up to 10 people to connect. Another benefit of Google Hangouts is that it does allow users the opportunity to have private video chats that are not recorded to YouTube and are only visible to the participants you invite into the conversation.

It is important to note that there are numerous other video conferencing options available, both free and for purchase. Some Counselor Education programs may pay for services such as GoToMeeting, and you will find that you use that video conferencing product consistently across all of your online courses while in the program. Other programs may have fewer resources and lean more toward those programs that do not require fees. Regardless of fee structure, it is common for these programs to require some level of downloads and registration in order to participate. For example, before being able to use Skype, you will need to log in to the company's website, download the necessary software and then register (i.e., create a Username and password). Typically the registration process is free, but it is important to consider that these steps take time and these processes would need to be taken care of prior to the commencement of your scheduled meeting.

There are some helpful tips to keep in mind when using video conferencing technology. First, feedback can be an issue, particularly when there are numerous people engaged in a conversation. For this reason, it is useful to mute your microphone when you are not talking so that your movements and noises do not cause additional interference. Furthermore, it can be particularly helpful for users to purchase an external headphone and microphone set. This equipment is not particularly expensive but makes the experience more pleasant as users will be able to hear and speak more easily with the group. One complaint about this type of program is that when someone speaks the voice is broadcast through another user's speaker, which then is picked up by that user's microphone, and then rebroadcast to the group. Having numerous people doing this can cause great frustration for everyone involved. Simply muting the microphones of anyone not talking creates a silent space for a colleague's voice to be shared just like in a face-to-face class.

Lighting is another issue that can have a positive or negative impact on a user's experience with video conferencing. Be sure to place your light source in front of you, not behind you, so that your face is illuminated and shadows are minimized. A tip to remember when planning group meetings is that sometimes, institution-purchased video conferencing software will include a number of layers of login for security measures. For students in rural settings or areas where fast Internet is more limited, the commercial programs such as Skype or Google Hangouts may require less bandwidth and operate more quickly and easily than the institution-purchased software.

One of the most important tips for successful video conferencing is to try it early, test it out, and make sure that all of the necessary software is downloaded and your equipment is working. It is stressful to try to log into an online course video conference 5 minutes before it starts and find out that a 15 minute download is required before you can enter. Planning ahead and being prepared will almost always result in less frustration, reduced anxiety, and increased chances for success.

Navigating Ancillary Resources and Tools

In addition to planning ahead and diligent practice, there are many other online tools that will help to enhance your potential for success in online Counselor Education classes. From day one in the graduate program, you are developing your professional identity and professional community of support. This is a process that takes place in a number of dimensions, including face-to-face, in daily life and online. You will begin to connect with each other through Google+ Communities, share resources through Pinterest, and build your professional resumes through LinkedIn.

Campus-based computer labs and virtual labs offered by your institution are other good sources of support. These labs contain a treasure trove of programs and professionals ready to provide technical support and direction to you. Virtual labs are often a new resource for graduate students. By hosting a virtual lab, some universities have been able to provide a wider range of specialized software programs. User licensing agreements for specialized software are sometimes quite expensive, and it would be very costly to try to provide specialized software to every single student. This issue has long been addressed by having campus-based computer labs that contain computers with specialized software loaded on the hard drives. Thankfully, institutions are committed to online learning and meeting the needs of online students and virtual labs have been developed to bridge the gap between campus-based labs and online students. Virtual labs are cloud-based computing options that allow you to log in and use a campus-owned or licensed program. When you log into a virtual lab, it is as if you have taken her seat at a computer in a campus-based lab, only in the comfort of your own space. The specialized software is only available if you are logged into the virtual lab.

With all of these ancillary support tools, it is certainly up to you how much you invest yourself in the process of using these to connect with other professionals and professional online resources external to what is required for coursework. We assert, though, that these tools and resources provide invaluable opportunities to savvy students. You can find creative ways to publicize your counseling programs as professionals. Many programs use Twitter to share professional information, scholarship opportunities, and job prospects with students and graduates. Google has a host of products that are available for free and can be used to enhance your experience, including Google+ Communities, Google Drive, which allows for shared document development and editing, and GoogleScholar, which is a searchable database of a vast quantity of professional scholarship from all disciplines. These online tools, combined with cloud-based storage, allow you access to the resources necessary to develop a trove of professional resources that will enhance your service-delivery as professional counselors. By learning to utilize these resources effectively as a student, you will be prepared to enter the field with confidence and enthusiasm.

Summary

Professionals who enter the field of counseling enter with confidence and enthusiasm, and it is important that you start your graduate program with the same attitude. Online learning may be a new experience for you, but if you come into it with excitement and a willingness to try new things and trust the process, you will likely be surprised by the extent of your abilities and potential for success. It is important to maintain an open line of communication with your faculty instructor and let him or her know early in the process if you are having difficulty navigating any of the technology tools and requirements. Also, use your resources! For just about any question you may have there are forums discussing challenges and process on the Internet. It may take time to sift through the maze of information available and find the best answer, it is likely someone before you has asked the same question. Be diligent about preparing early and connecting with your classmates, and you will find that many of your questions can be resolved quickly and without undue anxiety. Confidence and comfort in the online classroom come with practice, preparation, and a willingness to embrace a sense of adventure.

About the Authors

Kylie P. Dotson-Blake is an associate professor in the Counselor Education program at East Carolina University (ECU) in Greenville, North Carolina. During her tenure in the Counselor Education program at ECU, she has designed and developed online sections or hybrid sections for many Counselor Education courses. She has focused her curriculum development, in part, on embedding service-learning and community engagement projects in online courses. She has published and presented on the topic of embedding service-learning in online graduate coursework, and her work highlights the positive benefits students experience from being able to initiate and implement service and engagement projects in their home communities. Dr. Dotson-Blake and Dr. Glass have published many activities to support online learning in numerous textbooks and have coauthored the book *Online Group Activities to Enhance Counselor Education*.

J. Scott Glass is a professor in the Counselor Education program at ECU. Prior to his appointment at ECU, he taught at Elon University and Mississippi State University at Meridian. Dr. Glass received his Bachelor's degree from North Carolina State University and attended East Carolina University for his master's degree in Counselor Education. He then earned his PhD in Counseling and Counselor Education from the University of North Carolina at Greensboro. As the Program Coordinator of the Counselor Education program at ECU, he shepherded in the era of online education, developing many online and hybrid courses and encouraging other faculty to do so as well. Dr. Glass' areas of interest include online learning, adventure-based counseling, group work with all ages, processing, and issues related to diversity in counseling. He has served as the president of the North Carolina Counseling Association and served on the ASGW editorial board for over 10 years. He has had numerous presentations at the international, national, and state levels on topics related to adventure based counseling and group work.

References

Anderson, T. (2003). Modes of interaction in distance education: Recent developments and research questions. In M. Moore & G. Anderson (Eds). *Handbook of distance education* (pp. 129–144). Mahwah, NJ: Erlbaum.

Atkinson, C. (2011). *Beyond bullet points: Using Microsoft PowerPoint to create presentations that inform, motivate and inspire* (3rd ed.). Redmond, Washington: Microsoft Press.

Beatty, B., & Ulasewicz, C. (2006). Faculty perspectives on moving from Blackboard to the Moodle learning management system. *Tech Trends, 50*(4), 36–45.

Chandra, S. (2007). Lecture video capture for the masses. ITiCSE '07 Proceedings of the 12th annual SIGCSE Conference on Innovation and Technology in Computer Science Education, pp. 276–280.

Chandra, S. (2011). Experiences in personal lecture video capture. *IEEE Transactions on Learning Technologies, 4*(3), 261–274.

Coates, H., James, R., & Baldwin, G. (2005). A critical examination of the effects of learning management systems on university teaching and learning. *Tertiary Education and Management, 11*, 19–36.

Darabi, A., Arrastia, M. C., Nelson, D. W., Cornille, T., & Liang, X. (2011). Cognitive presence in asynchronous online learning: A comparison of four discussion strategies. *Journal of Computer Assisted Learning, 27*, 216–227.

Dunderstadt, J. J. (2001). The future of the university in the digital age. Proceedings of the American Philosophical Society. 145(1), 54–72.

Goldman, D. (2014). What is the cloud? *CNN Money.* Retrieved from http://money.cnn.com/2014/09/03/technology/enterprise/what-is-the-cloud

Hrastinski, S. (2008, November). Asynchronous & synchronous e-learning. *Educause Quarterly*, 51–55.

Lee, G. (2014). *Cloud networking: Understanding cloud-based data-center networks.* Waltham, MA: Morgan Kaufmann.

Lonn, S., & Teasley, S. D. (2009). Saving time or innovating practice: Investigating perceptions and uses of learning management systems. *Computers & Education, 53*, 686–694.

Moridani, M. (2007). Asynchronous video streaming vs. synchronous videoconferencing for teaching a pharmacogenetic pharmacotherapy course. *American Journal of Pharmaceutical Education, 71*(1), Article 16.

Muilenburg, L. Y., & Berge, Z. L. (2005). Student barriers to online learning: A factor analytic study. *Distance Education, 26*(1), 29–48.

Palloff, R. M., & Pratt, K. (2003). *Collaborating online: Learning together in community.* San Francisco, CA: Jossey-Bass.

Palloff, R. M., & Pratt, K. (2005). *The virtual student: A profile and guide to working with online learners.* San Francisco, CA: Jossey-Bass.

Perron, B. E., & Stearns, A. G. (2011). A review of a presentation technology: Prezi. *Research on Social Work Practice, 21*(3), 376–377.

Poole, D. M. (2000). Student participation in a discussion-oriented online course: A case study. *Journal of Research on Computing in Education, 33*(2), 162–177.

Poynton, T. A., & Baker, T. D. (2007). Free tech tools. *ASCA School Counselor, 44*, 22–29.

Richardson, J. C., & Swan, K. (2003). Examining social presence in online courses in relation to students' perceived learning and satisfaction. *Journal of Asynchronous Learning Networks, 7*(1), 68–88.

Slagter van Tyron, P. J., & Bishop, M. J. (2009). Theoretical foundations for enhancing social connectedness in online learning environments. *Distance Education, 30*, 291–315.

Swan, K. (2001). Virtual interaction: Design factors affecting student satisfaction and perceived learning in asynchronous online courses. *Distance Education, 22*(2), 306–331.

Young, A., & Kaffenberger, C. (2013). Making DATA work: A process for conducting action research. *Journal of School Counseling, 11*(2). Retrieved from http://jsc .montana.edu/articles/v11n2.pdf

PART I

Getting Started

3

Managing Family, Work, and School

Melissa Wheeler and Laura Shannonhouse

Chapter Overview

This chapter serves as a way to help you conceptualize the delicate balance of family, work, and school. After a brief overview of the life of an online student, two wellness models grounded in counseling theory are described, along with the basic steps for developing wellness plans, and evaluating outcomes. Application of these concepts will be discussed throughout the chapter. Finally, student experiences are offered as a means to showcase potential ways of balancing family, work, and school.

Learning Outcomes

- Understand models of wellness and how they relate to life as a student
- Awareness of one's own wellness strengths and areas for growth
- Develop strategies to positively impact wellness growth areas
- Generalize learning to working with clients on their wellness

Guide to Success

1. While reading about the wellness models, reflect upon your personal wellness.

2. Analyze areas of strengths and potential areas of growth in your personal wellness.

3. When considering your wellness plan, make a list of people you can rely on to hold you accountable and/or assist with your wellness goals.

Introduction

Balancing family, work, and school can be a challenge for graduate students enrolled in online education programs. Those training to become professional counselors have additional workloads due to the intensity and rigor in counselor preparation. Professional counselors are charged to provide client-centered services that foster wellness for all persons (Chi Sigma Iota, n.d.). In fact, engaging in self-care is discussed as a professional responsibility of all counselors in the American Counseling Association's *Code of Ethics* (2014). In order to support client wellness and engage in personal self-care, one must first identify one's own wellness strength and growth areas.

The Life of an Online Student

Online counselor education programs can be great choices for students who desire to pursue advanced degrees due to the flexibility these programs provide for completing professional studies while still allowing for life to happen. The structure of online learning environments will vary depending on the program offered; however, there is a common factor in that all online students have assignment deadlines, and the work can be fit into an existing schedule and completed anywhere with Internet access. In contrast, graduate students in traditional campus courses must report to campus each week for at least 3 hours per course, not including the time required commuting to campus.

While the flexibility of online education is an advantage, the structure of online learning can also present challenges. In traditional on-campus programs, students have a clear boundary of when they are required to be in class so it may be easier to set boundaries with friends, family, and work responsibilities. A significant amount of learning occurs in the classroom with students responsible for readings and assignments outside of class. In contrast, online counseling graduate students may feel challenged in the areas of setting boundaries and finding time to complete coursework. Students may find it harder to communicate to partners or children that time usually spent doing other tasks must now be set aside for school work. In an exclusively online course, learning can occur through readings, interactions with peers on discussion boards, pretaped lectures, weekly Web meetings, and assignments. The 3 hours traditional students spend on-campus per course each week are included in the assigned tasks in an online course. While online students generally have flexibility around where and when they complete course work, they can still expect to devote the same amount of time in class and outside of class as a traditional on-campus student.

It is common for online students to continue following schedules similar to life before graduate studies while adding on the demands

Table 3.1   Daily Schedule of Online Student

6 a.m.	Wake up, shower, get dressed, make breakfast, get kids ready for school
8 a.m.	Arrive at work
5 p.m.	Leave work; pick up kids from day care/afterschool or head to next obligation
5 - 7 p.m.	Take kids to extra curricular activities; commute home; gym; errands; church
7 p.m.	Dinner
7:30 - 9 p.m.	Help kids with homework; chores; spend time with partner; connect with friends
10 p.m.	Put kids to bed (Don't forget their baths!)
10:30 p.m.	Reading for graduate courses, homework, and research for graduate assignments
Midnight	Go to bed (Wash, rinse, repeat.)

of their graduate counseling program of study. Adding reading time, research time, and writing time to an already busy schedule may seem like a daunting task. How does anyone add time to an already exhausting schedule? To understand this, an examination of a typical schedule of an online graduate student has been provided in Table 3.1.

Your schedule may closely resemble this or it may be different depending on your life circumstances. Classroom teachers may well have a stack of student papers to grade at home in addition to completing their own homework for graduate school. You may even have to be at your job earlier than 8 am! If you live in a rural area, travel times may be extended due to the distance between work, school, and home. Learning how to evaluate your personal wellness may position you to better balance family, work, and school while positioning you for success in an online counselor education program. The following is a brief introduction to two models of wellness grounded in counseling theory. As wellness is integrated into the identity and ethical responsibilities of professional counselors (American Counseling Association, 2014), understanding the following theoretical background may likely be of both personal and professional interest to you.

Introduction to Wellness

Wellness, in contrast to the medical, "illness-oriented" model that conceptualizes problems as deficiencies from normal or average functioning, emphasizes optimal growth and development. Remediation of problem issues may be reconceptualized as resolving normal, developmental challenges through positive lifestyle choices, or, as stated by Remley (1991) and emphasized by Myers (1992), "We do not believe that people must first be diagnosed with an illness before they can be treated with counseling services . . . all people can benefit from counseling, fully functioning people who experience everyday stress in their lives . . ." (Myers, 1992, p. 138). Diagnosis and the treatment of pathology, essential to the medical model, becomes less central as professional counselors focus on making choices that promote optimal functioning. This is a powerful concept, as positively impacting your wellness now can have a lasting impact on your remaining lifespan, as well as positively impact those in your life such as your family. Professional counselors have embraced an identity around wellness-centered developmental approaches. But, to understand how to apply such an identity in practice through your own life and truly understand your own wellness and generalize that learning to your work with clients, it is important to more clearly define wellness.

Wellness Definition and Models

Wellness "requires conscious choices to engage in healthful behaviors" and results in "helping you live your life more fully in all areas" (Myers & Sweeney, 2006, p. 3). Wellness "involves the integration of mind, body, and spirit" (Myers & Sweeney, 2006, p. 3). Two wellness models, the (a) Wheel of Wellness (WoW; Myers, Sweeney, & Witmer, 2000) and (b) the Indivisible Self Model (IS-Wel; Myers & Sweeney, 2005a), offer a framework for structuring interventions to enhance your own well-being, as well as the wellness of your future clients who may struggle from a variety of problem issues (Myers & Sweeney, 2005a; 2008).

The Wheel of Wellness. Using Adler's Individual Psychology as a foundation and incorporating the findings from empirical studies on health, longevity, and quality of life across disciplines, Myers and colleagues (2000) developed a theoretical model that integrates 17 specific areas into a holistic conceptualization of wellness. Five life tasks were found central to healthy human functioning: (a) Work, (b) Friendship, (c) Love, (d) Self, and (e) Spirituality, with the latter hypothesized to be the central aspect of wellness, incorporating both individualized components of meaning and purpose making as well as religious/spiritual beliefs (Myers & Sweeney, 2005b). As spirituality is core to many racial/ethnic groups across the world, Myers and Sweeney (2005b; 2008) argued that the Wheel of Wellness model is generalizable to many populations. Further, through its simple visual depiction (Figure 3.1), this model is useful for teaching about the holistic nature of wellness and working on specific aspects of wellness.

The Indivisible Self-Model of Wellness. The IS-Wel (Myers & Sweeney, 2005b) emerged from research on the wheel model and illustrated Alfred Adler's concept of holism, as the self cannot be divided. Supported through structural equation modeling, the IS-Wel components are highly interrelated and grouped into five second-order factors, or "selves." Changes in any one area of wellness results in changes to other areas, which may be for better (through positive lifestyle choices) or for worse (through maladaptive behavior). As an example, consider how working long hours consequently may challenge your ability to devote time to relationships with family and friends, and it may even be that those relationships were important to your

Figure 3.1   The Wheel of Wellness

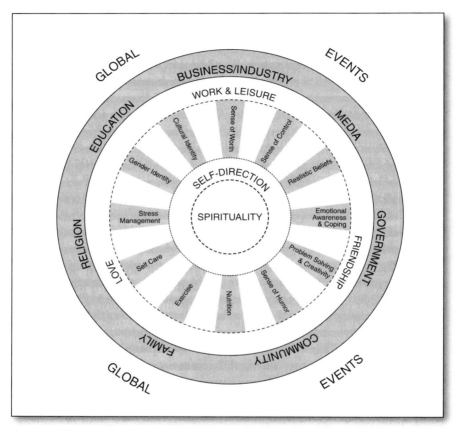

Source: Myers, J. E., Sweeney, T. J., & Witmer, J. M. (2000). The wheel of wellness counseling for wellness: A holistic model for treatment planning. *Journal of Counseling and Development, 78,* 251–266; reprinted with permission.

exercise habits. This integration is depicted in the model (Figure 3.2) through dashed lines between the Indivisible Self and the second-order selves.

Seventeen third-order factors, or wellness components, are nested within the second-order selves, and include those areas originally presented in the WoW. These include: (a) The Creative Self (i.e., Thinking, Emotions, Control, Work, Positive Humor), defined as one's intrapersonal and interpersonal characteristics that distinguishes oneself from others, (b) The Coping Self (i.e., Leisure, Stress Management, Self-Worth,

Figure 3.2   The Indivisible Self

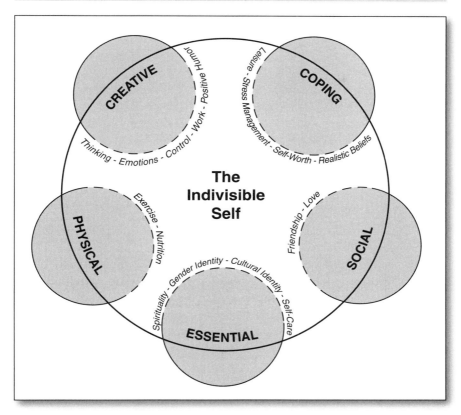

SOURCE: Myers, J. E., & Sweeney, T. J. (2004). The indivisible self: An evidence-based model of wellness. *Journal of Individual Psychology, 60,* 234–244; reprinted with permission.

and Realistic Beliefs) that includes the skills and resources that buffers one from life stressors and enhances quality of life, (c) The Social Self (i.e., Friendship and Love) that reflects experiences with and satisfaction from quality mutual relationships with others, (d) The Essential Self (i.e., Spirituality, Gender Identity, Cultural Identity, Self-Care) that involves meaning-making processes that result from experiences one has in relation to self, others, and life, and (e) The Physical Self (i.e., Exercise and Nutrition) that includes health promoting behaviors in the service of overall bodily well-being (Myers & Sweeney, 2004; 2008).

Myers and Sweeney (2008), through their summary of wellness research, found wellness was a critical factor in relation to career/job satisfaction, relational success, self-esteem/self-worth/mattering, and cultural identity development. Additionally, outcome studies showed the effectiveness of wellness approaches in improving stress management and college success (for an exhaustive list of these studies see Myers & Sweeney, 2008). This is, however the first time wellness has been used to conceptualize the needs of online students in managing family, work, and school.

Promoting Wellness of the Online Student

As with most counseling approaches, wellness approaches can be applied to work with individuals, groups, families, or communities. In this case, we are considering wellness approaches among counselor-trainees in an online counselor preparatory program. Within any of these interventions, a common four-step paradigm is usually applied. As described by Myers and Sweeney (2005b), wellness counseling involves (a) introduction of the wellness model, (b) assessment, (c) development and implementation of a personal wellness plan, and (d) evaluation and follow-up. Within all four steps, counselor-trainees are empowered to make lifestyle choices, whereby each choice leads toward greater wellness, more positive lifestyle choices, and positively impacting the rest of one's lifespan. The application of these four steps in practice is further elaborated below.

Introduction of the model. We become more committed to wellness when the concept is personalized; thus, wellness counseling often begins with exploring your own personal meaning of wellness and your self-assessed wellness strengths and growth areas. The visual depiction of a wellness model can facilitate this process, allowing you to see the components of your wellness, while discussing what those components look like and how they are interrelated in your own life. You are encouraged to provide examples to support the definitions and any modifications needed to personalize the factors to your own family, work, and school context.

Along with self-definition, self-direction is also central to wellness counseling; personal decision-making and choices are key concepts. You are encouraged to explore how your own lifestyle choices and deci-sions, in small and more significant ways, contribute to (or detract from) your overall wellness. Presenting wellness in each area as a continuum from low to high may also be helpful. While negative lifestyle choices may move you toward lower wellness, positive lifestyle choices create movement toward higher wellness. Again, positively impacting your wellness now can have a lasting impact on your remaining lifespan.

Assessment.   While discussing wellness components, self-assessment is needed to personalize the meaning of each factor. This can be accomplished formally, with a measure such as the 5F-Wel, or informally, through the exercise below. Given the large number of factors, we encourage you to select one or two areas that are most present and important to you. By focusing on too many factors, the potential for positive change declines significantly.

Assessing your schedule. You are encouraged to first take a moment to consider your current schedule. Create a chart of your daily schedule similar to the one provided at the beginning of the chapter. Now, further divide your schedule by adding in moments when you are attending to your family, responsibilities, self-care, and any other important aspects of your life. You may even want to label each moment with the corresponding self from the IS-Wel model. Identify areas of strength in your current wellness routine. Take a moment to review your wellness surrounding family, responsibilities, stress, and relationships. Are you stronger in one area than in another? Are there areas where your selves overlap?

Consider the example from our introduction.

Assessing your stress. Stress can manifest itself in varied ways among individuals. Indicators of stress in your schedule may not be as readily apparent as working long hours, but can be incremental and have a cumulative effect on your wellness. Assessing symptoms of stress can be done using a symptoms checklist or through an informal examination of your thoughts, feelings, and emotions throughout the day. As you were assessing your own schedule, did you notice a particular period of the day when you usually feel rushed, anxious, irritated, or overwhelmed? Do you notice somatic symptoms like stomach discomfort, racing heart, or tightening of your shoulder muscles when you consider these areas? Are there times during your day when you notice an increased sense of worry or that you cannot seem to concentrate? All of these symptoms could be a sign of stress. Take a moment to see if you can identify your actions, emotions, or surroundings prior to these stress indicators. Recognizing when these indictors of stress arise and what events precede stress reactions can help you be intentional about implementing positive lifestyle changes.

Table 3.2   Daily Schedule of Online Student Identifying Wellness Life Tasks

6 a.m.	Essential Self, Social Self, Physical Self	Wake up, read devotional, shower, get dressed, make breakfast, get kids ready for school
8 a.m.	Creative Self	Arrive at work
5 p.m.	Social Self	Leave work; pick up kids from day care/afterschool or head to other obligation
5 - 7 p.m.	Social Self, Essential Self, Physical Self	Take kids to extra curricular activities; commute home; gym; errands; church
7 p.m.	Physical Self	Dinner
7:30 - 9 p.m.	Creative Self, Social Self	Help kids with homework; chores; spend time with partner; connect with friends
10 p.m.	Essential or Coping Self	Put kids to bed (Don't forget their baths!)
10:30 p.m.	Creative Self	Reading for graduate courses, homework, and research for graduate assignments
Midnight	Essential Self	Go to bed (Wash, rinse, repeat.)

While stress and schedule typically emerge for online students, we encourage you to go through each of the five selves in Figure 3.2: (a) Creative Self, (b) Coping Self, (c) Social Self, (d) Essential Self, and (e) Physical Self. Typically, individuals immediately understand which wellness components are strengths, and which are weakness areas. There are many possible choices for enhancing wellness, and after a thoughtful selection of which area(s) you would like to focus on, you are encouraged to develop concrete goals to positively impact the area of wellness you have identified. When assessing your wellness, you are also taking stock of your own resources and supports, as well as needs to position you for success.

Developing and implementing a wellness plan. During wellness counseling, it is important to link any presenting issues or problems with wellness components, so that barriers to achieving goals can be identified and discussed. You may find maintaining a wellness plan easier if you choose to focus on increasing wellness in only one area at a time. Note that increasing positive contributions to your wellness in one area will positively impact other areas. We will guide you through this process while examining a few common growth areas for online students.

Wellness and family. Throughout the online graduate school journey, graduate students juggle many responsibilities and tasks. It is not uncommon for students to feel overwhelmed by family responsibilities as they juggle work, family, and school. On the opposite end of this spectrum, it is also not uncommon for students enrolled in online graduate programs to simultaneously feel disconnected to their family as family activity time is replaced with study time and responsibilities are traded off to accommodate the graduate student's schedule.

Whether beginning a journey to be a professional counselor through an online program or wrapping up the journey to be a professional counselor, family plays a valuable role in personal wellness. Through interactions and relationships with family, our Social Self can be positively and negatively enhanced. The Coping Self can be tied to family through our personal self-worth and leisure activities involving family. For graduate students who are married and/or have children, nutrition and exercise (Physical Self) may be closely tied to family rituals in the same way spirituality, cultural identity, and self-care (Essential Self) are part of our nuclear and extended family rituals. Family interactions often involve activation of our Creative Self through emotions, thoughts, control, work and positive humor. One's personal wellness is interconnected with family interactions and family wellness.

Developing ways to involve family in your personal wellness plan as well as ways to increase the wellness of the family unit can be a great way to stay connected throughout a busy graduate school career. Consider ways in which family strengthens the goals of accomplishing life balance and seeking optimal wellness. Does the family routine involve time to reconnect, share successes and stresses, and support each other? For most individuals, family connections are a valuable resource for stress management and reconnecting with our value systems (Coping and Essential Selves).

When assessing and developing personal wellness plans to manage responsibilities, stress, and relationships, family members can be an important resource to leverage in your plan and an accountability source to keep the plan on track. For instance, if one finds themself overwhelmed by home responsibilities (i.e., preparing meals, laundry, cleaning), family members can be brought in to share these tasks thus provide a form of stress management (Coping Self) by allowing time to focus on other areas of wellness such as work (Creative Self) or self care (Essential Self). Children can be assigned chores; spouses can develop a meal preparation schedule; and/or the family can schedule a weekly chore hour and compete to see who can finish the most in the allotted time—all of which are ways to involve family in your personal wellness plan. When the graduate student has an impending research project that requires focus, extended family members can be a valuable resource for childcare, assistance with other responsibilities, or even help proofreading for clarity. Involving family members in our wellness plans can also illuminate ways in which the family's overall wellness can be improved.

Managing responsibilities. Prior to enrolling in an online counselor education program, most individuals have a schedule determined by their life commitments to self, work, family, and community. Pursuing graduate studies online brings a new set of responsibilities. Students must find ways to fit homework, reading, research, and assignments into an already hectic schedule. How does one manage the addition of graduate schoolwork and the increase in time spent in the creative self?

Setting a realistic schedule. If your life is anything like the average person's, you return home from work tired and your evening does not work out the way you planned, even though you had the best of intentions. Setting a realistic schedule begins with being honest about your current responsibilities and barriers to successfully accomplishing your goals. To begin this exploration, create a list of recurring activities in the day or week that cannot be moved. Next, create a list of responsibilities that are flexible and can be moved to another day depending on added life and coursework responsibilities (some weeks will require more time online and with readings than others). Review your course syllabi and write down due dates for your assignments. Once these lists are created, step back and reflect on what strengths you have in your life that support accomplishing these responsibilities and what barriers might arise while trying to accomplish your tasks.

Once you have answered these questions, you can begin plotting your schedule. Start slowly by planning out one day with tasks that cannot be moved, add in flexible tasks, note any potential barriers to accomplishing this schedule, and try to plan ahead for what you could do when barriers arise. Take notes during the day regarding what was accomplished for the day and what barriers arose that you had not planned. It can be helpful to repeat this activity for a week to evaluate the stability of the week's schedule. Reflect on the week's accomplishments. Did you feel stressed at any point? Did you accomplish everything you scheduled? Are any resources available to help you accomplish your schedule?

Time management. Setting realistic expectations is only one cognitive key to managing responsibilities while time management is a skill that can help ensure responsibilities are completed efficiently and on time. While in graduate school, effective time management will help with goal accomplishment and time saved can incrementally add up to more time for increasing wellness in other areas. After setting a realistic schedule, carefully analyze the time spent on task, moments of inactivity, and any moments where accomplishing more than one goal at a time may be possible. Try to locate moments when your time is not being used efficiently. Managing time effectively involves re-envisioning life's responsibilities by being creative in how and when tasks are accomplished. How can one practice effective time management and still practice wellness?

Effective time management involves careful preparation. Keeping your school tools close by will help you utilize moments of inactivity and take advantage of multitasking moments. Whether you have your laptop or tablet with you or a textbook and a paper notebook, utilize those small moments of time to accomplish your school tasks. For instance, many parents take their children to after school activities (Social Self and Creative Self) and then wait while their child participates in this activity. As an online graduate student, this time spent waiting could also be utilized to read for class or begin composing papers (Creative Self). Some employers allow their employees an hour-long lunch break (Physical Self); this time can be spent completing class assignments (Creative Self). Additionally, incorporating the family by setting family homework time when everyone is working on homework together can be a great way to spend time with loved ones (Creative Self and Social Self), instill a value for education (Essential Self), and hold yourself accountable for getting work done. Using your resources wisely can help you better manage your time as a worker and student while keeping your stress level at a minimum.

Managing stress. The best stress management plans are enacted well before an individual becomes stressed. As an online graduate student, you can expect for life emergencies to happen while you are enrolled in your counseling program. Work related deadlines, family illness, Internet connection problems, or personal issues may arise that cause additional stress in your life. Earlier in this chapter, you may have identified additional barriers to accomplishing your work. Whether barriers are predictable or unpredictable, undoubtedly, anyone can still feel stressed when a well-planned schedule is interrupted.

To combat stressors, consider the strengths in your life and how they might be leveraged on your stress management plan to increase overall wellness. Family and friends can be strengths to help reduce stress or even resources to help share the workload when our schedule becomes tightened. Students may find that taking a mental break (Essential Self) by spending time with their family (Social Self) can help refocus efforts on assignments (Creative Self). Reviewing your time management plan can help regain a sense of control over the day or scheduling time buffers by intentionally scheduling extra study time during your week to be used when needed (Creative Self). Choosing one activity that you enjoy to be incorporated in your weekly schedule as a point of self-care (Essential Self) can also provide an effective stress management (Shallcross, 2011).

Finally setting realistic expectations about how much work can be accomplished can help manage stress reactions (Coping Self). Realistic expectations could mean giving yourself permission to earn a grade of B on an assignment to help relieve stressors. Knowing how much work you can truthfully complete and setting this as an expectation versus trying to complete a week's worth of readings and assignments in one night can also be an effective form of stress management. Keep in mind that your professors are invested in your growth as a professional counselor as well. Reach out to your professors when life stressors arise and inquire about possible extensions if allowed. These strategies can help reduce stress through the utilization of strengths and help get a well-planned wellness routine back on track.

Managing relationships. Establishing relationships is a cornerstone stage in the counseling process (Hackney & Cormier, 2013), and this skill is transferrable to our daily lives. As discussed previously, our Social Self encompasses our experiences with this network of supportive friendship and love (Myers & Sweeney, 2004; 2008). Prior to entering graduate studies, the ability to build and maintain relationships could help provide a network of friends, family, and colleagues who are reciprocally supportive. This network can be a strength during graduate studies by providing support, active listening, and as an accountability check for an established wellness plan. Managing these relationships often requires work on the part of both parties, which can add stress to a graduate student's complicated life. We will examine ways to maintain these relationships and maintain personal wellness. Our focus will be on relationships outside of our immediate family as a review of wellness in the context of family has already been explored.

Using the IS-Wel as the foundation of our exploration, consider ways that your relationships currently contribute to your wellness. Spending time with close friends can be a stress management technique that incorporates the Social, Creative, Coping, and Essential Selves. Walking with others and conversing about the trials and triumphs of the day can incorporate wellness in the Physical, Social, Creative, and Coping Selves. Providing a listening ear to a friend in crisis may be a daily or weekly occurrence for you and be part of your identity (Essential Self and Coping Self).

When you begin graduate school, you may find that your time for these activities becomes limited due to increased time spent in the creative self due to your graduate schoolwork. To successfully manage these relationships, examining the impact of these relationships on your wellness should be established. Does the time spent energize you, or does it feel more like work? If you notice any of the stress indictors present before, during, or after interactions with an individual, this may be an indicator that this relationship is stress producing. Is there a way to change this relationship so that it is a source of strength and wellness instead?

Managing relationships as a graduate student enrolled in a counseling program can be difficult. You may find yourself using the skills from your counseling courses in interactions with friends. Establishing boundaries around these relationships can not only be a key to your personal wellness, but is also ethically important to avoid dual relationships (American Counseling Association, 2014). As professional counselors, we cannot ethically provide counseling to our friends or family; however, we must take the lead in communication and advocacy around avoiding these dual relationships. Being transparent with important individuals in our life about the type of relationship we can have and monitoring when our helpful interactions are nonreciprocal and unbalanced can help regulate stress. Being comfortable with and knowing when to respectfully say no to event invitations or requests for favors from close friends can be an important skill used in our self-care practice. Most importantly, when you find a close relationship does not contribute to your wellness, take a moment to reflect on the IS-Wel model to consider whether or not this relationship can be reestablished in a way that promotes optimal wellness.

Evaluation and follow-up. As is true of any behaviorally oriented plan for change, optimizing wellness is a process that includes continual evaluation of progress, examination of choices, discussion of barriers, and assessment of commitment. The goal is to help yourself (and your future clients) learn to focus on strengths rather than limitations. Over time, as you (and your clients) grow and change, goals will similarly evolve. Using a psycho-educational model to teach wellness components has allowed you to see how change in one area contributes to changes in others, and has helped you review and internalize the components of holistic wellness. This process can lead to *self-perpetuating growth*, whereby your wellness choices lead to positive lifestyle changes that result in more positive choices. In order to clarify further, three student experiences are provided that model wellness planning or lack of planning.

Student Experiences

The following case studies were chosen to demonstrate the application of wellness approaches in three individual students in one online training program. Emphasis is placed on the areas of wellness that may have been compromised, and on particular wellness issues that could arise for online graduate counseling students. For all cases, the authors provide details or insight from their experiences with similar cases and in facilitating wellness among counselor-trainees. The reader is charged with using these examples as strategies for case conceptualization from a wellness-oriented framework, to promote personal growth and development and optimize wellness in one's own life.

The Case of Jesse: Elementary School Teacher

Jesse is an elementary school teacher in her mid-30s who is entering her first semester in an online counseling program to pursue her dream of being a school counselor. She has been married for 8 years and has two children, one 6 years old and one 3 years old. Prior to entering graduate school, Jesse's overall wellness would be considered well-balanced. Her Coping, Physical, and Social Selves are addressed by her routines with her family and friends that include walking with her family when she gets home, cooking dinner for her family, and meeting once a month with other neighborhood moms for a "Moms' Night Out." Jesse would say her Creative Self thrives at work with her students and when she is with her children. Along with her monthly moms' meeting, Jesse's Essential Self is fulfilled with weekly church attendance.

Three weeks into her graduate program, Jesse's life has changed. Her spouse reports that she has been irritable and has snapped at the children twice in the past week. Jesse has her first major assignment due at the end of the week, and she has fallen behind on her readings. To catch up, she declined to attend this month's mom's night and she has had trouble fitting in her daily walk with her family.

In Jesse's Introduction to Counseling class, her instructor teaches about the Wheel of Wellness and the Indivisible Self. Jesse evaluates her own schedule and wellness routines to see where she may incorporate some of the ideas from class. Immediately she notices that her Coping Self has been neglected as she is no longer walking nightly with her family and she missed her monthly night with friends. In turn, this has affected her Creative Self as she is having a hard time concentrating on her work and controlling her emotions with her family. She is also worried about the effect this has had on her Physical Self.

Jesse's instructor asks that each member of the class identify a wellness area that they might be able to increase. Jesse chooses to focus on her Coping Self, particularly stress management through better time management. Her goal for the week is to increase her time management by multitasking more. Jesse makes an effort every day to bring her tablet with her so she has instant access to her courses and her ebooks. While she is waiting for her children as they participate in after school activities, Jesse reads. When she is at the doctor's office, she works on her courses. She takes any free moment she finds to jot down thoughts about assignments and to do her course readings.

(Continued)

(Continued)

After a week of this routine, Jesse has noticed a change in her schedule. The extra moments of reading have added up in her daily schedule, and Jesse was able to incorporate her family walks back into her schedule. Not only has this impacted her Physical Self, but she has also noticed an improvement in her Social and Creative Selves. Jesse is feeling emotionally positive again and no longer snaps at her family members. By targeting one area of wellness (Coping Self), Jesse has impacted other areas of wellness (Physical Self, Social Self, Creative Self, and Essential Self) therefore improving her overall wellness.

The Case of Alex: Internship Issues

Alex is single, in his mid-20s, and works one full-time and one part-time job. He has completed most of his required courses in an online clinical mental health counseling program. Prior to and during graduate school, Alex would report his overall wellness to be "okay." Working two jobs to help pay off student loan debt coupled with his graduate studies has increased the amount of time spent in his Creative Self. To counterbalance this, Alex goes to the gym for an hour each morning before work to relieve stress (Physical Self, Essential Self, and Coping Self), and he spends at least 1 night a week with friends or family (Social Self).

Alex has felt stressed during his online counseling program but has never felt the level of stress he felt during his first week of internship. Alex's program requires that he earn at least 4 hours per day for 5 days a week throughout the semester in order to be certain he will meet the minimum internship hours required. Alex had already arranged to only work at his part-time job on the weekends but says he still feels crunched with full-time work, internship, and supervision for his internship course. Alex continues to go to the gym every morning and feels he cannot say no to his friends when they invite him to go out after working his part-time job.

By the sixth week of internship, Alex's wellness has slipped on the back burner. He has fallen behind on his work for his internship course (Creative Self), he is overwhelmed at work (Coping Self), and has isolated himself from colleagues (Social Self), and he has cut his daily trips to the gym (Physical Self, Essential Self). He has noticed an increase in somatic symptoms such as tightness in his muscles and chest, racing heartbeat, and exhaustion. By Week 7 of his internship, Alex has caught a virus and can barely get out of bed. After conversations with his advisor, Alex withdraws from internship to allow himself time to heal and work on a wellness plan to take him through internship in a future semester.

The Case of Andrea: Family Emergency

Andrea works full-time at a local lawyer's office. She is a single mother in her late 30s pursuing her clinical mental health counseling degree. Andrea is in her fifth course in the program and feels she has adapted her wellness routine to her graduate course work and her daughter's busy after school schedule. She often completes readings and assignments for her graduate classes at a local coffee shop while her daughter is participating in after-school activities (Creative and Coping Self). She and her daughter create meal plans and grocery shop on Sundays (Social, Essential, and Coping Self) so that they can cook together during the week (Social Self). Andrea completes most of her schoolwork while her daughter is also doing homework, but she sets the boundary to always go to bed by 11 pm (Coping and Essential Self).

Andrea's semester is progressing as she planned when she receives a call from her sister regarding their mother who has fallen ill. Andrea was asked to check in on her mom since she lives an hour from the hospital and her sister lives four hours away. The prognosis on her mother is not hopeful, so Andrea wants to be sure to spend as much time with her mom as possible.

For the next week, Andrea has been spending most of her time after work at the hospital or traveling to and from. Andrea has seen a reduction in wellness in her Coping, Social, and Physical Selves due to her daughter staying with friends and the absence of home cooked meals. Andrea feels stressed to complete her schoolwork on time, and she has a hard time concentrating on tasks related to work or school (Creative Self).

Andrea's mother passes after only a week in the hospital. Grief stricken and hoping to get back on track with her schoolwork, Andrea logs on to finish a course assignment only to realize she does not have enough time to put enough work into her assignment to earn an A. She panics. Before she realizes what has happened, Andrea has e-mailed her professor to say that this assignment is too hard and she wants to quit.

Andrea's professor is aware of the stress Andrea is under and schedules a phone meeting with her. Together, Andrea and her instructor discuss Andrea's wellness and how they can develop a plan to help her get back on track. Andrea chooses to focus on her Social Self by allowing herself to spend more time with her daughter. Andrea's professor agrees to give her an extension on her assignment so that Andrea may spend more time with her family and to help plan the funeral. Through this discussion, Andrea realizes she has been

(Continued)

(Continued)

over working to earn an A and that she can afford to earn a B on the upcoming assignment. Together Andrea and her professor work to complete a schedule of deadlines for Andrea to follow for the duration of the course and Andrea agrees to communicate once a week with her professor regarding her plan. Andrea immediately notices a difference in her stress level as a result of setting realistic expectations for her schoolwork and spending more time with her family.

Summary

This chapter focused primarily on the wellness of the online student. Counselor wellness is imperative if we are to be able to foster wellness in clients. Two wellness models were described, along with strategies for integrating wellness approaches through case studies. Specifically, we discussed ways in which counselors can assess their own wellness strength and growth areas, positively impacting one's own ability to balance family, work, and school, as well as evaluate outcomes. This is an intentional first step in enabling online counseling students to move in the direction of fostering wellness-centered treatment plans with their clients.

Additional Resources and Readings

8 ways to take control of your time. (n.d.). Bigfuture by *The College Board*. Retrieved from https://bigfuture.collegeboard.org/get-started/inside-the-classroom/8-ways-to-take-control-of-your-time

Hattie, J. A., Myers, J. E., & Sweeney, T. J. (2004). A factor structure of wellness: Theory, assessment, analysis, and practice. *Journal of Counseling & Development*, *82*(3), 354–364.

Ivey, A. E., Ivey, M. B., Myers, J. E., & Sweeney, T. J. (2005). *Developmental counseling and therapy: Promoting wellness over the lifespan*. New York, NY: Houghton-Mifflin/Lahaska.

Myers, J. E., & Sweeney, T. J. (Eds.). (2005). *Counseling for wellness: Theory, research, & practice*. Alexandria, VA: American Counseling Association.

Myers, J. E., Sweeney, T. J., & Witmer, J. M. (2000). Counseling for wellness: A holistic model for treatment planning. *Journal of Counseling and Development*, *78*(3), 251–266.

Shallcross, L. (2011). Taking care of yourself as a counselor. *Counseling Today.* Retrieved from http://ct.counseling.org/2011/01/taking-care-of-yourself-as-a-counselor/

Shannonhouse, L., Myers, J., Barden, S., Clark, P., Weimann, R., Forti, A., Porter, M. (2014). Finding your new normal: Outcomes of a wellness-oriented psycho-educational support group for cancer survivors. *Journal for Specialists in Group Work, 39*(1), 3–29.

About the Authors

Melissa Wheeler, PhD, NCC, ACS, is a distance clinical professor in the Department of Counseling and Special Populations at Lamar University in Beaumont, Texas. She has experience teaching a variety of online graduate level courses including introductory courses for new graduate students. Dr. Wheeler is excited to share her experiences helping students transition to the world of graduate school, while maintaining balance in their lives. Her research interests include supervision of counselors-in-training and the experiences of first-generation college students. Specifically, Dr. Wheeler is interested in research and strategies to support first-generation college students in the transition from high school to college as well as teaching counselors to best support these students throughout the career choice process. She has presented her work at state, regional, and national conferences to increase awareness around the experiences of first-generation college students.

Laura Shannonhouse, PhD, NCC, LPC, is an assistant professor at Georgia State University. Her research interests focus on multicultural training in counseling, with an emphasis on community engagement, crisis intervention and disaster response, aging, and development across the lifespan. Her research and clinical work have included working with marginalized populations in a variety of contexts both domestically (e.g., crisis center, cancer center, college counseling center, hospital, etc.) and internationally (e.g., illness-related trauma counseling in South Africa, grief work in day care center fire disaster in Mexico, disaster response in post-Katrina New Orleans, and Haitian refugees post-earthquake, etc.). Dr. Shannonhouse has disseminated her work through peer-reviewed publications and presentations at local, national, and international conferences, and received research and best practice grants from the Association for Counselor Educators and Supervisors (ACES), Southern

Association for Counselor Educators and Supervisors (SACES), and Chi Sigma Iota International. Dr. Shannonhouse is a Licensed Professional Counselor (LPC) in the State of North Carolina, a Nationally Certified Counselor (NCC), and an Applied Suicide Intervention Skills Trainer (ASIST).

References

American Counseling Association. (2014). *ACA Code of Ethics*. Alexandria, VA: American Counseling Association. Retrieved from http://www.counseling .org/resources/aca-code-of-ethics.pdf

Chi Sigma Iota. (n.d.). What is a professional counselor? Greensboro, NC: Author. Retrieved from http://www.csi-net.org/?page=Professional_Counsel

Hackney, H. L., & Cormier, S. (2013). *The professional counselor: A process guide to helping* (7th ed.). Upper Saddle River, NJ: Pearson.

Myers, J. E. (1992). Wellness, prevention, development: The cornerstones of the profession. *Journal of Counseling and Development, 71*(2), 136–139.

Myers, J. E., & Sweeney, T. J. (2004). The indivisible self: An evidence-based model of wellness. *Journal of Individual Psychology, 60*, 234–244.

Myers, J. E., & Sweeney, T. J. (2005a). *The five factor wellness inventory*. Palo Alto, CA: Mindgarden.

Myers, J. E., & Sweeney, T. J. (Eds.). (2005b). *Wellness in counseling: Theory, research, and practice*. Alexandria, VA: American Counseling Association.

Myers, J. E., & Sweeney, T. J. (2006). Counseling for wellness: Theory, research, and practice. Response to Charyton. Retrieved from: http://libres.uncg.edu/ir/ uncg/f/J_Myers_Counseling_2006.pdf

Myers, J. E., & Sweeney, T. J. (2008). Wellness counseling: The evidence base for practice. *Journal of Counseling & Development, 86*, 482–493.

Myers, J. E., Sweeney, T. J., & Witmer, J. M. (2000). The wheel of wellness counseling for wellness: A holistic model for treatment planning. *Journal of Counseling and Development, 78*, 251–266.

Remley, T. (1991, August). On being different, *Guidepost*, p. 3.

Shallcross, L. (2011, January 17). Taking care of yourself as a counselor. *Counseling Today*. Retrieved from http://ct.counseling.org/2011/01/taking-care-of-yourself- as-a-counselor

4

Understanding the Quality of Your Online Program

Amy L. McLeod

Chapter Overview

This chapter will provide you with some ways to understand and evaluate the quality of your online program. With all of the online options available to you, knowing how to evaluate the caliber of the program you have selected is crucial. You will need to be able to discuss program quality when you are ready to enter the job market with your degree in hand. Specifically, this chapter will address some of the essential variables for students that impact program quality and suitability. The chapter begins with a discussion about the role of a student as an educational consumer and then transitions to the various factors that may impact the decision to enroll in a counselor education program. Next, program-specific factors including graduation and retention rates, faculty experience, and degree requirements are explored. Lastly, formal measures of quality in counselor education are presented.

Learning Outcomes

After reading this chapter, students will be able to

1. Identify and describe their personal and lifestyle factors, educational/academic needs and goals, and career aspirations and describe how these variables relate to the quality of an online counselor education program

2. Describe program-specific indicators of quality including retention data, faculty experience and engagement in professional activities, and degree requirements

3. Explain the purpose of accreditation and understand the differences between university-wide and programmatic accreditation. In addition, students will be able to describe the benefits of accreditation

4. Understand various methods for formally assessing online program quality, including the Online Learning Consortium (OLC) Program scorecard and the Quality Matters rubric

Introduction

Welcome to online education! You have either selected or are in the process of selecting the counseling program that is the best fit for you. As an informed consumer, it is important for you to understand the quality of a counseling program and to be able to articulate that quality when you are ready to search for jobs in the counseling profession. You want to be able to answer the questions that may arise from others who are less familiar with online programs than you are. All of these elements are explored here so that current students have a full understanding of the quality of their existing program and so that prospective students may make informed decisions.

The Quality Counselor Education Program

Selecting a counselor education program is a personal process. There are many quality counselor education programs available, and selecting the right program involves careful consideration of personal and lifestyle factors; educational or academic goals and needs; and career aspirations (Lei & Chuang, 2010). Many counselor education programs have similar courses and degree requirements. Thus, some of the factors listed above may play more of a role in your decision than the actual program of study.

Personal and Lifestyle Factors

Logistical factors. Programs offer different delivery models for counselor training. Within the realm of online counselor education, there is a wide variety of online formats, ranging from fully online courses and programs to courses and programs that blend online and on-ground classroom experiences. Identifying your comfort level with technology and online communication, your ability to travel to a physical campus, and personal time constraints will allow you to select a program that fits your needs. Online counselor education programs are often a choice for students because they offer the advantage of a flexible schedule and remove the constraints of a more traditional, fully on-ground program. An online program can allow you the ability to pursue a graduate education that may have otherwise been impossible due to multiple life demands, including family and work responsibilities. If you choose to attend an online counselor education program that also involves time on a physical campus, the geographic location of the campus is an important factor to consider. Some students choose to travel from another state to attend weekend on-ground classes or on-campus residencies, while other students select a physical campus that is close to their home. If commuting to a physical campus, the cost of travel and hotel accommodations should be factored into your educational budget.

If you have already enrolled in a program, it is important to understand the different delivery models highlighted and to be able to articulate your rationale for selecting the model of your university. For example, you may have investigated various programs and determined that they all offered the same 60-credit hour degree in clinical mental health counseling. However, because you work full time and have a family, the ability to attend classes on-campus would have been a hardship. As a result, you selected a program that had the same academic requirements of other universities but offered you the ability to complete most of your coursework in an asynchronous fashion.

Cultural factors. The cultural diversity of the faculty and student body is another important personal factor for consideration. The American Counseling Association (ACA) *Code of Ethics* (2014) calls for counselor education programs to actively recruit and retain a diverse body of faculty and students. In addition to being comprised of a diverse group of people, the counseling program should also demonstrate a commitment to multiculturalism through actively valuing diverse worldviews and creating a safe and encouraging learning environment for all students to develop as counselors (ACA, 2014). While multiculturalism is a central value in the counseling profession, individual counselor education programs may vary in the degree to which they achieve the goals set forth by the profession (Shin, 2008).

Social factors. Social considerations are personal variables that are salient for many students. Some students choose a graduate program because they have friends, family members, or coworkers who also attend the program (Poock & Love, 2001). Having existing social contacts can certainly ease the transition into the counselor education program. However, new connections with peers and faculty can also provide a sense of community and support. In many online counselor education programs, students are geographically dispersed but come together for the common purpose of developing as counselors. Counseling programs can foster student connections through opportunities to participate in student organizations, such as Chi Sigma Iota Counseling Academic and Professional Honor Society International (CSI). Over 90,000 members strong, CSI is dedicated to advancing scholarship, research, professionalism, leadership, advocacy, and excellence in the counseling profession (Chi Sigma Iota, 2014).

There are many other student organizations that may be offered in addition to CSI. If a counselor education program does not offer a student organization that is of particular interest to you, you might consider approaching a faculty member for assistance in establishing a chapter of the student organization. Investigating the various opportunities for student organizations offered by each counselor education program can assist you in beginning to build a professional network in counseling. In many cases, it will be more important for you to engage in these types of activities in an online environment than in a traditional one. Because much of the learning in an online environment is asynchronous, you will have to work to develop your peer network and faculty relationships. It will be important for you to take advantage of opportunities for student leadership and social interaction in order to form the relationships necessary for an ongoing professional network.

Educational and Academic Needs and Goals

Online counseling programs are designed to be flexible and accommodating to students needs; however, there is no such thing as a "one-size-fits-all" program. When evaluating whether or not a particular program is a fit, prospective students may wish to evaluate the following educational and academic variables: program and class size, campus resources, course formats, degree requirements, and opportunities to become involved in teaching or research assistantships.

Program and class size. With regard to student numbers, overall size of the counseling program and average class size are important considerations. Program size does not necessarily impact program quality, as long as adequate resources are available. For example, consider how the faculty to student ratio may impact the educational experience that a program is able to offer. A program that has one full-time faculty member for every 10 students is able to offer increased amounts of faculty access and interaction in comparison to a program that has one full-time faculty member for every 20 students. Also keep in mind that overall program size is not necessarily related to the number of students in each class. Some programs that have a very large overall student population are also able to offer small classes, providing a more personalized feel.

Campus resources. Campus resources are another factor for consideration. Some online counselor education programs also involve some time on a physical campus. In these types of programs, you may wish to evaluate the technological resources available in classrooms (e.g., wireless Internet capabilities, interactive whiteboards, projectors), campus computer labs, the library, and student study areas. Technological support services are also important to success in an online counselor education program. In other words, is there someone available to help you when you have an assignment due and you cannot log in to the online classroom platform? Be sure to locate these types of resources at the onset of your program and to bookmark them in your Internet browser or develop a file of key contact information. For fully online counselor education programs, these types of resources may only be available online. Still, you should inquire about technological support services, technological requirements, and computer skills required to succeed in the online learning environment. You should also explore the availability of training opportunities that focus on how to effectively utilize the online learning environment. In many cases, universities provide an orientation to the online learning process and you should participate fully in this initial session.

Course format. Course format can be a critical component in student success, and it is important for you to understand the different types of delivery systems that are available. As mentioned previously, online counselor education programs are designed for flexibility and to meet the needs of a wide range of students, many of whom have busy schedules due to working full or part time and multiple life demands. Course formats generally fall into one of three categories: fully online courses; blended or hybrid courses that blend on-campus and online components; and fully on-campus courses.

Fully online courses meet all instructional contact requirements through an online educational platform. Fully online courses may have synchronous and asynchronous requirements. Synchronous learning involves students and faculty participating in an educational activity at the same time. For example, your program may use a live video conference and instant messaging to facilitate online synchronous engagement. Asynchronous learning, by contrast, allows students and the instructor to complete educational activities at a time of their choosing. Asynchronous learning may be one of the primary reasons that you selected an online program. Examples of asynchronous activities in an online educational platform include threaded discussion boards, blogs, and e-mail. In these cases, although you are engaging faculty members and peers, it is not in real time. You can post something to a discussion board and a peer may respond immediately because he or she is online at the same time or may respond a day later. The idea of asynchronous learning is that the classroom is operating on a continuous basis and the learning community is constantly evolving. It is important to note that a counselor education program may offer all of the courses required for a degree online, yet still require some face-to-face interaction at a designated physical location. This face-to-face engagement is often in the form of a residency. During the residency, students travel to a physical location for an intensive week-long educational session (we cover residencies in detail in Chapter 11). A counselor education program may require multiple residency weeks during the completion of the degree requirements. Students are typically responsible for transportation, food, and lodging costs associated with the residency. Be sure to investigate any residency requirements for your institution and prepare well ahead of time for the costs and time commitments.

Blended or hybrid online courses meet instructional contact requirements through a combination of online educational activities and on-campus activities. For example, a class may meet on-campus one night per week for 3–4 hours and in addition have weekly online assignments. Another popular blended or hybrid course format allows students to come to campus for intensive classroom experiences on the weekends, while participating in online activities each week of the course. The blended or hybrid course format is appealing to many students because it allows for flexibility and provides students with the opportunity to interact face-to-face with faculty and peers.

The most traditional course format is a fully on-campus course. Fully on-campus courses meet all instructional contact requirements through face-to-face interaction in a physical classroom. Participation in an online educational platform is typically not required in a fully on-campus course. While fully on-campus courses offer the least flexibility in terms of scheduling, they may be favored by students who are less comfortable with technology or who strongly value face-to-face interaction. In traditional course delivery, the group learning process or learning community typically only meets during the scheduled course time. Time between campus meetings is typically an individual process.

Teaching or research assistantship opportunities. Some counseling programs may offer students the opportunity to serve as a teaching assistant in a course. Typically, you are not able to be a teaching assistant at the educational level at which you are currently enrolled. So a master's level student could be a teaching assistant for an undergraduate course, but not for a master's level or doctoral level course. This distinction helps to prevent dual relationships within the learning community. For doctoral students, opportunities to serve as teaching assistants in master's level or undergraduate level courses provide invaluable mentoring opportunities that aid in development as a counselor educator. Because doctoral students do not take courses with master's or undergraduate students, the teaching assistant role is appropriate. Research assistantships allow master's and doctoral level students to collaborate with faculty on designing and implementing research projects. Students may have the opportunity to develop their research skills by assisting with instrument development, data collection, data analysis, or any other part of the research process. Teaching and research assistantships typically provide students with a partial or full tuition waiver and/or a stipend that offsets educational expenses. Because pursuing a graduate degree is an expensive endeavor, it could be important to investigate the potential for an assistantship in your program. Each program should have assistantships or other resources that may help in deferring the cost of education. However, the number of resources may vary from institution to institution.

Career Aspirations

Counseling program options. Regardless of whether you are enrolled in a graduate program or investigating the possibility, you want to be sure that your degree choice matches your career aspirations. For example, there are many different specialty areas within the counseling profession. The Council for Accreditation of Counseling and Related Educational Programs (CACREP—more on this organization later in the chapter) accredits the following types of master's level counseling programs: addiction counseling; career counseling; clinical mental health counseling; marriage, couple, and family counseling; school counseling; and student affairs and college counseling. At the doctoral level, CACREP accredits Counselor Education and Supervision programs (CACREP, 2009). Some of these degrees, like the clinical mental health counseling degree, offer a fairly general type of counseling training that could equip you to work in many settings with a diverse range of client populations. CACREP is the primary accrediting body for the counseling profession, and many licensure boards are including CACREP or CACREP-equivalent degree requirements in licensure laws. It is important to know your state laws and how your program fits within that legal framework. Accreditation is a lengthy process and programs may be at various stages. It is important to know if your program is accredited, pursuing accreditation, planning for accreditation, or deciding to remain independent of CACREP. Program accreditation doesn't relate directly to program quality but likely has implication for your ability to become licensed.

While accreditation is an important consideration, sometimes a degree targeted toward a specific counseling setting or specific client population might make it easier for you to find employment after graduation. For example, if you have determined that you are passionate about working with children or adolescents in an educational setting, then a degree in school counseling would probably be the most logical choice. In fact, some states require a school counseling degree, rather than other types of counseling degrees, to work as a school counselor in the public school system (American School Counselor Association, 2014). Keep in mind that counselor certification and licensure laws vary widely by state. Information regarding the number of credit hours required for licensure as well as specific course requirements can be obtained through state associations for licensed counselors. It is important for you to be very familiar with state laws and rules. You are ultimately responsible for making choices about degree programs. Pursuing a clinical degree and then discovering that you are not eligible for a position as a school counselor would be disheartening. Avoid this scenario and complete a thorough investigation of your counseling specialization and the scope of practice available upon graduation. Check with your state of residence for the most accurate information.

Academic reputation. The academic reputation of the counseling program you graduate from can impact your ability to gain acceptance into a doctoral program and/or find employment. Formal measures of academic rank are available through U.S. News and World report. However, these types of rankings may not be your best guides for decision making. National ranking like these are often tied to criteria that will not have a direct impact on the quality of your training. You can gain valuable insight into a counseling program's academic reputation in a more informal way by contacting counseling agencies in the community. For example, do local agencies routinely hire graduates of the online counselor education program you are considering? Do agencies provide practicum and internship opportunities for students from the counseling program of interest? Finding out how the network of professionals in your community perceives the academic rigor of the online counseling program can be far more important than national rankings in terms of preparing you to achieve your career aspirations.

In sum, a critical aspect of understanding the quality of an online counselor education program is determining if the program fits your individualized needs. No matter how rigorous and respected a program may be, if it does not meet your personal, academic, and career needs, then it is not the right program for you. Determining if a program meets your needs is one step in identifying a quality online counselor education program. Next, we will consider program specific indicators of quality.

Program-Specific Indicators of Quality

Retention and graduation rates. During the admissions process and throughout your graduate career, you may hear the terms *student retention rate, transfer rate,* and *graduation rate.* Student retention rate refers to the percentage of first-time students enrolled in a program who continue in that program the following academic year (Federal Student Aid, 2014). For example, if you were admitted to a master's level program in Clinical

Mental Health Counseling in the Spring semester of this year and were still enrolled in the program the following Spring semester, you would be counted toward the program's retention rate. Graduation rate refers to the percentage of first time students in a program who successfully complete all degree requirements within 150% of the published length of time for degree completion (Federal Student Aid, 2014). If the published duration of a doctoral program in Counselor Education and Supervision is 5 years, then the graduation rate would be calculated as the number of students who graduated within a 7.5-year time frame. This information provides you with a realistic estimate of your time to degree and the number of peers who follow the program of study to completion. Retention rates can be a good indicator of faculty involvement, resources, quality of instruction, and other variables that are important to graduate student success.

Using retention data to evaluate program quality. Counseling programs collect data on student retention rates, transfer rates, and graduation rates for program evaluation purposes and to comply with federal financial aid requirements (Federal Student Aid, 2014). These statistics can also provide prospective students with information about program quality. Low retention and graduate rates should raise a red flag about the merit of a counseling program. For example, a large majority of students pay for online counselor education programs with the assistance of student loan funding (National Conference of State Legislatures, 2013). If a student leaves the counseling program prior to the successful completion of graduation requirements, then the student has potentially incurred a large amount of educational debt and does not have a graduate degree. Without a counseling degree, the former student may have difficulty finding employment as a professional counselor and may also have difficulty repaying student loan debt (National Conference of State Legislatures, 2013). In addition to financial stressors, leaving a graduate program prior to degree completion can have serious emotional consequences for students. Students who leave graduate level programs may feel deep disappointment and shame as they struggle to restructure their lives and the professional expectations they held for themselves (Lovitts, 2001). Prospective students are advised to share their needs and expectations for the counseling program with faculty prior to admission to ensure expectations align with reality (Hoskins & Goldberg, 2005). If you are a current student, then we recommend evaluating your degree plan, speaking with a faculty advisor, and doing some self-reflection about your career goals.

Efforts to improve student retention. High-quality counselor education programs are aware of the stressors and barriers to graduation that students may experience and make conscious efforts to reduce these obstacles to student success. For example, nontraditional students may struggle to balance multiple life roles and demands with educational requirements (Carney-Crompton, & Tan, 2002). Of course, graduate studies have significant life implications for all students. As a graduate student, you have to take a realistic inventory of your life responsibilities and determine how graduate studies fit within that framework. In some cases, you may have to decide to let go of or temporarily suspend some activities that are nonessential. Faculty members often can help to make the process more palatable and can increase the retention of nontraditional students by facilitating support groups that promote peer connections, providing encouragement, and normalizing the difficulty of returning to school to purse a graduate degree (Gary, Kling, & Dodd, 2004). Additionally, psychoeducational groups on time management, study skills, academic writing, the use of technology in counselor education, and conflict resolution may also improve the persistence toward degree completion of nontraditional learners (Gary et al., 2004). Counselor education programs may offer online forums for these support and psychoeducational groups in order to accommodate the busy schedules of adult learners. If your program offers these types of resources, it is important to take advantage of them and maximize your potential for success. Unused available resources are too frequently a factor in student attrition.

Special efforts to improve the retention of racial and ethnic minority students are indicators of quality for online counselor education programs. It is important to note that students who are members of a cultural minority group are at increased risk of withdrawal before degree completion. Minority students often lack a feeling of connection to faculty and current students, particularly in educational institutions that are predominately White. These students may perceive the University environment as nonwelcoming or hostile and may experience prejudice and discrimination (Shin, 2008). While programs may make efforts to bridge gaps in cultural diversity, it is also important for you to consider how you can create a more inclusive environment. We encourage all students to facilitate a healthy respect for diversity and to advocate for those who may not have a clear voice.

Feelings of connection to the counseling program are related to persistence toward degree completion (Hoskins & Goldberg, 2005).

Counselor education departments comprised of a diverse group of faculty members can increase the comfort level of minority students (Rogers & Molina, 2006; Shin, 2008). Faculty participation in campus activities that promote diversity and multiculturalism can also facilitate minority student connection (Shin, 2008). In counselor education programs dedicated to the retention of racial and ethnic minority students, faculty make active outreach efforts. For example, faculty members may invite minority students to participate in social justice activities and research (Rogers & Molina, 2006), or provide formal and informal mentoring opportunities (Shin, 2008). Beyond academic opportunities, facilitating social engagement is also necessary to retain a diverse student population. Counseling faculty may provide opportunities for students to connect through lunch and learn workshops, potluck dinners, and inclusive planned social gatherings at conferences (Hoskins & Goldberg, 2005). Finally, retention efforts may involve collaboration with natural support systems for minority students, including historically Black colleges and universities (HBCU's), minority student organizations, and religious organizations (Gary et al., 2004; Rogers & Molina, 2006). While faculty members can make these efforts, it is also important for you to ask for the support you need. If a social group is important, consider asking a faculty member to help you facilitate one. Review faculty member research interests and ask to participate in a particular project. Look at campus-based resources and think about how you can create the same types of opportunities online.

Quality counselor education programs are committed to retaining the students who enter the program. Student support services should be evident for all counselors in training, particularly nontraditional learners and minority students. It is critical for counselor education programs to support the retention of these students in order to have a more diverse student body, who will contribute to the diversity of the counseling profession upon graduation. It is also critical for students to take an active role in creating the atmosphere necessary for academic and professional success. Make sure you investigate the available programs in your institution, advocating for the creation of needed programs, and make efforts to develop mentorship relationships with your faculty members.

Evaluating Faculty Experience, Research, and Service

Experience. When evaluating faculty experience, educational training, and clinical practice are variables to consider. With regard to educational experience, the 2009 CACREP standards outline the educational qualifications required of faculty members in counseling programs. Effective July 1, 2013, counseling faculty members are required to have an earned doctoral degree in the area of counselor education and supervision, preferably from a CACREP accredited doctoral program (CACREP, 2009). Mental health professionals with doctoral degrees from other disciplines (e.g., counseling psychology, social work) must have been employed full-time for a minimum of one year in a counselor education program prior to July 1, 2013, and must identify with the counseling profession as evidenced by involvement with counseling professional organizations in order to meet the CACREP (2009) faculty requirements. While this faculty requirement is relatively new for the counseling profession, it is common practice for professors to have a degree that matches the discipline they teach (Urofsky, 2013). In other words, psychology training programs typically hire faculty members with psychology degrees, just as social work training programs hire faculty members with social work degrees. The faculty training requirement for counselor education programs provides a direct benefit to students. Faculty members who have a degree in counselor education and supervision have specific training in developing new members of the counseling profession and are well positioned to mentor students as they develop their own professional identities as counselors.

The clinical experience of counseling faculty members can impact program quality as well. Many online counselor education programs advertise that their faculty members are practicing counselors with real-world experience. Professors who actively practice counseling certainly enrich classroom experiences. Their personal examples of work with clients can help bring course material to life. As supervisors, they are well prepared to help students develop their counseling skills and generate effective interventions for working with clients. They may also provide helpful career advice for students. Many of the practicing counselors who teach in counselor education programs do so on an adjunct or part-time basis. Prospective students should be aware that CACREP (2009) standards specify that accredited counseling programs must have at least three full-time faculty members and that core or full-time counselor educators must deliver the majority of course credit hours to students each year. These standards prevent counselor education programs from relying too heavily on part-time or adjunct faculty members. Just as practicing counselors who teach part-time are advantageous, full-time or core faculty members also provide unique benefits to students. In addition to teaching classes, full-time faculty members have responsibilities including providing students with academic advisement and ongoing feedback and support around academic and professional development. Some full-time counselor educators also maintain a clinical practice. Full-time faculty members may offer other specific advantages to students including increased accessibility, clear counseling identity, and detailed knowledge about departmental and university-wide policies and procedures. Finally, full-time faculty members provide programmatic oversight and control the direction of the counseling program (Urofsky, Bobby, & Pope, 2009). As a student, you can benefit by asking faculty members about their clinical experience and learning about the diverse practice areas that may be available to you. While clinical experience is not required to be a professor, it often provides for a richer educational experience. In sum, both practicing counselors who teach in counselor education programs on a part-time basis and full-time counselor educators who have devoted their professional careers to the development of new counselors can be wonderful assets to students. When evaluating program quality, consider the advantages that both types of instructors offer. Knowing the background of your faculty members can aid in your discussion about the quality of your program.

Research. Faculty research requirements vary widely among counselor education programs. Some counseling programs focus heavily on faculty research and grant writing, while other programs emphasize teaching and professional service. Regardless of the program's emphasis, most counseling faculty members engage in research to some degree. While faculty research may not be a direct consideration in your decision to pursue a master's degree program, it is likely a significant factor in the pursuit of a doctoral program. Counseling research is generally published in counseling journals. The flagship journal of the American Counseling Association is called the *Journal of Counseling and Development* (*JCD*). A subscription to the *JCD* is a benefit of ACA membership, which results in the *JCD* having the widest circulation of all counseling journals. Many of the divisions of ACA also have journals that focus on a specialty area of counseling. In addition to publishing research findings in counseling journals, faculty may present their research at counseling conferences. Each year, the ACA holds a conference. Many divisions of ACA also host annual or semiannual conferences, as do state counseling organizations. Attending conferences is a great way for students to sample faculty research and network with a group of counseling professionals. A good starting point for evaluating faculty research is to request a list of recent faculty publications and presentations. Students can also utilize the online library associated with their university to locate research publications authored by the faculty members in their counseling department. Regardless of your level of graduate training, it is important to have a working knowledge of the research being produced by your faculty members. The research strands of faculty members can give you some insight into faculty member interests and opportunities for involvement in their work. Faculty research efforts also provide an opportunity for specialized training and increased knowledge. As a graduate student, you should attempt to take advantage of all learning opportunities available to you.

Service. Faculty service is an important aspect of a faculty member's job description. When thinking about faculty service, the first thing that comes to mind may be providing direct counseling services to clients or educational support services to students. These are certainly functions of counseling faculty members; however, faculty service typically refers to departmental service, university service, professional service, and community service.

Departmental service directly benefits the counseling department and typically involves membership on committees that maintain and advance the quality of the counseling program. University service involves collaborating with faculty from other departments to fulfill responsibilities that promote the functioning and well-being of the university as a whole. Service to the counseling profession can take many forms. One type of professional service is involvement and leadership with professional organizations such as ACA, the regions and divisions of ACA, Chi Sigma Iota, and local organizations for licensed counselors. Or faculty may serve as editors or reviewers for professional journals. There are many forms of professional service, and what your faculty does can help bring you into the professional world as well. Finally, counseling faculty members also may provide services to their community by offering pro bono or free counseling services or participate in volunteer service projects such as providing workshops.

Dissecting Degree Requirements

Required credit hours. Before enrolling in a counselor education program, you should be familiar with the program's degree requirements. If you are already enrolled, then it is essential that you review your program of study. One factor to consider is the number of credit hours required for graduation.

Required credit hours may vary from program to program, depending on accreditation status, counseling specialty area, and state licensure requirements. For example, the Council for Accreditation of Counseling and Related Educational Programs (CACREP) requires a minimum of 48 semester credit hours or 72 quarter credit hours for accredited master's level career counseling, school counseling, and student affairs and college counseling programs (CACREP, 2009). Accredited master's level degree programs in the areas of substance abuse counseling; clinical mental health counseling; and marriage, couples, and family counseling must require a minimum of 60 semester credit hours or 90 quarter credit hours (CACREP, 2009). State licensure boards specify the minimum number of credit hours needed in order to satisfy the academic requirements for counselor licensure. Academic requirements for licensure vary widely from state to state and don't always match with national accreditation standards. For example, some states only require 36 credit hours for a degree in school counseling, while the CACREP minimum requirement is 48 hours. For the most accurate information, students should contact the professional licensing board in their state of residence. The number of credit hours required to earn a degree may influence the time it takes to complete the degree and the amount of tuition a student will expend. While number of credits doesn't directly relate to program quality, it is important to understand the national standards and how they relate to the ability to practice outside of your current state. If you decide to move to a new state in the future, a degree with less credits may not qualify you for practice in your new state.

Course content. In addition to evaluating the number of credit hours required by a degree program, prospective students must also consider the content of required coursework. The 2009 CACREP standards identify eight Common Core curricular areas required of all students: professional orientation and ethical practice, social and cultural diversity, human growth and development, career development, helping relationships, group work, assessment, and research and program evaluation. In CACREP accredited counseling programs, the Common Core curricular areas may be addressed through a class specifically devoted to a particular area or addressed throughout multiple classes in the program. For example, most counseling programs require a specific course on social and cultural diversity. Social and cultural issues are also integrated into all courses in the program. In addition to the core curricular areas, counseling programs may offer elective courses. Students may elect to take a course on a specialty topic of interest to them. Commonly offered elective courses include substance abuse counseling, human sexuality, spirituality in counseling, crisis and trauma counseling, play therapy, couples and family counseling, and consultation.

Regardless of how the content is delivered, it is important to ensure that the content matches requirements stipulated in state laws. As stated, laws differ from state to state but many require content from the eight core areas identified in CACREP. They also require specific field experiences. In some cases, licensure boards will accept courses from CACREP accredited institutions without question and will require an applicant to demonstrate CACREP equivalence for courses from nonaccredited programs. The Center for Credentialing in Education (CCE) evaluates transcripts to determine CACREP equivalence for licensure boards. Students are advised to research the specific course content needed for professional licensure and to ensure that the courses match for current requirements. If you plan to practice in multiple states, then you should investigate all relevant state laws.

Culminating program requirements. Many counselor education programs require students to conduct a research-based project and/or pass a comprehensive graduation exam after the completion of all required coursework. At the master's level, students may complete a thesis, which is a research project conducted with the support of faculty members. Alternatively, some master's level programs require students to pass a comprehensive graduation exam that covers the core counseling content areas or to complete a professional portfolio. The graduation exam is often a high-stakes test, meaning that even if a student has successfully completed all coursework, the degree is not awarded until the comprehensive exam is also passed. At the doctoral level, students are typically required to complete a dissertation. The dissertation is an original, self-directed research project. Doctoral students present their research to their dissertation committee in a meeting known as a dissertation defense. Doctoral students are also typically required to pass a comprehensive exam that covers counseling practice, research, and supervision. As in the master's program, the doctoral dissertation and comprehensive exam are high stakes assessments.

Preparing for these culminating degree requirements can be a highly stressful experience for students. Successful completion requires a great deal of preparation. Students are advised to begin preparing well in advance of due dates and testing dates. In addition, faculty support plays a key role is student success. High-quality counselor education programs provide ongoing support and mentoring as students complete the final aspects of their training programs.

Other program requirements. As mentioned previously in this chapter, counselor educators and supervisors serve as gatekeepers for the counseling profession, ensuring that counselors in training are meeting the professional standards for acquiring counseling knowledge and demonstrating interpersonal effectiveness and clinical counseling skills (ACA, 2014; CACREP, 2009). As such, most counselor education programs have academic standards that students must maintain in order to progress in the program. Examples of academic standards include requiring students to maintain a minimum grade point average (GPA), requiring students to retake a class if a grade below B– is earned, and implementing academic probation or program dismissal if a student has to repeat a specified number of classes. Prior to enrollment, a prospective student should reflect on his or her academic history, current level of motivation, and access to resources to determine if the requisite academic standards are attainable and realistic. During enrollment, students should remain vigilant about academic performance and be aware of the potential consequences for low performance.

Students in counseling programs are also required to adhere to the ACA *Code of Ethics,* demonstrate professional behavior, and maintain a minimal level of personal wellness (ACA, 2014). Counseling programs may provide students with feedback about their interpersonal effectiveness and professional presentation after each class, on a semiannual, or annual basis. If a student demonstrates a deficit in interpersonal presentation or demonstrates physical, cognitive, or emotional impairment, remediation and support are provided by counseling faculty. In order to succeed in a master's or doctoral level counseling program, students must commit to personal and professional growth and attending to their own wellness.

In sum, earning a graduate degree in counseling involves much more than taking classes, writing papers, and passing tests! By choosing to enter the counseling profession, you are committing yourself to personal and professional growth. Sacrifices of time, energy, and money are required. By graduation, you will likely feel exhausted and energized at the same time as you realize that you have transformed from someone with an interest in helping others to a self-aware, culturally competent, knowledgeable, and clinically skilled helping professional.

Formal Measures of Quality in Counselor Education

Up until this point in the chapter, we have discussed various informal methods for assessing the quality of an online counselor education program. This section provides information about formal measures of quality in counselor education. Accreditation status and ratings on the SLOAN-C scorecard and Quality Matters rubric provide students with more objective standards by which to measure online counseling programs.

Accreditation

Accreditation is, "a quality assurance and enhancement mechanism for educational institutions, colleges or schools, and/or academic programs" (Urofsky, 2013, p. 6). In the United States, there is not a governmental department devoted to the oversight of educational quality in higher education. As such, the accreditation process is a form of professional self-regulation (Urofsky, 2013). The process of accreditation requires colleges and universities, and specific educational programs to engage in a self-study or internal evaluation of program quality. Accreditation standards or criteria serve as the quality indicators by which educational quality is assessed. In addition to the internal evaluation of quality, the accreditation process involves an external peer review process (Urofsky, 2013). The internal and external quality evaluations serve as checks and balances for each other. The accreditation process can take up to 2 years for a program to complete.

University and programmatic accreditation. There are two basic types of accreditation: accreditation at the institutional or university level and accreditation at the programmatic level. Regional accrediting agencies provide accreditation for entire universities or institutes of higher education. There are six regional accreditors (Urofsky, 2013): the New England Association of Schools and Colleges (NEASC), the Middle States Association of Colleges and Schools (MSA), the Southern Association of Colleges and Schools (SACS), the North Central Association of Colleges and Schools (NCA), the Northwest Commission of Colleges and Universities

(NWCCU), and the Western Association of Schools and Colleges (WASC). These accrediting agencies evaluate educational institutions based on broad standards that may include institutional mission, administrative structure, resources and support for students and faculty, financial stability, and the physical resources of the campus (Urofsky, 2013). Institutional or university-level accreditation is a very important factor for students to consider. In order to receive federal financial aid, a student must be enrolled in an accredited college or university. In addition, students who wish to transfer credit hours from one university to another may have difficulty if transferring from a nonaccredited university. Employment after graduation may also present a challenge for students who attend a school that is not accredited. Nonaccredited schools may be viewed as "diploma mills," or low quality institutions that give degrees without requiring sufficient academic output from students.

Programmatic or departmental accreditation is also very important, particularly in the counseling profession. CACREP evaluates the quality of counseling programs based on 165 core standards and substandards (Urofsky, 2013). The CACREP standards address, "core and specialty curricular content, institutional support for the program, training facilities, clinical and supervision requirements, faculty and supervisor qualifications, student and faculty support and program identity" (Urofsky, 2013, p. 12). The benefits of CACREP accreditation are described below.

Benefits of CACREP. CACREP accreditation offers numerous benefits to students. First, CACREP accreditation is a widely recognized indicator of program quality. Prospective employers understand that counselors who graduate from CACREP accredited programs have been well-trained and have successfully completed rigorous academic requirements. In fact, many employment opportunity announcements in the counseling profession indicate a preference for CACREP graduates. Graduation from a CACREP accredited program may also improve your chances of passing the National Counselor Exam (NCE). Adams (2006) compared the NCE scores of graduates from CACREP-accredited programs with the scores of graduates from programs that were not CACREP accredited. CACREP graduates scored significantly higher on the NCE. Graduation from a CACREP-accredited program can also reduce post-master's requirements for licensure and certification. For example, in addition to passing the NCE, the National Board of Certified Counselors (NBCC) requires 3,000 hours of post-master's counseling experience and 100 hours of clinical supervision over a 24-month time period in order to earn the National Certified Counselor (NCC) credential. The requirement for post-master's experience is waived for CACREP graduates (NBCC, 2014). Finally, graduating from a CACREP-accredited program may provide you with the ethical foundation needed to stay out of trouble. Even and Robinson (2013) conducted a multiway frequency analysis of ethics violations and sanctions and found that fully licensed counselors who graduated from CACREP-accredited programs had a lower frequency of ethical misconduct sanctions than fully licensed counselors who graduated from programs that were not CACREP accredited.

CACREP-equivalent programs.   Clearly, CACREP accreditation is beneficial to students. What about a CACREP-equivalent program? Isn't that just as good? In short, the answer is no. CACREP accreditation requires a counseling program to carry out a lengthy and complex self-study that details how the program meets the standards identified by CACREP. The results of the self-study are submitted to CACREP. CACREP team members review the self-study document submitted by the counseling program. If the self-study document provides sufficient evidence that the program meets the CACREP standards, a site visit is scheduled. During the CACREP site visit, a team of CACREP reviewers comes to the counseling department and thoroughly reviews all aspects of the counseling program. The CACREP review team then makes a recommendation about whether or not the counseling program meets the accreditation standards. Finally, CACREP board members vote to determine if a program will receive accreditation. Once accreditation is received, counseling programs continue to evaluate student-learning outcomes and continuously update their program to remain in compliance with the most recent CACREP standards. The self-study and site review process is repeated each time a counseling program comes up for reaccreditation. In other words, the CACREP stamp of approval is not handed out without significant evidence that a counseling program meets the CACREP standards.

In contrast, there is no restriction as to which counseling programs identify themselves as CACREP equivalent. There is also no universal definition of what CACREP equivalent means (Urofsky, 2013). Typically when counseling programs advertise themselves as CACREP equivalent, they are referring to having course work that aligns with the CACREP core content areas. However, the CACREP standards are not limited to core curriculum (Urofsky, 2013). In fact, CACREP clearly states that there is not a legitimate usage of the terminology CACREP equivalent (CACREP, 2009). In fact, it is possible that a program may have applied for CACREP accreditation, been denied, and still advertise CACREP equivalency. Usage of CACREP-equivalent terminology may be misleading to students and is not an indicator of program quality.

Evaluating Online Education Programs and Courses

Online education has become increasingly popular over the last decade. In 2013, over 7 million students in higher education took at least one class online, which represents the highest rate of engagement in online education in U.S. history (Allen & Seaman, 2014). Institutions of higher education recognize the importance of online learning formats. According to recent survey results, over two-thirds of chief academic officials view online education as critical to the long-term strategy of their college or university (Allen & Seaman, 2014). Clearly, online education is a popular and vital means of providing student training; however, questions exist regarding the quality of online education in comparison to traditional face-to-face learning environments. Recent survey results indicate that nearly 75% of academic leaders view the learning outcomes associated with online education as equal to or better than the learning outcomes associated with traditional face-to-face instruction (Allen & Seaman, 2014). These survey results are informative and can be strengthened with data from assessment instruments designed to measure the quality of online learning. Two instruments that have been developed for this purpose are the Sloan Consortium (Sloan-C) scorecard and the Quality Matters rubric.

The Online Learning Consortium/Sloan Consortium (Sloan-C) and scorecard. The Online Learning Consortium (OLC) formerly known as Sloan Consortium (Sloan-C) is an organization that promotes effective practices in online education with the goal of making quality online education accessible and affordable for all learners (Moore, 2005). The OLC has identified five pillars of quality that assist colleges and universities in the ongoing process of identifying goals and tracking progress toward goals in order to improve learning outcomes (Moore, 2005). The OLC pillars of quality are learning effectiveness, cost effectiveness and institutional commitment, access, faculty satisfaction, and student satisfaction (Moore, 2005). The OLC publishes the *Journal of Asynchronous Learning Networks* and hosts conferences for online educators and online program administrators.

In addition, the OLC has developed a scorecard or rubric that provides a measurable assessment of the overall quality of an online education program. *The Quality Scorecard for the Administration of Online Education Programs* includes 70 indicators of program quality in the overarching categories of institutional support, technology support, course development and instructional design, course structure, teaching and learning, social and student engagement, faculty support, student support, and evaluation and assessment (Sloan-C, 2014). Educational institutions can rank their educational programs on a 0–3-point Likert scale for each of the 70 quality indicators. A score of 0 indicates that the specific quality indicator is not observed in the educational program and a score of 3 indicates that the program meets the specific quality criterion completely. A score of 210 on the *Quality Scorecard* is a perfect score and indicates exceptional program quality. Scores below 125 are considered unacceptable (Sloan-C, 2014). The Sloan-C scorecard is primarily used for internal program evaluation purposes. While it is highly unlikely that an online counselor education program would make their *Quality Scorecard* scores available to students and prospective students, the knowledge that a program is using the Sloan-C scorecard as an evaluation instrument demonstrates some level of commitment to providing continuously improving online education.

Quality Matters program and rubric. Quality Matters is another organization designed to promote quality and best practices in online education. The Quality Matters program offers conferences and continuing education workshops for online educators. In addition, online programs can purchase a subscription to Quality Matters that allows online courses to be submitted for a peer review process. Specially trained Quality Matters evaluators who have extensive experience in online education will review the submitted course and provide feedback about the quality of the course according to the Quality Matters rubric. The general standards addressed in the Quality Matters rubric are course overview and introduction, learning objectives, assessment and measurement, instructional materials, learner interaction and engagement, course technology, learner support, and accessibility (Quality Matters, 2014). The rubric also includes 41 more specific standards of evaluation for fully online and blended/hybrid courses. The goal is for each online course to successfully meet at least 85% of the indicators of quality outlined in the Quality Matters rubric (Quality Matters, 2014). When comparing the

Table 4.1   Guide to Success in Evaluating the Quality of Your Online Program

Goals/Challenges	Strategies for Success
Choosing a Program	
<ul><li>Decide what type of program works for you — fully online, hybrid, etc.</li><li>Check out student organizations.</li><li>Know the concentration you wish to pursue (e.g., school, clinical mental health, career).</li></ul>	
Understanding Program Indicators of Quality	
<ul><li>Ask about retention and graduation rates.</li><li>Investigate support for students in the program.</li><li>Read the CVs of the program faculty to get a sense of their areas of expertise.</li><li>Investigate the accreditation status of the program and decide what you need to be successful.</li></ul>	

quality indicators from the Sloan-C scorecard and the Quality Matters rubric, it is evident that the Quality Matters rubric focuses on assessing the quality of a specific online course, whereas the Sloan-C scorecard provides feedback about the overall online program quality. These formal assessment measures could be used in conjunction with one another, since they offer specialized functions in evaluation.

Summary

Evaluating the quality of an online counselor education program is a demanding task. There are numerous counseling programs available to students, some of higher quality than others. In order to identify a top-notch program that will offer a challenging yet supportive academic experience, prospective students must look beyond appealing marketing campaigns and investigate indicators of program quality. One of the first factors to consider when selecting a counseling program is how well the program meets a student's needs and goals. Personal and lifestyle factors including logistical, cultural, and social variables weigh into the decision-making process. Additionally, academic factors including class size and overall program size, course format, campus resources, and student opportunities influence program choice. In addition to meeting personal and academic needs, the online counselor education program should allow students to fulfill their career aspirations. By evaluating the specific counseling degrees offered by an online program and the program's professional reputation, students can make an informed decision as to whether or not the degree offered by an online counselor education program aligns with their career plans.

Programs specific factors including retention, transfer, and graduation rates; faculty experience, research, and service; and degree requirements are also indicators of program quality. Retention data can provide students with information about a program's efforts to support student success. Programs with low retention rates should raise concern about program quality. The faculty members in quality counselor education programs must meet specific training requirements. In addition, faculty members in high-quality counselor education programs are actively engaged in research and various types of professional service. Finally, various degree requirements were discussed. Students are advised to explore the number of credit hours and the specific course content required for licensure in each state. In addition, students should evaluate their own academic strengths and challenges and reflect on how their unique characteristics align with program requirements.

Lastly, this chapter discussed formal measures of quality in online counselor education programs, including accreditation and assessment instruments designed to evaluate online education (i.e., Sloan-C scorecard and Quality Matters rubric). Accreditation at the university and programmatic levels ensures that minimum quality standards are met. The Council for the Accreditation of Counseling and Related Educational Programs (CACREP) is the accrediting body for counseling programs. CACREP accreditation offers students numerous professional benefits. Organizations dedicated to promoting continuous quality improvement in online education were also discussed. The Sloan-C has developed a scorecard for assessing the overall administration of an online education program. Quality Matters has developed a rubric for assessing the quality of a particular online course. Participation in Sloan-C or Quality Matters evaluation is an indicator of program quality.

In sum, students can evaluate the quality of an online counselor education program using a combination of informal and formal data sources. In addition to gathering as much information about the program as possible, students should engage in self-reflection regarding their needs, goals, resources, strengths, and challenges. Choosing the right counselor education program involves finding a high-quality program that meets as many student needs as possible.

About the Author

Amy L. McLeod, PhD, LPC, NCC, is an associate professor in the Counseling Department at Argosy University–Atlanta. For the past 6 years, Dr. McLeod has served on the admissions committee for the counseling department and has met with hundreds of students interested in pursuing a counseling degree. She is aware of the wide variety of questions and concerns students have during the process of selecting a training program and is excited to provide information that may assist students in evaluating the quality of an online counseling program. In addition, Dr. McLeod has extensive experiencing teaching in the blended course format, which combines an online platform with face-to-face campus time.

Dr. McLeod is a member of the American Counseling Association (ACA), the Association for Counselor Education and Supervision (ACES), the Southern Association of Counselor Education and Supervision (SACES), and the Association for Assessment and Research in Counseling (AARC), formerly the Association for Assessment in Counseling and Education (AACE). Dr. McLeod has served on the AARC (formerly AACE) Executive Committee as the Secretary and Member at Large-Membership. Dr. McLeod's research interests include multicultural issues in counselor education and supervision, women's issues, and crisis assessment.

References

Adams, S. A. (2006). Does CACREP accreditation make a difference? A look at NCE results and answers. *Journal of Professional Counseling, 34,* 60–76.
Allen, I. E., & Seaman, J. (2014). *Grade change: Tracking online education in the United States.* Babson Park, MA: Babson Survey Research Group.
American Counseling Association. (2014). *ACA Code of Ethics.* Alexandria, VA: Author.
American School Counselor Association. (2014). *State certification requirements.* Alexandria, VA: Author. Retrieved from http://www.schoolcounselor.org/school-counselors-members/careers-roles/state-certification-requirements

Carney-Crompton, S., & Tan, J. (2002). Support systems, psychological functioning, and academic performance of non-traditional female students. *Adult Education Quarterly, 52*, 140–154.

Chi Sigma Iota. (2014). *Our mission.* Greensboro, NC: Author. Retrieved from http://www.csi-net.org

Council for Accreditation of Counseling and Related Educational Programs. (2009). *The 2009 standards.* Alexandria, VA: Author. Retrieved from http://www .cacrep.org/doc/2009%20Standards%20with%20cover.pdf

Even, T. A., & Robinson, C. R. (2013). The impact of CACREP accreditation: A multi-way frequency analysis of ethics violations and sanctions. *Journal of Counseling and Development, 91*, 26–34. doi: 10.1002/j.1556-6676.2013.00067.x

Federal Student Aid. (2014). *Glossary.* Washington, DC: Author. Retrieved from https://studentaid.ed.gov/sa/glossary

Gary, J. M., Kling, B., & Dodd, B. N. (2004). A program for counseling and campus support services for African American and Latino adult learners. *Journal of College Counseling, 7*, 18–23.

Hoskins, C. M., & Goldberg, A. D. (2005). Doctoral student persistence in counselor education programs: Student-program match. *Counselor Education and Supervision, 44*, 175–188.

Lei, S. A., & Chuang, N. K. (2010). Demographic factors influencing selection of an ideal graduate institution: A literature review with recommendations for implementation. *College Student Journal, 44*, 84–96.

Lovitts, B. E. (2001). *Leaving the ivory tower: The causes and consequences of departure from doctoral study.* Lanham, MD: Rowman & Littlefield.

Moore, J. C. (2005). *The Sloan Consortium quality framework and the five pillars.* Needham, MA: Sloan-C. Retrieved from http://sloanconsortium.org/ publications/books/qualityframework.pdf

National Board of Certified Counselors. (2014). *Requirements for the NCC certification.* Greensboro, NC: Author. Retrieved from http://www.nbcc.org/Certification/ NationalCertCounselor

National Conference of State Legislatures. (2013). *For-profit colleges and universities.* Washington, DC: Author. Retrieved from http://www.ncsl.org/issues-research/educ/for-profit-colleges-and-universities.aspx

Poock, M. C., & Love, P. G. (2001). Factors influencing the program choice of doctoral students in higher education administration. *NASPA Journal, 38*(2), 203–223.

Quality Matters. (2014). *Higher Ed Program Rubric.* Annapolis, MD: Author. Retrieved from https://www.qualitymatters.org/rubric

Rogers, M. R., & Molina, L. E. (2006). Exemplary efforts in psychology to recruit and retain graduate students of color. *American Psychologist, 61*, 143–156. doi:10.1037/0003-066X61.2.143

Shin, R. Q. (2008). Advocating for social justice in academia through recruitment, retention, admissions, and professional survival. *Journal of Multicultural Counseling and Development, 36*, 180–191.

The Sloan Consortium. (2014). *A Quality Scorecard for the Administration of Online Education Programs.* Needham, MA: Author. Retrieved from http://online-learningconsortium.org/consult/quality-scorecard

Urofsky, R. (2013). The Council for Accreditation of Counseling and Related Educational Programs: Promoting quality in counselor education. *Journal of Counseling and Development, 91,* 6–14.

Urofsky, R., Bobby, C., & Pope, V. (2009, May). Faculty requirements in the 2009 CACREP standards. *Counseling Today, 51*(11), 68–69.

5

Professional Identity and Professional Engagement

R. J. Davis and Wendy Greenidge

Chapter Overview

This chapter will provide you with an understanding of a professional identity as a beginning counselor. Because your professional identity is rooted in the professional activities you select, this chapter will focus largely on your professional engagement. Membership in professional organizations, development of a professional network, and your professional comportment as a counseling student are part of professional engagement and discussed further in this chapter. Finally, maintaining that professional commitment outside of the counseling program in areas such as social media is also discussed.

Learning Outcomes

After reading this chapter, students will be able to

1. Understand the importance of a clear professional identity

2. Articulate a plan to establish a professional identity

3. Describe and access professional counseling organizations at local, state, and national levels

4. Identify sources of continuing education and professional growth conferences

5. Explain the value of collaboration with other counseling professionals

Introduction

You have made the decision to commit to an online counselor education training program. In that decision, you have considered your opportunities for success, the impact on your family, and the career path you hope to take. Now it is time to look at not just getting a degree in counseling, but truly becoming a counselor. Becoming a counselor means developing and maintaining a professional identity that advances you in the field.

Building a Professional Identity

Few things are more important to a counselor or counselor educator than knowledge of self; to really know yourself and to be comfortable in that knowledge; and to live congruently. How do we come to know ourselves? Throughout your program you will be, or have been, asked to reflect, analyze, evaluate, and to take perspectives other than your own. These behaviors are most likely second nature to you by now. However, these are not the only ways to know one's self or to establish identity. Our actions also define us and make us who we are as individuals and for many, as professionals. Building your professional identity is done with intent, purpose, and agency. Your actions as a professional counselor or counselor educator shape your professional identity. Having a clearly established professional identity is one way for others to know you more deeply and on a different level.

It is exciting to think that you can take your new skills and professional credentials in a myriad of directions. Paying attention to your interests, the areas of counseling that draw you in, is important as you make the transformation from graduate student to professional. Spend some quality time reflecting on how you will engage. What things might you need to do? Think about how you can locate others with the same interests. Are there specific credentials you need or can pursue? Building your professional identity begins with knowing who you are as a counseling professional.

As a new counselor, you can accomplish this task in a number of ways including getting involved in professional counseling and mental health organizations, engaging in advocacy efforts, collaborating with professionals that have similar interests, attending conferences, and seeking out and participating in continuing education activities. Much of the information you will need to begin is available online. Do your research and create a plan.

By getting involved with professional counseling and mental health organizations, you communicate your interest to others. This is one way for them to know you as a professional. Being active in the organizations confirms their impressions. You become known for your involvement and commitment. Others will begin to associate you with specific organizations, services, or activities. Your professional identity begins to solidify.

Engaging in advocacy efforts supports your emerging professional identity in a number of ways as well. Advocacy efforts are typically group endeavors. Working with and meeting other counseling professionals promotes a shared identity and is a great way to establish your reputation within professional circles. Communities benefit as well as you become known as a reliable and valued resource or expert. Many counseling professionals take leadership roles in advocacy efforts that promote social justice or social change.

Attending professional growth conferences and participating in continuing education activities further supports your identity as a professional counselor or counselor educator. As you build your network of professional relationships, you also expand and refine your repertoire of skills and services. You stay connected and current. Professional growth conferences are also an excellent source of information about job opportunities that may interest you.

As a counselor educator, the establishment of a clear professional identity will benefit you in your quest to secure a position in higher education. It will serve to set you apart from other potential candidates and communicates your commitment and dedication as well as professional interest areas to potential employers. Candidates with clear professional identities are perceived as motivated and engaged. One form of engagement may begin at your place of employment. For example, many institutions of higher learning encourage and often require the new professional to engage in activities such as committee work for their department, college, and the university. Taking an active role in academic initiatives and engaging with colleagues across disciplines is often seen as an essential activity for those seeking promotion and tenure. In addition, engagement of this type builds relationships that may lead to collaboration on research and other scholarly activity including publication, which we will discuss later.

Creating a strong professional identity is important to the counseling profession as well as an endeavor that is promoted by leading counseling organizations and accrediting bodies. Several years ago, the American Counseling Association and over 30 of its partners began the difficult process of creating a strategic plan to define a strong professional identity for counselors that would guide the profession into the future. One of the core principles in that plan, *20/20: A Vision for the Future of Counseling*, is that a shared professional identity is essential (Kaplan & Gladding, 2011; Sheperis & Sheperis, 2014). In the broad view, we are a united group of counseling professionals with diverse interests and specialties assisting clients with a variety issues in a number of ways to support mental health and promote wellness. Creating your personal professional identity as a counselor or counselor educator strengthens this view.

Professional Affiliations

Many of us have probably heard the expression "you are known by the company you keep" at some point in our lives. Conventional wisdom of this type is often passed on to us by our parents and teachers. The adage holds true for counselors and counselor educators as well. Professionals in many fields belong to organizations created to support or promote specific vocations and professions. This tradition harkens back to the guilds created by various craftsmen and artisans of the past. The benefits of being affiliated with professional organizations that help define your professional identity are many. They include the sharing of resources and information, networking with like-minded individuals, access to career centers, opportunities for advocacy or leadership, and assistance avoiding potential pitfalls such as stagnation and possible feelings of loneliness associated with working in isolation. For these reasons and others, counselors and counselor educators affiliate and engage with the various professional organizations created to advance or support the practice and science of counseling on local, state or regional, and national or international levels.

Affiliation without engagement is neither helpful nor professional. In other words, it is not enough to simply join a professional organization. You have to get involved. Engagement at the local level may take many forms, including hosting community mental health events, offering services pro bono, and belonging to local mental health organizations. You find counseling professionals volunteering their time to sit on community advisory committees or participating in community-wide efforts. Look around you. What are the issues that interest the community, and where do they intersect with yours or those of your clients?

Building relationships within the local community is beneficial as well. These relationships are typically built on service and interest area. Community mental health organizations as well as civic organizations often utilize advisory boards or create task forces whose members are drawn from local professionals. This is an excellent avenue for engagement at the local level and an opportunity to become affiliated with networks of professionals that share common goals and interests. Conduct a needs assessment in the community. What are the community needs and what resources are in place to address them? Compiling a list of community needs or issues, the resources available or those lacking, and potential contacts is a great place to start. Utilizing the resource database you created, you can reach out to specific groups or agencies based on your interests or areas of expertise. Your goal is to create a network and to get involved. Begin by introducing yourself, communicating your interests, and working to establish connections within the group. Join with them. Volunteering, attending the group meetings and functions that are open to the public, and offering yourself as a potential resource are all appropriate and often rewarding ways to affiliate and engage at the local level.

The next level of recommended engagement or affiliation in professional organizations for the new counselor or counselor educator is at the state level. In the United States, professional counseling organizations both large and small exist in all states. These organizations exist to support counseling professionals within the state by providing leadership and professional services, advocacy for clients and resources, and mental and behavioral health needs assessment, as well as promoting optimal development and wellness.

At the state level, these professional counseling organizations are generally focused on special interest areas closely mirroring national organizations along with the issues within the specific state. For example, the

National Career Development Association (NCDA) which is one of the founding divisions of the American Counseling Association (ACA), is represented at the state level with the same focus on career development. In Ohio, the state level organization for this interest area is the Ohio Career Development Association (OCDA), in Texas it is the Texas Career Development Association (TCDA), and so on.

Engaging at the national or international level in professional counseling organizations is accomplished in much the same way. National organizations have been created for most recognized specialty areas. Increased attention is being focused on international engagement. Organizations such as the National Board of Certified Counselors (NBCC) and the American Counseling Association work with groups around the world. Counseling professionals across the globe are coming together at conferences to share research, collaborate, and build interest networks. Examples of international counseling organizations include the International Association for Marriage and Family Counselors (IAMFC) and the International Association of Addictions and Offender Counselors (IAAOC). Opportunities for engagement and leadership are available within these organizations. Information about national and international organizations can be found on their websites and through related publications including professional journals and newsletters published by the organizations.

Continuing Education and Professional Growth Conferences

As mentioned earlier, there are multiple ways to develop and refine one's professional identity. Pursuing continuing education opportunities and attending professional growth conferences are highly encouraged and often expected. For example, requirements for maintaining licensure typically include an obligation to complete a certain number of continuing education units or CEUs within a given time period. Engaging in ongoing professional development supports the concept of lifelong learning. In addition to gaining new knowledge and skills, you may find new areas of interest or avenues of research you would like to explore. Conveniently, most professional growth conferences provide multiple opportunities for professional development and gaining CEUs by attending presentations or workshops, and they are often hosted by the very organizations to which you belong.

Conferences can be energizing. Meeting other counseling professionals expands your professional network. Larger conferences often provide career centers, opportunities to interview, and information about employment. The following are a few examples of leading counseling organizations that hold large conferences that draw master clinicians, counselor educators, researchers, and graduate students from around the world:

- American Counseling Association
  http://www.counseling.org
- Association for Assessment and Research in Counseling
  http://aarc-counseling.org/resources
- Association for Counselor Education and Supervision
  http://www.acesonline.net
- American School Counseling Association
  http://schoolcounselor.org
- National Career Development Association
  http://ncda.org/aws/NCDA/pt/sp/home_page

Participating in continuing education and attending professional growth conferences help build your professional identity. These activities are typically expected and often required. Continuing education enables counselors to maintain higher standards of care for their clients or students. Professional growth conferences can be enriching experiences that stimulate growth and often a sense of renewal.

Thinking Like a Professional

Making a successful transition from graduate student to new professional involves a shift in your thinking (Gibson, Dollarhide, & Moss, 2010). This shift includes how you view yourself, how you self-monitor or evaluate your attitude, and how you interact with others. According to Nugent and Jones (2009), your professional identity becomes personal. The study and practice of counseling is transformational in many ways. Changes in thinking occur. Similarly, you must change how you think as you transform from graduate student to professional. As a student, you rely on your instructors for their knowledge. Later on, you may turn to your supervisors for help in refining your skills or to your mentors for guidance when making career decisions. At some point, you close the circle and turn to yourself. You take charge of your own learning and development. Self-evaluation becomes a component of your process.

A part of your transformation requires an internalization of our code of ethics and our guiding principles of autonomy, nonmaleficence, beneficence, justice, and fidelity. In the same sense that self-awareness is understood to be good for the individual, a professional self-awareness will benefit you in a number of practical ways.

One practical consideration is how you communicate with other professionals. Professional communication is simply that, professional. For example, e-mail is considered a primary form of communication for most professionals. It is important to remember that e-mail is not face-to-face communication. In addition, tone in e-mails can be easily misinterpreted. Often, an e-mail sent by you to another professional is the first impression you make. Professional e-mails commonly have a greeting followed by whatever information is being shared or requested and some form of closure. Naturally, the communication should be free of errors such as misspellings. Sending e-mails in haste can also send unintended messages about you. Remember that e-mails or written communication are representations of you as a professional. Be courteous, conscientious, and professional in all your communications with others. For more information about professional e-mail communication, see Chapter 7.

In addition to your communication, your appearance is important as well. Professionals dress the part. One way to ensure that you are dressed professionally is to think about the forum, setting, occasion, or event. Consider the purpose of the activity and who will be in attendance. What is your role and how do you wish to be perceived? Being appropriately dressed for whatever occasion, whether it be a fundraiser, business meeting, or block party, communicates important messages about you as a professional. These messages include an attitude of care, situational awareness, and intentional preparation.

Performance of your work is another important consideration. Successful professionals continuously strive to improve, expand their knowledge base, and refine their skills. They meet deadlines, show up on time, and work well with others. Failure to produce, prioritize, and plan becomes obvious to others rather quickly in professional environments.

Your interaction or engagement with others, or perhaps more importantly the lack thereof, is also a part of thinking like a professional. Take a look at the professionals around you. You may find that some are described as team players, while others may be more loners. You may even know some professionals who would be described as mavericks. You will want to spend time with people who are committed professionals who can motivate or inspire you. It is not a good idea to isolate yourself. Being collegial is appreciated and often expected.

As you can see, thinking like a professional requires careful thought and planning. It also involves a type of management of your professional self or persona. The advent of social networks such as Facebook and LinkedIn have increased the importance of this aspect of thinking like a professional. What can someone learn about you by searching for you on social networking sites? When questioning who is googling you, the answer is anyone and everyone, including potential employers, colleagues, and clients.

As your thinking begins to shift and your behavior becomes more intentional with regard to your career, a positive attitude will serve you best. Be supportive of your new professional self and confident in your professional identity. Apply what you know to your own situation. Reframe that situation if necessary. You are not just seeking a job, you are beginning a new adventure and you possess the knowledge and skills to be successful.

Collaborating With Other Professionals

A great way to further establish and refine your professional identity is to collaborate with other professionals. Collaborating also keeps you connected and up-to-date. It can stimulate ideas and generate solutions to problems that may elude an individual working in isolation. In other words, it is good for you and keeps you current. As you build relationships within the professional community, seek out others with similar interests and explore opportunities for collaboration.

Engaging in advocacy efforts, conducting research, writing for publication, and partnering to provide services are all potential forms of collaboration that should be considered. You may choose to work with a local agency to create a public event or hold a workshop on a specific topic. You may partner with a coworker to offer a specific counseling service. Faculty members can collaborate on research and publication. Creating or being part of a writing team can keep you inspired and make you productive. For counselor educators, working together makes it easier to meet tenure and promotion goals in academic environments. In addition, collaboration can aid in problem solving and mirrors a professional activity known as consultation (Trippany-Simmons, Rush-Wilson, Patton, & Perepiczka, 2015).

Discovering or creating opportunities to collaborate with other professionals can benefit your clients or students as well. There are interest networks, task forces, listservs, and advocacy groups that you can join that bring people together, serve specific populations, and whose clients have common goals. The array of topics and potential interest areas is vast. Collaboration can add to your scope of competency and expand your area of expertise.

Consider making collaboration a prominent component of your professional counseling identity. Getting started is as easy as going online and accessing websites of professional counseling organizations such as ACA or the websites of organizations in your area. Reflect on your interests. As you begin to build your network of colleagues, seek out opportunities for collaboration that reflect those interests.

Professional Conduct

Protecting the Public

A primary responsibility of all counseling professionals is to protect the public. This protection is provided in several ways. Counselors and counselor educators are essential to the process of safeguarding the public.

As a counselor, you will adhere to mandatory reporting laws. Although laws vary from state to state, most have provisions for reporting abuse of vulnerable populations including children and the elderly. Reports are generally required to be made to the appropriate authorities within 48 hours. Many such reports may be made over the telephone, but some may require a face-to-face interview. You will be expected to know the laws in your state and to follow protocols established in the organizations or agencies in which you work. These are legal as well as ethical obligations.

Another form of protecting the public is gatekeeping. Counselor educators serve this function in academic settings and are required to do so by the ACA *Code of Ethics* (2014) and the Council for the Accreditation of Counseling and Related Educational Programs (2009). Gatekeeping requires counselor educators to monitor, evaluate, and assess the fitness of a counseling student to enter the profession (Bernard & Goodyear, 2004). Many students come to counseling programs because they wish to help others. However, not all students who begin counseling programs should become counselors. Fortunately, many such students realize at some point that counseling may not be the best way for them to realize their goal of helping others. Some students seek out faculty members for guidance or assistance in exploring other areas of study. In other less fortunate situations, it may become clear that the individual does not possess the skill or disposition to be a professional counselor. Counselor educators protect the public and the profession by not allowing these individuals to enter the profession. All counseling programs have processes in place to remove students should it become necessary.

Professional Dispositions and Rubrics

Professional dispositions and rubrics are part of most counseling programs and may be used in other settings as well, as both can be used as assessment tools. Students and employees are often assessed at different points in their programs or different times of the year.

Counselor educators use professional disposition documents to assess student performance. The dispositions typically include a list of desired characteristics arranged in checklists which are closely aligned with ethical codes and professional standards. Students are expected to develop and grow as they progress through their program. The dispositions often provide for the evaluation of skill acquisition. These dispositions are typically reviewed by faculty to monitor this growth. It is a good idea to have a clear understanding of these dispositions so that you can work to ensure that you meet or exceed program expectations.

As a student, you are familiar with rubrics being used as a guide for grading your work, but they can be used in other ways as well. Counselor educators are often evaluated with rubrics. These evaluations are common components of tenure and promotion reviews. Faculty are expected to engage in a range of activities including teaching, scholarship, and service. A typical evaluation rubric would have certain percentages assigned to each area. For example, faculty may be expected to spend 40% of their time teaching, 40% on scholarship, and 20% on service. While teaching is primarily course delivery, it may also include course development. Examples of scholarship include conducting research and writing for publication in peer-reviewed journals. Service is often defined in several ways including service to your university or department, the community, or the counseling profession. Service may come in the form of committee work, engaging with area professionals, or making presentations at professional growth conferences. Using rubrics to guide this evaluation process will help you manage your time and monitor your activities as a counselor educator.

Ethical Functioning in an Online Environment

Ethical functioning in an online environment includes more than just following the rules of etiquette. Counselors and counselor educators are trained to adhere to ethical codes. You are expected to apply these ethical codes and other codes specific to your program to your behavior in the online environments. Academic honesty is expected. Your integrity as a counseling professional is evidenced in your behavior and should be above reproach. Your work as a student is a representation of you as a professional. Students in graduate programs are expected to understand and avoid plagiarism. Cheating in any form can be cause for dismissal.

You have been trained to follow ethical guidelines. In addition, you have been trained to use ethical decision-making models that can be used in any number of situations. Apply what you know. Regardless of environment or program, counselors and counselor educators follow these guidelines. More information on online etiquette can be found at www.albion.com/netiquette/corerules.html.

Patience in an Online World

The advent of computers and Internet technology brought many changes to the classroom and workplace. It will be some time before the impact of these changes is fully understood. Certainly, there has been an impact on the immediacy of communication. Students and instructors may hold some unrealistic expectations in this regard. A general guideline and common professional courtesy is to expect a response or to respond within a 48-hour window. A measure of patience will serve you well in online environments and most other environments as well.

In addition, your verbal and written communication should be professional at all times. Communicating with other professionals, students, or clients should be done with care. Hastily prepared reports, terse responses, or sloppily written e-mail are unprofessional.

Understanding the Student Evaluation Process

Students in most counseling programs are regularly evaluated. These evaluations are used for several purposes, but primarily to identify areas of strength and areas requiring more focused development. In most counseling programs, you can expect to be informed of this process and to have results of evaluations shared with you.

Typically, graduate level counseling students are expected to maintain a specific grade point average (GPA). Students falling below the required GPA are sometimes placed on probation or remediation plans. This process can be guided by faculty advisors or program committees created for that purpose. However, grades are not the only consideration.

As mentioned earlier, students are evaluated for disposition as well. Certain components of the evaluation are designed to measure ethical and psychological suitability. In this manner, student evaluations are a component of the gatekeeping process to safeguard the public.

A Professional Approach to Appealing Grades and Other Decisions

Much of this handbook is created to guide you in your development as a counseling professional. Being a professional often includes knowing and following specific steps in a process. The process of appealing a grade or other decisions, such as suspensions, should be handled professionally and according to procedure. These procedures are typically outlined in a program handbook.

It is not uncommon for strong emotions to be involved in situations involving grade disputes. Professionals keep their emotions in check. Sending angry or unprofessional e-mail only complicates matters and copying others not immediately or directly involved causes additional problems. Your interests will be better served by taking a methodical approach, remaining professional in your communication and demeanor, and following the procedure.

Typically, the first step is to contact your instructor of record. Asking for additional feedback on a grade or clarification is a great way to begin. Share your concerns with your instructor and give them the opportunity to respond to you. Another option would be to request a meeting to discuss the issue. Some programs utilize grade appeals committees that generally consist of faculty members, and the issue may be referred to the committee to decide the matter. If outcomes are still unsatisfactory, the next step may include requesting a meeting with the program coordinator or the department chairperson depending on the program's procedure. It is somewhat uncommon for issues to move beyond the specific department. However, some program procedures include provisions for meeting with the college dean or university provost.

It is your responsibility to determine the appropriate steps to advocating for yourself at your particular institution. In some cases, students have sent initial e-mails to the university president and skipped all of the elements in between. This approach typically reflects poorly on the student. University presidents are fully aware that there are multiple perspectives to every story and don't jump into action because they receive an e-mail from a student about a course grade. The typical response is for the president to send a copy of the e-mail to the college dean, who then forwards the e-mail to the department chair. This process occurs until it reaches the instructor in question. In the end, the same process occurs as if the student e-mailed the instructor directly. However, the process is delayed because of the multiple layers involved, and each person in the chain had to take the time to manage the issue.

There is nothing wrong or inappropriate about wanting to appeal a grade or important decision. If you find yourself in this situation, work to remain calm, cool, and collected. Document your actions and keep copies of communications for your files. Regardless of the ultimate decision, maintaining your professionalism in all aspects of the process is essential.

Social Media and Online Presence

With increasing social networking platforms and the growing number of users, it is imperative that you are mindful of how you conduct yourself on social media. It is widely known that more and more academic institutions and potential employers are scrutinizing the accounts of individuals before offering employment and acceptance into academic programs. No matter how many privacy settings you activate on your accounts, your information is never completely private. Keep this in mind as you begin your journey in graduate school.

There are hundreds of social media sites available. Some of the more popular ones include Facebook, Twitter, Instagram, LinkedIn, Pinterest, Vine, YouTube, and Tumblr. It is almost impossible to expect that you will not have to interact with others through social media. The key is to remember that your social media profile should be an extension of who you are. Instead of spending time carefully hiding personal things with the privacy settings, just post responsibly! Always ensure that you are representing yourself, your academic institution, and future employers well.

A common error for students is to inappropriately vent about aspects of an academic program on social media. They may rant about instructors, assignments, group projects, or peers. Remember, grievances are better resolved when presented directly to the individuals involved rather than played out on social media. The repercussions are too vast. Likewise, the issues may never be resolved, as the individuals involved remain unaware of how these things are affecting you. Going directly to your instructors allows them to address your concerns in a timely manner. Take some time to play the tape all the way through before making a post. By ranting about a particular professor, course, or program, you are sending a negative message to the public about what you are learning. Instead of promoting yourself and your knowledge base, you end up downplaying your own qualifications through criticisms on social media. You also portray yourself as someone who complains rather than someone who is solution focused. By pursuing your graduate degree in counseling, you are entering a new phase and must consider how your profile represents your professional side to the public.

There are several great examples of how social media can be used appropriately. Many cohorts of students in online programs also develop private Facebook groups to network with each other and build a community of support as they progress throughout their programs. In these groups, students share resources, remind each other of upcoming deadlines, create study groups, and exchange ideas. However, it is important that these groups do not replace the role of your instructor. Relying on peers for answers to course questions is inadvisable. Remember that they are pursuing the same degree you are. Instead of posting questions in a private student-only forum, post the question to the course discussion board and invite the response of the course instructor. You are then able to gain an official response, and all students can benefit from the information. Likewise, ensure that the group remains professional in their communication about the course, program, and instructor. Again, any grievances with either of these should be communicated directly with the instructor so they may be resolved in a timely manner. Airing issues out on social media platforms, which your instructor, advisor, and peers have no immediate access to, does very little to solve the identified issues.

Building a Professional Online Profile

One of the more common ways of navigating the online social media world is to keep your professional and personal profiles on social media sites separate. Having a personal account as well as a professional account allows individuals to tailor the content of their profiles to suit the intended audience. The personal account (which still needs to remain appropriate) can be used to post personal and family content such as photos, personal updates, and other more intimate information. The professional page is reserved for potential employers, academic settings, and interacting with peers and colleagues.

There are many social networking sites that can be used to create a professional online profile. The most common and effective use of social media for professional connections to date is LinkedIn. LinkedIn is the world's largest professional network with (as of February 2015), 300 million members in over 200 countries and territories around the globe. The goal of LinkedIn is to connect the world's professionals in order to make them more productive and successful. When you create an account, you immediately get access to people, jobs, news, updates, and insights that help you be great at what you do. It is relatively easy to create a profile and get started with creating your professional online profile. It allows you to become visible to others who can then seek you out for potential employment or collaborations. Social media can also be used to follow experts in your field and remain abreast with the ins and outs of what's happening in real time.

Professional Contact Information

A large part of your professional identity lies in how you communicate with faculty, peers, and other counselors. One piece of that communication is your professional e-mail address. You may not have thought about a professional e-mail when you opened your e-mail account so many years ago, but it may be time to retire fluffybunny123$@yahoo.com! Now, there is no reason you cannot keep that e-mail for personal use, but it will be worth investing time in developing another address for professional contacts. As a student, it is often tempting to use your university address. However, remember that you will not always have access to that address. When it comes time to secure employment, a stand-alone address that you can control is in your best interest. See Chapter 7 for more information on developing professional contact information.

Summary

Developing a professional identity starts before you become a professional. In fact, it is an activity to consider before you start school. Crafting and maintaining this identity takes intentionality. You will want to align yourself with those who are successful and begin to develop an online professional presence. This chapter outlined some specific activities you can begin now and maintain throughout your career to become the professional counselor you desire.

About the Authors

R. J. Davis, PhD, NCC, LPC-intern, is an assistant professor and coordinator of the Clinical Mental Health Counseling program at Lamar University. R. J. Davis' teaching career began in secondary education with a decade of experience working with and teaching multiple subjects to diverse populations. Davis' experience as a counselor comes from his service as a university career counselor and later as a director of a counseling and training clinic. Davis is active in service to the profession in his current role as president of Texas Counselors for Social Justice and past president of Texas Career Development Association. Davis is also an active member of state and national counseling associations and has presented at state, national, and international conferences including the Texas Counseling Association, Texas School Counseling Association, Texas College Counseling Association, the American Counseling Association, Association for Counselor Education and Supervision, the Association for Assessment and Research in Counseling, and the Online Learning Consortium. In addition, R. J. Davis is a contributing author to *Foundations of Clinical Mental Health Counseling* (Pearson).

Wendy L. Greenidge is an assistant professor in the Department of Counseling and Special Populations at Lamar University with over 15 years of experience in the field of mental health counseling. She is a Licensed Mental Health Counselor (LMHC) and holds several certifications in many subfields of counseling. Wendy is a Fulbright Scholar Alumna with a strong interest in improving online counseling programs as well as establishing and improving international mental health programs. Her research interests primarily focus on increasing utilization of professional counseling services through culturally appropriate interventions. More specifically, her work examines the psycho-cultural correlates of help-seeking in international populations and develops strategies for reducing the barriers to help-seeking.

Wendy is also interested in counselor wellness, play therapy, family counseling, and infusing technology and expressive therapies in counselor education programs and counseling practice. She has published numerous articles on her interests, presents at the local, national, and international level and facilitates mental health workshops internationally. Wendy also serves on several international counseling associations and journals such as the *Caribbean Journal for Psychology*. She has worked in various professional counseling settings including inpatient, partial hospitalization, outpatient programs, in-home counseling, K–12, and college counseling settings, substance abuse, and marriage and family agencies. She enjoys working with children and families.

References

American Counseling Association. (2014). *Code of Ethics*. Alexandria, VA: Author.

Bernard, J. M., & Goodyear, R. K. (2004). *Fundamentals of clinical supervision*. Boston, MA: Pearson Education.

Council for Accreditation of Counseling and Related Educational Programs. (2009). *CACREP accreditation standards and procedures manual*. Alexandria, VA: Author.

Gibson, D. M., Dollarhide, C. T., & Moss, J. M. (2010). Professional identity development: A grounded theory of transformational tasks of new counselors. *Counselor Education and Supervision*, *50*(1), 21–38.

Kaplan, D. M., & Gladding, S. T. (2011). A vision for the future of counseling: The 20/20 principles for unifying and strengthening the profession. *Journal of Counseling & Development*, *89*(3), 367–372.

Nugent, F. A., & Jones, K. D. (2009). *Introduction to the profession of counseling* (5th ed.). Upper Saddle River, NJ: Pearson.

Sheperis, D. S., & Sheperis, C. J. (2015). *Clinical mental health counseling: Fundamentals of applied practice*. Upper Saddle River, NJ: Pearson.

Trippany-Simmons, R., Rush-Wilson, T., Patton, J., & Perepiczka, M. (2015). Consultation and referrals. In D. S. Sheperis & C. J. Sheperis (Eds.), *Clinical mental health counseling: Fundamentals of applied practice* (pp. 179–200). Upper Saddle River, NJ: Pearson.

6

Navigating a Digital Textbook or Online Lab

Belinda J. Lopez, Rachael Ammons Whitaker,
Patricia A. Harris, and Lisa A. Wines

Chapter Overview

This chapter will provide a greater understanding of various aspects of navigating through a digital textbook and online lab. First, the chapter begins with the positive and negative aspects of renting or purchasing textbooks, followed by a discussion on vendors and digital libraries. Next, the benefits and functions of an online lab are visited with information on notes and highlighting. Also, a guided navigation of an e-text, including necessary functions such as creating, storing, editing, retrieving, printing, or searching for created personal notes, is discussed. Further, an explanation of other forms of practical use for students such as accessing embedded media and understanding learning outcomes within the e-text, information, and techniques are presented to specifically help filter through chapters and pages. In conclusion, the importance of using the content of each textbook to prepare for future certification and licensure is discussed.

Learning Outcomes

After completing this chapter, students will be able to

1. Describe the difference between renting and purchasing textbooks

2. Understand how digital libraries can serve as an efficient environment for learning

3. Describe the purpose of an online counseling lab and their benefits

4. Understand the various note-taking processes for instructor and students in an e-text platform and locate instructor notes from categories placement

5. Understand the components of an online chapter including search functions, embedded media, learning outcomes

6. Explain how to use the textbook or lab to prepare for certification or licensure

Introduction

Textbooks are vital to the world of higher education and are a requirement in your program of study. You likely remember carrying around a heavy backpack full of texts, notebooks, highlighters, pens, and other needed supplies. Now, students are typically offered a variety of formats for acquiring and using the texts necessary to complete their program, which may include all digital. That heavy backpack could be reduced to a single tablet or laptop. Learning how to navigate these choices is part of becoming an online student. Let's take a look at some of your potential options.

Renting Versus Purchasing

Renting textbooks can be a financial benefit, therefore, many opt to rent instead of purchasing books. First, make sure to do comparative shopping and evaluate options before making a purchase. The average price of new textbooks can range from $95–$250, which can easily add up each term. The yearly cost can be as much as $1,200. This trend continues to steadily increase every year. Smart shopping is the key, so understand that you have choices.

Renting can cost as much as 50% less than the retail price of a textbook. For graduate students that do not plan to keep their books, renting is ideal. Before anyone decides to rent textbooks, it is important to read and understand the fine print.

1. The textbook must be returned by the designated date or late fees might be applied.

2. The textbook must be free of stains and markings.

3. Lost or stolen textbooks can be costly.

4. If purchasing from an online vendor, be aware of shipping and other associated charges.

5. Be aware of scams, and order rentals from reliable vendors.

Purchasing textbooks is still the preferred method for many. Purchasing can have benefits, although this option might be more costly. Often, students keep their textbooks for personal reasons such as highlighting, note-taking, and as a future resource. For those considering selling, the buyback price can be as much as 75% on the return, or as little as zero dollars. At times this might be more economically feasible than renting. Campus bookstores offer both new and used textbooks. Online marketplace vendors often display variable pricing from their sellers including the book's condition. A word of caution on trying to resell the textbook, especially when the book is damaged, marked, or a new edition will be released the next term. The chances for getting any money back are minimal. Used textbooks are in popular demand as compared to new textbooks. The best recommended strategy is to do your research and shop early. Before anyone decides to purchase textbooks, it is important to understand return policies.

1. For a full refund, the textbook must be returned by a designated date.

2. The textbook must be in its original packaging.

3. If purchasing from an online vendor, be aware of shipping and other associated charges.

4. Be aware of scams, and order only from reliable vendors.

Vendors

Traditionally, higher education vendors have been the university bookstores. Today, various book sellers offer textbooks and complete book bundles with supplementary materials in digital format. In this competitive market for textbook sales and profit, many companies are gaining popularity. For convenience, major book vendors are located in large cities and sell at retail and half price to the public, while others have remained solely with the online market. Most vendors have joined the bandwagon of online sales. The counselor education student is not restricted to purchase from the university bookstore anymore. The student has the option of driving to the store or searching online for competitive textbook prices. Whether the student chooses to drive to or call, many vendors provide the service of ordering for immediate availability or mailing to the doorstep. For example, Maria needs a textbook for her first counseling course and is comfortable with technology. Her preferred book format is an e-text that is available in minutes. On the other hand, Ray is new to computers and prefers a traditional hardcopy that will be mailed to his home. Graduate students have a plethora of choices and need to be consumer savvy and aware of unreliable vendors.

Digital Libraries

Many remember going to the public library every 2 weeks to check out books, as well as the musty odor that permeated throughout the building. Not all are familiar with accessing information on a card catalog or from the computer database. Brick-and-mortar libraries still exist, but because of the digital age, many students are taking advantage of the available technology for learning. The computer age has opened up a world of opportunities for learners. Textbooks and other course materials that are essential to education are available in digital format. What if you are able to access the information that you need 24/7 without leaving the comfort of your home? Digital libraries are easy to access from practically anywhere as long as you have Internet or Wi-Fi available and an electronic device to access the information.

What are digital libraries? They are libraries without walls, and are also known as electronic or virtual libraries. The idea of storing information and retrieving it later started more than 50 years ago. A digital library is a collection of information that is stored in digital format and is viewed as an extension of library services. A digital library is a better way to receive information and books from all over the world in an electronic format. From the Library of Congress to the university and local libraries, electronic content is accessible anywhere Internet is available. With the increased use of electronic devices and computers, collections of books, chapters, journal articles, magazines, and newspapers can be found in digital format. Information that is available at a traditional library is also available through the digital library. Reference works and encyclopedias are also available, and the newest versions are often available immediately or through the inter-library loan process.

A few years ago, our university counselor education program and a vendor partnered to bring students a digital library that is convenient and saves students on the purchase price. The DL offers access to a complete digital library of the required counseling e-text curriculum at one low flat subscription price. Special access codes for e-texts and labs are available in the school bookstore, or directly online. The customized DL provides an all-access subscription to the required texts and labs across the program for a low cost of approximately $200 for 6 months. For students like Ray that prefer a hardcopy, each individual text costs from $75 to $140. Labs can be purchased for a low cost of $15 to $40. Imagine having access at the touch of your fingertips. DL's provide helpful guides to help students around the library. Special apps are available for android tablets and other devices that are compatible with electronic device browsers, but DL system supports may require faster processors and hard disk space for optimal viewing. The digital process provides a seamless transition from traditional ways to a more efficient and effective method that facilitates learning. Students comment that the DL has saved them money and time and is easy to navigate.

Deconstructing an Online Lab

If you search the Internet for online counseling labs, you may be directed to virtual biology labs studying the social sciences or actual labs where counseling takes place and counselors in training (CITs) hone their skills at centers or universities. In the digital world, however, and for our counseling program, a counseling lab describes a shell used to house course content or additions to the course acting as an ancillary resource for a course. This counseling lab, associated with a course or book purchase, is designed to aid and enhance the course content as a digital lab used in conjunction with an online course.

Online labs are a valuable component to education as book companies, publishers, and authors seek to aid student retention, offering additional resources by coupling a course with a lab. Studies have shown that

> online labs allow opportunities for student success by delivering consistent, measurable gains in their courses. Best practices are identified with these new technologies across disciplines including counseling. Better retention rates and better learning outcomes

with technology enhanced instruction are the results of integrating effective digital resources. (Pearson, 2015, p.1)

Book publishing companies are always looking at best practices and technological ways to aid instructors who teach students. In addition, the offer of an ancillary resource, such as a counseling lab, has given counseling programs who adopt digital library options many opportunities to aid the students financially. Thus, this is a win-win situation for programs that are considering the costs of program improvement, student retention, and instructors' use of valuable time as they try to meet students' needs with labs that offer customized teaching tools. Lastly, students win when they get the best educational experience at a reasonable cost!

Counseling programs can decide which courses will best benefit from the use of the lab with a course. Labs are designed for various reasons and usually the course content outlines the objectives students need to master. For example, counseling labs can be constructed to house practice exams for certification within a practicum course. (You will read more specifics on labs for certification preparation later in this chapter.) Another course may utilize counseling videos to watch and learn about various counseling techniques. An example of incorporating videos is the Individual Theories and Techniques counseling course. Counseling students who are discerning their personal theoretical orientation find videos showing the skills demonstrated from different counseling theories. The lab allows individualized viewing and modeling from a set of created scenarios, in this case, examples in the use of techniques in counseling theories. Students can watch and reflect upon the videos and their rationale for choosing a particular orientation. The additional information of video viewing, reflective assignment, and instructor assessment of students' work can be located in a counseling lab and can help the instructor enhance students' understanding of an important portion of the Individual Theories and Techniques course. The grades can even be exported in the central course grade book if points are allocated for any of this work.

Why is a counseling lab beneficial to students if there are a plethora of free YouTube videos or even websites of various counseling theories and techniques? Why pay a counseling lab fee that costs approximately $15.00 for the extra resource? I would like to share a company's rationale for the additional resource, which is provided in the "Engage Students Effectively With Immersive Content, Tools, and Experiences" box.

Counselor educators, course leads, and instructors desire to find ways to help students learn and retain their subject matter in the online world of education. Counseling labs can be customized for each course

Engage Students Effectively With Immersive Content, Tools, and Experiences

The funny thing about the "one-size-fits-all" approach to learning technology is that it doesn't fit anyone particularly well. With MyLab & Mastering, you and your students will get precisely what you need to succeed: teaching and learning tools that are personalized, customizable, and always engaging.

Each MyLab & Mastering product is designed for a particular course, with a range of discipline-specific features that have been thoughtfully created to maximize engagement and relevance. And due to their very differences, each MyLab & Mastering product is uniquely suited to deliver clear learning gains, and help you and your students break through to better results. (Pearson, 2015, p.2)

and personalized for individual needs. Piggy-backed, if you will, with a counseling course already aligned with national Council for Accreditation of Counseling and Related Educational Programs (CACREP, 2009) standards, state standards, competencies and domains, the online counseling lab truly becomes a laboratory to experiment and aid learning of the course content. Counseling courses are modified in a 3-year cycle, but counseling labs have more flexibility in order to deliver additional material useful to students beyond the scope of preset courses.

Yet, it is at the program's discretion if counseling labs are created and used. Programs may or may not opt for the use of counseling labs in their programs. Initially, instructors avoided the additional shell creation, and counseling labs were underutilized. However, the shift is evident as Best Practices indicate that "the way educators integrate a learning technology is the single most significant element that affects resultant outcomes" (Pearson, 2015, p. 1). Book publishers who offer counseling labs are discovering students' desire for rigor in their online courses. They want to study the extra material personalized per course. Online labs are used for homework, assessment, and graduate tutorials. Thus, with a desire for additional technology resources as part of Lamar University's counseling program goals, the clinical mental health and school counseling programs began to offer online counseling labs to many of our courses.

Online labs are available as part of course requirements or to anyone with a book purchase and an access code. Students may be able to register through their learning management systems (i.e., Blackboard) if the counseling lab is linked. Students will be given an access code created by the instructor if a counseling lab is required for the course. For example, using MyCounselingLab as an enhancement of counseling course assignments, the MyCounselingLab course shell will be set up by the instructor or course developer/lead. Students are directed to the "MyLab" shell to complete assignments or view video resources, customized for that particular course. An instructor can post announcements, e-mail registered students, upload any additional resources, and grade assessments. Used in conjunction with their course, the MyLab allows options for instructors in every course.

For the purpose of ease, the instructor will have an online lab access code for you if the lab is a course requirement. When a course requires a lab, some book companies do offer temporary access codes for students' individual book purchases as an entrance to the labs with an approximate 2-week time span if they are purchasing an individual book from another source. This keeps the students on track in a fast paced course schedule. The syllabus will list the required book(s) and post the online counseling lab requirement with its access code. You should gain entry just as you would an online course start date. The instructor will have set up the counseling lab as they prepare each course-for-course launch.

Students who buy individual e-texts can find the access codes in the front or back of the book, and the access code is usually on paper and shrink-wrapped with the book. You can also buy an access code for a book previously used, but you will want to ask about stand-alone access codes for purchase at the campus book stores. They will contain a card and instructions. You can also purchase access codes from the book vendor. In some cases, you can pay with a credit card for a signature access, but this varies with book companies, so you will have to ask about their online lab offerings and fees.

Once you gain access to the lab, you will be greeted by a similar format of your central course. Instructors like to welcome you and direct you to the left menu, similarly to how a learning management system course such as Blackboard is set up. Since the course is somewhat customized by the instructor, these menus may vary. In general, however, you are given online lab-learning outcomes and objectives the instructors or course leads want for you. Working with the central course syllabus, you will know week to week when to attend the online lab. For example, let's say in Week 2, the learning outcome your instructor wants you to achieve is that you will be able to identify the parent and child role in two examples from the videos for Week 2. You will locate Week 2 videos in the online lab and view the videos on Transactional

Analysis (TA) techniques in action. The instructor may have grouped several videos that pertain to these or other techniques. After you watch them, the instructor will have a reflective assignment or a multiple-choice section of what you learned from viewing the videos. If you are not graded on this assignment, then perhaps you will be given a grade for online course work completion. Perhaps, you will be asked to upload your reflection into the Blackboard central course shell for a grade. As such, the resource has assisted your understanding of TA and the counseling techniques associated with it.

Online labs are designed to enhance student success in an online platform. Instructors are challenged to interact with students in a regular, consistent fashion. Online labs aid in these discussions by offering additional information about the course that strengthens or bolsters the course content. By doing so, online labs can accomplish what students are desiring—more affordably priced resources and successful learning outcomes.

Instructor Notes

Counselor educators in an online program use several options to interact with students in their course. From simple e-mail correspondence in order to respond to students' questions to weekly webinars where students come together and discuss the content of a course as a group, an instructor will optimize their opportunities for student engagement. Another instructor option is Instructor Notes. Added to the readings in an electronic textbook (e-text), notes can aid student comprehension and retention of the material. There are times when instructors will want to share their ideas on a specific part of the reading from an e-text they are using in a course. The use of instructor notes communicates to the student that the noted material is important.

If an instructor has added notes, they can be easily found and identified. As you read through the assigned chapters, you will find a thumbtack or pushpin icon that opens to a specific instructor note. You can access it easily by clicking on the icon, which opens the note box at the spot of the note in the reading. An instructor may draw your attention to the paragraph itself with a colored highlight or add special notes (I call them bonus notes) that may include test hints or any customized material the instructor desires to share with the class regarding that portion of the text. Hyperlinks can be added in the box as well.

You will find the instructor note icon usually located in the e-text toolbar. After you launch your eBook or e-text, these icon tools will catch your attention as you proceed in the assigned reading. You may also access the instructor notes through the digital library. Using Pearson's Digital Library homepage drop-down menu as an example, instructor notes under the name "My Notes" will be available as long as the instructor has shared the notes with students (Pearson, 2015).

Instructor notes can also be categorized. Instructors may assign a note to a pre-existing category, or a new category can be created. You will be directed to find a category in the e-text platform. Categories can be thought of as a form of an outline. This can guide your study habits and direct you to those specific areas instructors deem essential. Counseling students have shared their enthusiasm with their instructors during live webinars about the benefits of instructor notes, speaking positively about how the added statements or clues regarding the topic at that juncture have enhanced their learning. Students' perceptions in course evaluation comments are that the instructor is actively involved in assisting online students, reading along with them, commenting, and advising them. Fortunately, the notes remain in the course if the instructor has kept the course active, making notes accessible for later times. An instructor may modify the shared notes as the e-text edition is updated, which makes this ancillary resource a valuable tool. Thus, instructor notes can enhance your learning experience by answering many of the questions you may want to ask in these notes.

Personal Notes/Highlights

The benefit of making personal notes or note-taking has historically been known to assist the reader in processing and retaining information presented within the textbook. Personal notes made within an e-text provide students with a way to organize and document their thought processes, while being exposed to the content of the textbook. Understandably, students may wish to create notes that allow preparation for them to ask questions of their course professor. Additionally, students can use personal notes as a study guide for assessment preparation or for comprehensive examinations in the course or during their program. Finally, personal notes can be used to pinpoint relevant information in order to complete course-related assignments. The following section will describe approaches to creating a note within the digital e-text.

Creating a Note

There are many reasons one may choose to create a note. There is an electronic way of completing this task, which is beneficial to the user. In order to create a note, select the appropriate icon available on the navigation toolbar. Once that occurs, the cursor automatically becomes a floating push-pin, allowing the user to then hover over the preferred content. Select the identified point of reference by clicking your mouse, thus allowing a blank note to appear with the words self-study in the upper left-hand corner. This is where information can be input into your note, along with being able to change the font by making it bold, italicized, or underlined. Another option is for you to highlight your note, paste it in the box creating an URL, and attach that link to a webpage if desired. Ultimately, you will see an indicator present on the screen, which signals the reader a stored note has been created.

Storing and Accessing a Note

Storing a note is described as saving the input information within the e-text. This allows the user to access their documented thought processes at a later time. Once the option to create a note and information into the note has been entered, the user can click on the save button. In doing so, the note has been saved and the title changed from self-study to private note. At that time, finalizing your saved material can be done by closing out the note screen.

Notes can be stored in one of two places: (1) along the left side of the toolbar under the notes section or (2) at the visible marker. When accessing your stored notes through the notes section under the left toolbar, you will need to use the navigation tool to determine which notes you are trying to access. There, you will notice options such as table of contents, notes, bookmarks, glossary, or index. By selecting the notes option, a downward arrow symbol known as a caret automatically turns downward with the option to open notes manager. If you select any of the stored notes, and click on the open notes manager, a box will appear. Within this box is a list of saved notes (private notes) with the title and chapter of the book, the date, and options to edit the note. The other way to access the note is at the visible marker. Accessing your stored note at the marker is designed for quick referral or reference. By clicking on this marker, it provides the actual note recorded with no other information available to the user.

Users may wish to retrieve their stored (saved) note, which is conducive to accessing a personal study guide of the actual textbook. There are two ways to retrieve a saved or stored note within the e-text or online digital textbook. By selecting the e-text, users can select the My Notes tab, which alphabetically lists each of the e-text. Once the preferred e-text is selected, a list of stored notes will appear for that textbook ordered by page number. There, users can review their note and either edit, print, or export the note.

Editing a Note

An option available to users is to edit saved or stored notes. The reason a user may desire to edit or change a note varies, and within an e-text, there are two paths to getting this accomplished. Once an e-text has been selected, along the left side of the navigation toolbar is a notes option. The user can click on each saved note, which takes the user directly to the section of that book where the note was saved. There, users can read what is in that part of the e-text, along with clicking on the icon and selecting the edit button. Another way to edit a note is to select open notes manager by double-clicking. The notes manager screen will appear and users can select the pencil icon to revise the former information entered.

Printing and Exporting a Stored Note

Printing or exporting stored notes is a convenient way to access the notes in a tangible way. This can be done individually or all notes can be exported in totality in order to print. Once you access the notes manager, and limit the search by page numbers, you can select find. All notes within that page range will appear. Users can select a note and then the printer icon. The other option is to export all notes collectively, and print or save the exported notes.

Embedded Media

Digital textbooks have media embedded or videos to aid users in the understanding of content or concepts presented within the course. This embedded media can be accessed within the labs and are associated with the learning outcomes. Expanding or enriching your knowledge base, relative to that particular learning outcome, is critical through the option made to review that represented learning outcome in the video or vignette. Another way to access embedded videos or media is in the digital library. Users can select videos, which are compiled in global categories such as addictions, career, assessment, ethics, school, or theories. For example, if you select career development, videos will be organized by topics appropriate to this area such as analyzing interest, counseling and unemployed adults, or career assessment interpretation.

Understanding Learning Outcomes

Learning outcomes associated with a course are essential to provide a roadmap that clearly delineates what students should know at the end of each textbook chapter. Learning outcomes are a description of what knowledge, skills, or principles were learned by the student. Learning outcomes are found in the lab section of the digital library. Once you launch the lab, an option for course content is available along the left side of the navigation screen. Upon selecting your choice, the caret (also known as a chevron) will drop down and a list of learning outcomes will appear. Users can read the learning outcomes, as it helps the user to know what information should be learned along with providing suggestions toward information the user may study or use to create a saved note. Another option is to click on the learning outcome, which provides a list of standards for professional practice in the area of marriage, couple, family, school, and clinical mental health counseling. Finally, assignments and activities can be chosen that allow the user to watch embedded media and to answer questions in a short-answer response format.

Deconstructing a Chapter

Deconstructing a chapter within a textbook might seem like a fairly simple task; however it might be to the readers' advantage to look deeper when considering electronic textbooks (e-text). Typically, having a structured format for working through chapters in an e-textbook helps acquire and organize larger volumes of vital information. Whether a textbook is online or a traditional hardcopy, there are generally similar concepts and deconstruction techniques. However, online textbooks typically have more functions in order to organize, highlight, and identify specific information. For the purposes of this section, we will look at deconstructing an e-textbook, also known as digital textbooks or e-texts.

Electronic textbooks are typically defined as traditional hardcopy textbooks but accessed in an online capacity. E-texts have a multitude of advantages; cheaper cost for student and University, access to multiple features to help organize information, smaller impact on the environment due to saving paper, and access to unlimited knowledge that can be linked to the concept through the electronic version. These concepts might contain embedded videos, discussion forums, professional links, images, additional websites, labs, and/or tools to enhance learning with the click of a button. This particular information will walk you through chapter objectives, learning outcomes, headers, sub-headers, figures, tables, terms, glossaries and multimedia as part of an online learning consortium with e-texts.

Before we began looking at the specifics, let's review techniques to become familiar with the chapters and information. First and foremost, the reader should become familiar with the e-text, learning to access the text and generally filtering through chapters and pages. Another general goal is having a basic understanding of chapter breakdown and content. On many occasions, there may be videos or tutorials to help utilize the e-text to its fullest capacity. For this specific reason navigating e-text for the first time may require a little more set up and prep time before diving into the information. Try to familiarize yourself with being able to skip to specific pages or chapters as well as the search functions when wanting to locate specific information. Many e-texts have search, footnotes, and hyperlinks to access information within the text. Once you feel familiar with the technology, you will feel more comfortable with navigating the information for deconstructing the chapters. See Table 6.1.

After becoming familiar with the basic technology within the e-text and e-chapters, students can begin to deconstruct a specific chapter. Deconstructing a chapter can allow for chapter organization and mind mapping. Mind mapping refers to organizing the information within your memory while working through the e-text. The following will discuss information that might help students organize these textual concepts (see Table 6.2 for an overview of deconstructing a chapter).

Chapter Objectives

Chapter objectives are an easy way to get a quick glance at the information to come. These objectives can also be extremely beneficial in directing you to specific information. Identifying components of the chapter and what the reader should understand after reading is the main goal. You can often think of chapter objectives as a roadmap for the information to come.

Table 6.1   Things to Consider When Starting Deconstruction of
a Chapter/E-Text

E-Text Access	How will you access the information? Do you need Internet to access all information within the chapters? Will you download the e-text to a laptop, computer, and/or smart device, or will you access the chapters via passwords protected site? Organizing quick access can be extremely beneficial.
Chapter and Page Navigation	Learn to access specific chapters and page numbers. Typically this information can be accessed in multiple ways through searching or tabs.
Table of Contents	Explore and learn how to navigate the table of contents and the E-textbook and chapters. This will also help with chapter and page navigation.
Glossary	Learning to use the e-text glossary can help you access terms and vocabulary definitions embedded in the text. Many times, you will see hyperlinks or footnotes that might indicate such tools.
Page View	Depending on the publishers, you may be able to view more than one e-page at a time. This can depend on personal preference. Viewing one or multiple pages at a time might be an option.
Bookmarks	Exploring bookmarks can help you easily identify pages with important information to the reader. Typically bookmarks allow you to jump to a specific section.

Using this roadmap can also test your knowledge after reading to see if you gained knowledge of the objectives identified. It is important as a student to observe chapter objectives within the e-text, and also chapter objectives the instructor may have identified. What students will read, gain, and study are the basis of learning objectives.

Chapter objectives are also great ways to highlight/notate important information you may need in the future. Be sure to check the functions within your e-text. Many publishers allow you to add notes or use highlight functions for organization purposes. This can allow you as a student to quickly scan information and notes that you may have added in the chapter objectives instead of digging through the chapter for specific information.

Learning Outcomes

Learning outcomes are statements that specifically acknowledge what the reader will learn. The outcomes are used to express knowledge and specific skills obtained though this information. Typically you will see chapter objectives as broad headings and learning outcomes as specifics to knowledge gained. Learning outcomes can serve a multitude of objectives. They can focus the information for desired knowledge outcomes. Learning outcomes can help identify specifics within chapters and units. These outcomes can also serve as specific guidelines for content and knowledge evaluation. Often learning outcomes are defined as measurable objectives. This means that they describe an observable action. Learning outcomes can be defined in course syllabi as well as the beginning of e-chapters or e-text.

So what is the difference between learning objectives and learning outcomes? Again, objectives are typically defined as intended results and learning outcomes are defined as achieved or measurable. Both objectives and outcomes aid in maximizing the content within the e-text. Let's look at an example to better understand learning objectives versus learning outcomes. A sample learning objective might be stated as, "At the conclusion of this chapter, students will be able to understand the difference between learning objectives and learning outcomes." A sample learning outcome might be stated as, "The student will successfully write learning outcomes and learning objectives on the chapter quiz." Understanding the differences between learning objectives and outcomes will aid the reader in deconstructing the chapter through e-text.

Headers and Subheaders

Headers and subheaders are used to visually represent specific information within sections of an e-text. Headers are typically just a one or a few words to give the reader an idea of what the section content encompasses. The short phrases are not in-depth, but give the reader guidance throughout the chapter layout. Headers are usually always uniform throughout the e-text. Subheaders can be slightly longer since they are typically expanding on information indicated in the header. The format of these may vary depending on writing style. Visually subheaders are smaller in font than headers; however, both are conveying importance in information.

While headers and subheaders might be a familiar concept they can be different when using e-text. These heading systems can possibly be links to paralleling information. Meaning, since headers and subheaders indicate targeted information they may also be linked to additional supporting material. When becoming familiar with the e-text this might be an important concept to explore. In some publishing companies, you can actually click on headers and subheaders to link you to additional resources pertaining to that specific information. Headers and subheaders are speedy ways to decode targeted information within sections and e-chapters.

Figures and Tables

Figures and tables are popular forms of visually representing information to students. Figures and tables are typically eye-catching and easy ways to get a snapshot of the information presented. E-texts tend to display more figures and charts due to accessibility through hyperlinks to such information. Figures can be visually represented through graphs, charts, photos, drawings, maps, and symbols. Tables most often visually represent numbers or text within columns and rows. Often tables will have legends to understand the information represented. Using tables can help the reader visually grasp qualitative and quantitative data with ease. Figures and tables in e-text have the ability to be "live" or "in motion." This means figures and tables within chapters can be continuously updating or moving to represent information. This concept can give a new and exciting visualization to a variety of information. For example, think of tables/charts that represent the items on the stock market, gas prices, or Yahoo news feed. Then consider this type of information pertinent to your chapter embedded within your readings. Figures and tables within e-text can provide valuable and visually interesting information.

Terms and Glossary

Terms and glossaries can be unique to the e-text world. These are important concepts to understand when you first began using electronic textbook systems. However these two concepts can provide a multitude of information. Terms are typically words embedded within the text. Important terms may be highlighted or have footnotes to indicate specific information. Some text may have certain terms defined through art, different fonts, or side notes if the author believes it is important information for the reader to understand the content. For example, a word may be highlighted and when right-clicked, a full definition and picture may be displayed. Glossaries are typically defined as the main presenting vocabulary throughout the e-text. The glossaries are typically at the end and represented in alphabetical order, however with most e-text, the glossary is easily accessed through additional tabs or links. Terms and glossaries embedded in e-chapters and e-text give easy access to the vocabulary comprehension for better content knowledge.

Multimedia

The use of multimedia might be one of the most distinguishing aspects of online learning in e-text. Multimedia is typically defined as something that is played or recorded. For the purposes of online learning, this could be in the form of videos, websites, text, audio, images, animation, or any interactive content. Multimedia is traditionally embedded into the text as supplemental forms of learning and concept reiteration. Using multimedia in a variety of ways allows the reader to understand and experience the textual information through multiple facets that engage the learning concepts and outcomes. Imagine reading about a specific theory and then being able to watch an interview with the actual creator or learning about particular skills, and then being able to view an animated role-play demonstration. Multimedia is at your fingertips through the access of e-text. Identifying multimedia for your e-text can enrich the learning process through many features.

Table 6.2   Deconstructing a Chapter Chart

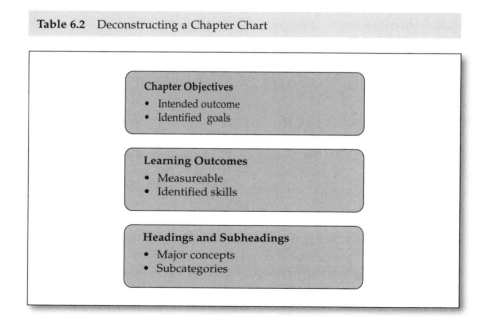

Table 6.2

Figures and Tables
- Charts
- Visual representations
- Data

Terms and Glossary
- Identified terminology
- Alphabetical listings of terminology

Multimedia
- Videos
- Images
- Animations

Using E-Textbooks to Prepare for Certification and Licensure

Preparing for certification and licensure exams can be a stressful time. Learning to prepare for these tests early can benefit you when beginning to prepare for testing. Certification is defined as an individual meeting specific criterion for a private organization. Typically practitioners will seek certification for self-promotion in attempts to identify oneself as part of a select group. Licensure is defined as state or government agencies that grant individuals permission to be referred to as licensed. Obtaining licensure in some professions is mandatory in order to practice. Understanding state laws for certification and licensure for individuals will help prepare for such tasks. Using the multitude of concepts you have learned throughout this reading can help you prepare and organize. Knowing early on the tested areas and subjects allows for you to identify specific information through your e-text when taking the courses.

Using the variety of tools provided through your virtual publisher can also be extremely helpful when accessing information after the course/courses have passed. Many e-text will provide labs with additional information or e-links for preparing you for certification and licensure in specific areas and states. Saving this information for later use could aid in the preparation for certification and licensure. Being aware at the start of your studies of state and national requirements when it comes to certification and licensure will be tremendously helpful with preparation.

Summary

One of the most important components of a course is the textbook. Textbooks provide content information that can serve as a foundation for the course. When planning to purchase a textbook, careful consideration should be taken to ensure that you obtain the best possible price. Just as you would when shopping for clothing or food, a smart graduate student should be familiar with their options for renting and purchasing a textbook, and the role vendors' play to facilitate the process and save you money. On the other hand, digital libraries provide quick and easy access to electronic textbooks at affordable low prices.

Two resources found in the online world are instructor notes and online counseling labs. Instructor notes can aid the student by identifying those important concepts or elaborating on a key element of the particular chapter in the e-text. Course instructors use this to "speak" to students via notes so that students will know what is important to learn in the course. In a similar fashion, customized online counseling labs created for the enhancement of the major course can be the vital resource that aids student understanding and learning of key concepts in a required course.

Navigating digital textbooks, or e-texts, have options available for executable functions. These functions allow a user to create, store, edit, and print notes. Additional features of a digital textbook consist of optional embedded media that provide users with learning outcomes. All of these options make it less challenging to interact with the text and to develop a system of managing your personal notes. Moreover, online textbooks (e-texts) typically have extra functions in order to organize, highlight, and identify specific information. Learning to navigate and access the text and generally filtering through chapters and pages and becoming familiar with the basic technology will initially take a little extra time. Understanding the functional elements and utilizing the e-text to its fullest capacity will ensure a successful learning experience. It is also important to understand that early preparation and planning is the key to passing your certification and licensure exam. Utilize the tools each e-text offers, and this proactive effort will pay off in the end.

About the Authors

Belinda J. Lopez, PhD, NCC, LPC-S, CSC, is an assistant professor and Coordinator for the School Counseling Program in the Department of Counseling and Special Populations at Lamar University. She earned her doctorate in counselor education from Texas A&M University-Corpus Christi. Her research interests include school counselor supervision, mattering and wellness, and multicultural issues.

Rachael Ammons Whitaker is currently a visiting assistant professor and field experience coordinator for the school counseling program at Lamar University in Beaumont, Texas. She has worked as a behavioral therapist, behavioral interventionist supervisor, and school counselor before pursuing counselor education. In 2014, Rachael was awarded the national Courtland Lee Multicultural Excellence award from American Counseling Association. Rachael's professional obligations currently consist of Southeast Texas Counseling Association legislative liaison, Association for Assessment and Research in Counseling social media chair, and peer reviewer for the Journal of College Counseling and the Journal of Asynchronous Learning Network. She currently supervises Lamar interns placed at Wheatley School of the Early Childhood Program in Port Arthur, Texas, providing mental health services to underserved children and families. She provides individual therapy for several refered child and adolescence clients at Lamar's Cardinal Clinic. Rachael continues to implant herself in education and clinical sides of the counseling profession. Her current research involves beliefs and implementation in the American School Counseling Association National Model, best practice in autism spectrum disorder, and online counselor education.

Patricia A. Harris has been a Clinical Instructor at Lamar University since the development of the Online Counseling Degree Program in 2011 and the Counseling and Special Populations (COSP) Department. She has been an educator for over 20 years serving as a Certified School Counselor at two SE TX high schools while teaching campus based graduate counseling courses as an Adjunct Professor at Lamar. Patricia is a Licensed Professional Counselor, National Certified Counselor, and a National Certified School Counselor. She is a trained EMDR therapist working with clients in the Cardinal Community Clinic using EMDR to complete her certification. Dr. Harris was featured in the 2013 Summer edition of the Association for Spiritual, Ethical, and Religious Values in Counseling (ASERVIC)'s *Interaction* newsletter.

Dr. Lisa A. Wines is an assistant professor in the Department of Counseling and Special Populations here at Lamar University. Dr. Wines comes to us with over 15 years of professional experience in education, inclusive of elementary, secondary, and post-secondary levels. She is a certified school counselor and a licensed professional counselor intern. Her major focus consists of counseling children and adolescents, with evolving experiences in study abroad programming, hospitals, and private practice settings. Her research interests are in the area of qualitative research methodology and explorations of school counselor phenomena, bringing commitment to developing practical, application-based literature for the counseling profession at large.

References

Council for Accreditation of Counseling and Related Educational Programs. (2009). *The 2009 standards*. Alexandria, VA: Author. Retrieved from http://www.cacrep.org/doc/2009%20Standards%20with%20cover.pdf

Pearson. (2015). *Instructor notes*. Retrieved from http://help.pearsoncmg.com/etext/viewer4/en/ipad/welcome.htm#NotesAndHighlights

7

Interacting Productively With Faculty and Peers

Wendy Greenidge

Chapter Overview

This chapter will provide you with some practical guidelines for successfully interacting in the online learning environment, the online etiquette, and suggestions for interacting productively and professionally with faculty and peers. We then address how to successfully utilize the online discussion board as well as how to utilize various online platforms and social media to facilitate a positive online environment and enhance student satisfaction and success in online learning programs.

Learning Outcomes

Upon completion of this chapter, you will

1. Become familiar with online etiquette especially as it relates to online learning

2. Understand how to interact positively on online discussion boards

3. Understand how to foster a positive online learning experience and facilitate success

4. Learn how to create and maintain a professional online presence

Introduction

Enrollment in online academic programs continues to increase dramatically across the United States, with more and more traditional institutions embracing the trend. While online education is not best suited for, or preferred by everyone, it does have appeal to a broad audience of prospective students. Some of the conveniences and advantages that online programs provide include flexibility, increased options in varying geographical locations, anytime-anywhere studying, accelerated courses, lower costs, and self-paced learning to name a few. While some people believe that online academic programs offer an easier, less rigorous form of learning, the exact opposite is true. Online learning has proved to be just as effective as traditional face-to-face learning and in many cases can be more intensive than traditional classrooms due to the accelerated nature in which courses are presented.

Success in online learning programs depends on many factors including being equipped with the knowledge and skills needed to be effective in the online environment. This chapter therefore seeks to provide you with the resources and support needed to be effective in your online counseling program. More specifically you will be introduced to the fundamentals of successfully interacting with others in an online learning environment. This chapter will also highlight important netiquette (online etiquette) guidelines to facilitate an increase in online productivity, satisfaction, and foster a successful online environment.

Online Etiquette

Netiquette refers to rules of etiquette that apply to online communication. Many individuals are very familiar with online and social technologies yet lack the understanding of how to appropriately and effectively use these in an online academic and professional setting. Just as communication in face-to-face or campus based classes follow unwritten but acknowledged standards, so do online programs. However, communication in online programs may become a bit more challenging than in traditional classrooms. With the absence of visual cues and immediacy in providing clarification in online programs, misunderstandings and misinterpretations are frequent. Learning how to account for this deficit and make full use of the techniques and strategies that will be presented here becomes paramount. Netiquette rules and guidelines offer a much needed baseline to ensure professionalism in online interactions.

It is common practice for instructors to clarify their behavioral expectations (e.g., respecting diversity, engaging in appropriate scholarly discussion, acknowledging different perspectives) of students during the first week or orientation of a course. These are also typically highlighted in course syllabi. As soon as these become available to you, it's recommended to devote some time to reviewing these expectations as well as your roles and responsibilities and those of your instructor. Be sure to consider what these expectations look like in practice and to seek input if you are unsure.

Juanita is a new online student in a school counseling program at Avatar University. She hasn't been in school for over 20 years but wants to make a career change. In her first discussion board posting for class, Juanita noticed that another student made a comment about the need for more Spanish-speaking counselors in her home area. Juanita replied to the student and stated that she thought that all counselors should be bilingual to meet the needs of those students who spoke English as a second language. Several members of the class disagreed with Juanita, and she became angry with their opposition. In her next post, she typed, "COUNSELORS CAN'T BE PREJUDICED."

What happened in this situation that could be addressed through appropriate netiquette and scholarly behavior? First, counselor educators encourage students to base comments in research. Informed opinions are much more appropriate than personal opinions for a scholarly discussion. It might have been a much different discussion if Juanita replied to the initial post in the following manner, "Sarah, I agree with you about the need for more Spanish-speaking counselors." Gonzalez (2015) conducted a study that demonstrated a higher academic success rate for Mexican-American high school students in schools with a Spanish-speaking counselor. Gonzalez's study makes me think that this would also be true for other schools with Spanish-speaking populations of students.

When interacting with your faculty and peers online, one rule of thumb is to always assume good intent of an individual posting a comment or sending a message (Pallof & Pratt, 2001). With the absence of visual and auditory cues, it is easy to misunderstand messages as they lack the emotional richness of context. As a result, it is advisable to delay responding to perceived attacks for at least 24 hours (West, 2010). Failure to adhere to this may result in flaming (posting critical and angry messages), which only serve to create a negative and hostile online environment.

E-mail Communication

It is imperative that e-mail exchanges remain professional at all times. This becomes a bit more difficult when a student seeks to present a complaint or dissatisfaction with some aspect of the course. In these instances, after drafting an e-mail, it is recommended that you allow someone else to review your message to ensure it's professional, or you may delay sending the e-mail until some time as lapsed. Please note that e-mail messages should be sent from the official e-mail address assigned to you by your academic institution to ensure that communication is documented and that it is not blocked by institutional filters. It is also good practice to review your official account daily, as this is the medium your instructors will most frequently use to communicate with you.

The subject of your e-mail message should always accurately reflect the purpose of your message. Including your course and section number in the subject line of your e-mail also facilitates a speedy response from your instructors (e.g., CNDV 5381 M02 Assignment One or CNDV 5381 M03 Grades). Many instructors facilitate several courses per semester and including this information in your e-mails, precludes them from having to review each of their class lists to determine which class you're enrolled in and what specific assignment you're alluding to, for instance. In the body of your message, always begin with a salutation. Address your instructors appropriately (e.g., Dr. Smith, Professor George, Ms. Andrews) unless they direct you to do otherwise. It is inappropriate to address your instructor by his or her first name.

E-mails should be constructed using standard English. The use of slang, shortened versions of words (most commonly used in social media), Internet slang and acronyms are strictly prohibited in academic settings. All communication should be constructed in a professional manner using complete sentences and correct grammar and spelling. Always review your e-mails once or twice before sending. Remember once you send the e-mail, you may have the option to retract or recall your message; however, the recipients still have a copy of the original message.

If you intend to address more than one item or issue in your e-mail, please ensure that these are clearly delineated. One way to do this is to address each issue in a separate paragraph. You may also number your items so that the recipient knows there is more than one issue. In online courses, students should be patient with delays in communication. Typically instructors will state how quickly you can expect to receive a response (e.g., within 24–48 hours). However there may be delays due to illness, holidays, the weekend, etc. For some common netiquette guidelines related to online courses, see Table 7.1. These guidelines are applicable to all forms of communication in an online learning environment: e-mails, discussion boards, videoconferencing, and others.

Table 7.1   Guidelines for Netiquette in an Online Course

Guideline	Rationale
Respect others and the opinions of others	In our increasingly diverse world, it is almost a guarantee that you will be in class with individuals with differing opinions, values, and cultures. When embraced and treated with respect, these differences serve to enrich the learning the experience.
Refrain from writing in ALL UPPERCASE	This is generally used to signal dissatisfaction and anger. When communicating with faculty and peers, stay away from this as you will be perceived as being disrespectful and unprofessional.
Revise before submitting	One of the benefits of online learning is that you can review and revise your material before submitting. Take advantage of this benefit by reviewing your work before posting.
Avoid acronyms	Acronyms (e.g., BTW) can be confusing to people who are not familiar with them.

(Continued)

Table 7.1 (Continued)

Guideline	Rationale
Avoid Internet lingo and text speak	Avoid the use of Internet lingo such as "ur" instead of your, "l8r," short for later and "idk" that is typically the shortened form of "I don't know." These are not tolerated in professional and academic settings and will reflect poorly on your writing skills. For many, the use of these acronyms on social media has become second nature; as a result, it is advisable to critically review your assignments and posts and correct any errors before submitting.
Write concisely	In online courses, participants are required to engage in lots of reading. Your peers are more susceptible to read your posts if they are concise, clear, and well written. You may also break texts into shorter paragraphs and leave a space between each paragraph. Many institutions offer writing labs to assist students with improving their writing skills. Take advantage of the resources that are available to you.
Identify sources	Always identify the source(s) of your material, otherwise your work will be flagged for plagiarism. Plagiarism simply means that you presented someone else's work as your own. Most institutions have a zero tolerance for plagiarism and sanctions range from deduction of points to expulsion from the course or program. It is expected and recommended that you will first review reading materials from various sources to assist with your course assignments. In these cases you are to paraphrase (put in your own words) your findings and indicate the source(s) of all materials used in your assignment papers and discussion posts.
Contribute substantial responses	When responding to the posts of your faculty and peers, provide substantial responses to maintain the flow of the discussion. Responses such as "me too" are inadequate.
Check in on comments	After posting a comment or response, always return to your posting frequently to see if anyone has responded.
Pause	Wait 24 hours before replying to an attack. In some cases, it may be more prudent to report the incident to your instructor before responding to the attack.

Guideline	Rationale
Clarify	As in face-to-face classes, expect occasional conflict. However do not confuse confusion with conflict.
Attend to language	Be considerate with your language. Remember that the lack of auditory and visual cues and feedback don't allow you to see the effects of your writing on others.
Be prompt	Replying to others quickly allows for a continuous scholarly discussion.
Post frequently	Post frequently. Remember your discussion posts are often the only forms of communication you have with your peers. Going too long without interacting will leave others wondering whether you are listening or committed to the course.
Privacy	Consider the privacy of others. Seek permission before reposting material from another to third parties.
Test technology	Test your technology ahead of scheduled postings and communication to ensure that it works. No matter how competent you are with online technologies, they *will* sometimes fail. Be patient. (West, 2010)
Be polite	Finally, be pleasant and polite. Don't use offensive language, and don't be confrontational for the sake of confrontation.

Lack of Anonymity in an Online Environment

While many social media sites offer privacy controls, one's privacy and level of anonymity is never 100% foolproof. Anonymity means that the identity of the author of a message is not shown. This is often used to make it difficult or impossible to discover who the real author of a message is. Pseudonymity is also used, and this refers to those instances where the author uses a name other than their own. Many individuals on social media may employ either strategy for various reasons. They may create Facebook or Twitter accounts for instance with fake identities or use a name other than their own.

It is important to recognize that there is no anonymity when enrolled in online courses. Your full name is always displayed in classroom forums and will be visible to your instructors, teaching assistants, and all others enrolled in the course. Students do not have the option to use pseudo-identities or, in many cases, to use fake photos as the official university photo is typically the default. This is another great reason to avoid irresponsible behavior and to communicate appropriately with your instructors and peers. When participating in an online classroom, you should consider it the same as if you were sitting in a classroom on a university campus.

Students should also exercise more control over personal information disclosure due to the lack of anonymity in online learning environments. In other words, be wary of the amount of personal information shared online in your courses. Students generally have complete control over how much and what types of personal information is shared with others. There is enough flexibility to introduce yourself at the start of a course and share your thoughts, beliefs, and values throughout the course, without divulging information that's too personal. There is generally no need to disclose sensitive information such as physical addresses, birthdates, phone numbers, or other related information in an open forum.

Effective Online Discussion Board Interaction

In many cases, participation on course discussion boards is compulsory and accounts for a large portion of a final grade. Therefore you do not have the option to simply avoid participation as a means of securing anonymity. The challenge is in finding ways to balance the amount of personal information shared while remaining authentic.

How to Make a Professional Post in a Discussion Forum

Many online academic programs use discussion boards to facilitate interaction and increase a sense of community among students. There are several uses of the discussion board; however, in many cases students are required to submit numerous discussion posts throughout each course. These posts are often closely monitored and graded by the instructor, and it is imperative that students remain professional on these discussion boards and practice guidelines for submitting appropriate content. Although you may have a wealth of experience with submitting posts on social media forums, the expectations, rules, and writing style for educational settings are much different.

When working on your discussion posts, ensure that you have devoted adequate time to successfully fulfill the requirements of the post. Many of the errors that will be highlighted below easily occur when students are rushed and pressed for time. Then, the likelihood of errors increase and the quality of your posts may be severely compromised.

Before you begin to draft and submit your discussion posts, spend some time reviewing expectations, rules, and discussion board guidelines for this specific course. Ensure that you fully understand what is being asked of you. Never assume that the rules and expectations are the same for every online program or online course.

After reading the instructions for your discussion post, begin thinking in paragraphs, not sentences. Avoid overly brief responses. It is impossible to effectively address a college-level discussion board assignment with one or two sentences. Review the rubric and instructions for the assignment and ensure that you sufficiently address each aspect in your submission. You will shortchange no one but yourself by not being fully committed to the course.

Make time to carefully read the posts from your instructor and peers before posting yours. The title of your discussion post should reflect the specific assignment. Some instructors provide guidelines for the subject line of your discussion posts. Be sure to pay attention to these. All discussion posts should include a reference list of sources that you used to help formulate your post. Remember that strong discussion posts are informed by various resources such as textbooks, credible online sources, library sources, and personal experiences. If your discussion assignment is based on readings, spend adequate time reviewing course lectures, articles, textbook chapters, and other resources. Restate the central points in your own words and present your opinion or reactions to these. Remember to include a reference list at the end of each of your posts. This is especially important if you are required to submit all assignments in APA (American Psychological Association) format.

Participate in the online discussion board frequently throughout each week. For best practice, your initial posts should be submitted early in the week, and your response posts should be scattered throughout the week—on several days. Ensure that your discussion posts are well developed and fully address all aspects of the assignment. Your post should also demonstrate a careful analysis of the posts of your peers and instructor and extend meaningful discussion by building on previous posts. Make every attempt to advance the discussion through factually correct, reflective, and substantive contributions. Submit discussion posts that are clear, concise, easy to read, and free of grammatical and spelling errors.

When asked to provide a reflection, think about what you've learned and how it may impact your beliefs, behaviors, and your current and future careers. If there is a maximum number of words for your discussion posts, ensure that your entire post addresses the topic in a concise and relevant manner. Adding fillers to ensure you meet the maximum is obvious and frowned upon by your instructors and peers.

Often you will be required to respond to a few of your peers. Always go above and beyond the minimum requirements. For instance, if you are required to respond to at least two peers, try to respond to four or more. One of the goals of the discussion board assignments is that you not only interact with many of your peers, but that you also learn from the input of your peers and gain diverse perspectives on the topic being explored. In a traditional classroom setting, you would more than likely interact with and hear the perspectives of more than two classmates. The same applies with online learning—make a deliberate effort to use the discussion board to maximize your learning experience. This will offset the feeling of isolation, and the more you participate and interact with your peers, the more you will feel motivated and involved.

Pay close attention to the formatting of your posts. Correct grammar and spelling are expected at *all* times in academic and professional settings. Avoid internet slang, acronyms, and online abbreviations such as "ur" instead of the word *your*. Ending your sentence with a period so others know you have finished your thought is great practice. Leaving a space between paragraphs also better organizes your submissions. Students may use a word processor such as Microsoft Word to first type out their responses, review, check for spelling and grammar before posting on the discussion board. Mechanics are usually accounted for in your discussion posts grades. With this being said, it is not your responsibility to identify and correct the spelling and grammatical errors of your peers. Leave this up to your instructor.

Remember those reading your posts are doing so in the absence of auditory and visual cues. Ensure that you are projecting the intended message. Refrain from posting comments that don't add anything to the discussion. Avoid submitting excessively lengthy posts. This decreases the likelihood that it will be read in its entirety by your peers. Also refrain from posting irrelevant information, links, comments, thoughts, or pictures.

Ensure that your question hasn't already been addressed and received a reply before posting it. In a traditional classroom, you would not repeat a question, right after it was asked and addressed. The same applies with online classrooms. Similarly, review course resources such as the Resources Page, FAQ, or search the Internet to determine if an answer to your question is easily obtainable.

Always read the most recent comments before replying to a discussion post. The issue might have been resolved and opinions may have changed.

Comments that would not be appropriate in a traditional face-to-face classroom are also inappropriate in an online learning environment. Be forgiving of your peers when they make mistakes. We all err at times. Being polite and respectful fosters a safe and open environment where individuals feel free to be themselves. Communicate with warmth— remember you are communicating to people, not to the computer. Empathy also goes a long way in ensuring appropriate posts. Put yourself in the shoes of your peers and instructor and ask the following questions: How do I sound to others? How do I think they will respond to my posts? Do you think anyone will be offended by my posts? Are there any revisions that can be made before I submit? Always present with a respectful tone and remember to include "please" and "thank you" when appropriate and when soliciting assistance from your peers and instructors.

Use descriptive and specific subject lines. This helps others decide whether your particular words of wisdom relate to a topic they care about. Common reasons for low scores on discussion posts include

- Failure to strictly adhere to the guidelines and norms for discussion posts.
- Posts were off topic.
- All areas of the assignment were not addressed. Students often miss parts of an assignment especially when there are multiple requirements.
- Post was not clear, accurate, precise, or relevant.
- Posts were inflammatory and inappropriate.
- Too many spelling and grammatical errors.

Before you post, ask yourself . . .

- Would you say this to someone?
- Who is going to see this?
- Am I mentioning someone else?
- Would they mind I posted this?
- Would I want this said about me?
- Is it a fact or opinion?
- Is the fact truthful?

Engaging in a Scholarly Debate Versus an Argument

Classrooms, both traditional and online, are often filled with students from various backgrounds and cultures as well as students with differing values and opinions. When embraced, these serve to enrich the classroom experience and enhance learning. However, if diversity of opinions is not embraced, students can often become defensive, and handle the differences in inappropriate ways.

Online discussion boards provide great avenues for students to interact with their peers online as well as to reflect and refine attitudes, beliefs, and values without fear of offending others or experiencing embarrassment or feeling exposed. Students who are new to online programs, often struggle with the different expectations as compared with what they're used to in general communication on social media. Students are often required to dialogue about key topics related to the subject matter. Many students tend to veer toward the side of caution by only submitting "safe" and agreeable responses. While we expect respect and concern for others, we also encourage constructive scholarly debates on the presenting topics. It is absolutely possible to adhere to all the netiquette guidelines and still engage in healthy scholarly debates. During these interactions it is expected that there will be scholarly debates about the issues under review. Care must be taken to avoid engaging in arguments that lead to nowhere and only serve to create a hostile environment.

So what are the key differences between scholarly debates and arguments? Scholarly debates move online discussions from mere superficial postings to generating depth in online learning forums. Scholarly debates consider and respect the opinions of others while offering new perspectives. On the contrary, arguments dismiss the opinions of others, while presenting the opinion of the author as the sole acceptable position. Arguments are defensive and often divisive while scholarly debates seek to build on the position of others rather than attack and tear them down. Arguments tend to be self-centered with neither side willing to respect the view of the other. Scholarly debates do not result in peers ganging up on each other, they are not demeaning, and they offer solutions.

With increasingly diverse classrooms, it is inevitable that some of your peers may have differing opinions and values. There are appropriate ways of voicing disagreement with another's post. Engaging in attacks, flaming, criticism, and demeaning language are all inappropriate and unsuccessful. Use these opportunities to demonstrate your maturity and ability to argue a point using assertive yet polite language. Consider the difference between "This is nonsense! You obviously have no idea what you're talking about" versus "Thank you for sharing your thoughts on the topic. I have a different view however . . ." The former ignites contempt and hostility, while the latter fosters a safe environment where individuals are free to share their perspectives without fear of being attacked. If you feel the need to disagree, do so politely while simultaneously acknowledging valid points presented in your peer's argument.

Appropriately Advocating for Yourself in an Online Environment

When you communicate online, whether via e-mail or on discussion boards, your words are written and most likely stored somewhere in cyberspace. Likewise, your messages and posts can be easily copied and forwarded to nonintended third parties. With this in mind, it is always a good idea to ensure that you always represent yourself in the most professional manner so that your words don't come back to haunt you later. Instructors appreciate feedback from students and are happy to assist in facilitating your learning. As a result, we look forward to and welcome students who advocate for themselves and their learning experience. The key is to be able to do so in a professional and timely manner.

It is a good rule of thumb to adhere to the same high standards of behavior online that you would follow in a traditional face-to-face classroom. Standards of behavior may be different in some areas of cyberspace, but they are not lower than in real life. In traditional classrooms, students who interact with professors are generally very cautious about their tone, language, and manner in which they approach the instructor. The same applies with online learning. It is easy for some to forget that there are human recipients behind these computers and that the same standards of behavior and ethics should be applied. Your message of concern, suggestions, and general feedback will be more palatable to your instructors and other intended recipients if it's presented in a professional manner. All netiquette guidelines that we covered earlier also apply here.

When advocating to your instructors, be concise paying attention to linking your requests to the objectives and goals of the course and specific assignments. Communicate in a timely manner. Your instructor will be more likely to assist if you've allowed him or her adequate time to do so. Be mindful of the instructor's time and other responsibilities. If you are experiencing difficulty with course expectations, communicate this to your instructor promptly. The instructor has no other way of knowing your specific needs unless you let them know. Be precise and prompt when stating what you're struggling with. This allows your instructor to respond in a timely manner.

As discussed earlier, ensure that your subject line reflects the general message conveyed in the body of your e-mail. When advocating for yourself, state the issue in a polite and respectful tone and where appropriate offer strategies for resolution. For instance, if you are disputing a grade, offer examples of where you provided the information requested, ask for more specific feedback so you may learn from your mistakes, and when appropriate generate possible solutions for increasing your grade such as resubmitting the assignment, writing an additional paper, etc. This conveys the message that you remain open to feedback, you accept responsibility for the areas in which you erred and you're willing to work hard at improving your grades. Consider the difference between the scenario just presented and the case where a student sends an angry e-mail to the instructor demanding that the grade be revised. Always think about how your message will come across to the reader, in the absence of visual and auditory cues. Think about strategies that will make your instructor more apt to work with you.

Many instructors offer individual consultations via videoconferencing, the phone, or for those nearby, in person. Take advantage of these opportunities. Inform your instructors if you need additional guidance, resources, or feedback. When presented in a professional manner and a tone that communicates your investment in your learning, instructors are very amenable to your requests. Of course, you also want to ensure that you take some responsibility for your learning and demonstrate your attempts at finding a solution to the issue presented.

There is typically a chain of command for addressing issues and concerns in an online learning environment. This differs based on the institution, but they all have one thing in common: you always begin with the instructor of the course in question. This allows the instructor to become aware of the issues or concerns you are experiencing and provides him or her the opportunity to remedy the situation. If after a reasonable time has elapsed the issue is still unresolved or not to your satisfaction, you may then approach the next in command, which may be the Program Coordinator or the Department Chair for instance. It is your responsibility to determine the appropriate steps to advocating for yourself at your particular institution.

Social Media and Online Presence

With increasing social media platforms and the increasing numbers of accounts, it is imperative that students are also mindful of how they conduct themselves on social media. It is widely known that more and more academic institutions and potential employers are scrutinizing the accounts of individuals before offering employment and acceptance into academic programs. No matter how many privacy settings you activate on your accounts, your information is never completely private.

There are hundreds of social media sites available. Some of the more common ones include Facebook, Twitter, Instagram, LinkedIn, Pinterest, Vine, Snapchat, YouTube, and Tumblr. As of February 2015, there were over 1.39 billion monthly active Facebook users, and 890 million log onto Facebook daily. It is almost impossible to expect that students will not also have social media accounts where they interact with others. The key is to remember that your social media profile should be an extension of who you are. Instead of spending time carefully hiding personal things with the privacy settings, just post responsibly! Always ensure that you are representing yourself and your academic institution well.

One common error that students often make is to inappropriately vent about aspects of their academic program on social media. They may rant about instructors, assignments, group projects, peers, etc. Remember, grievances are better resolved when presented directly to the individuals involved rather than played out on social media. The repercussions are too vast. Likewise, the issues may never be resolved as the individuals involved remain unaware of how these things are affecting you. Going directly to your instructors gives them an opportunity to address your concerns in a timely manner.

There are several great examples of how social media can be used appropriately. Many cohorts of students in online programs also develop Facebook groups, for instance, to network with each other and build a community of support as they progress throughout their programs. In these groups, students share resources, remind each other of upcoming deadlines, create study groups and exchange ideas. It is important that these groups however, do not replace the role of your instructor. Likewise, ensure that the group remains professional in their communication of the course, program, and instructor. Again, any grievances with either of these should be communicated directly with the instructor so they may be resolved in a timely manner. Airing issues out on social media platforms that your instructor, advisor, and others have no immediate access to does very little to solve the identified issues.

Building a Professional Online Profile

One of the more common ways of navigating the online social media world is to keep your professional and personal profiles on social media sites separate. While we discussed the elements of social media in Chapter 5, we believe that the information is important enough to review again here. Having a personal account as well as a professional account allows individuals to tailor the content of their profiles to suit the intended audience. The personal account (which still needs to remain appropriate) can be used to post personal and family content such as photos, etc., while the professional page is reserved for potential employers, academic settings, and interacting with peers and colleagues.

The counseling profession is a relatively small world, and it is easy to begin your professional network through social media sites like LinkedIn. In fact, we encourage you to create a professional LinkedIn profile now that you are preparing to advance your professional career. You can even search for the authors of this textbook and make connections right away. While social sites like Facebook are not appropriate connections for faculty and students, professional sites like LinkedIn are useful.

As we stated in Chapter 5, LinkedIn is the world's largest professional network with (as of February 2015), 300 million members in over 200 countries and territories around the globe. There isn't a better way for you to create an immediate connection to the counseling profession. Having a professional LinkedIn profile will already set the stage for job hunting when the time comes.

While job pursuit is a key factor in developing a social media profile, it can also be used to keep up with thought leaders in the counseling profession. By following discussions and posts by thought leaders, you will be sure to be aware of the most current developments in the counseling profession. When you see something that is particularly interesting, you can then share it with your online peers. Thus, your efforts help to educate your peers about the most up-to-date information.

Creating Professional Contact Information

In online programs, your instructors and peers often don't have the luxury of meeting you in person or observing you in a classroom setting. As a result, more emphasis is placed on the manner in which you present yourself in your exchanges throughout the course. First impressions count, and often you only get one opportunity to make a first impression. In the online world, your first impression may be with the e-mail message you send to your instructor.

Many academic institutions will assign every student a university e-mail account and address. This e-mail address should be used when communicating with your instructors and classmates. In the event that you do not have an official university account or your instructors allow messages from your personal accounts, ensure that your e-mail address is professional. It's highly inappropriate to contact your instructors using an e-mail address such as sexyeyes69@abc.com or unbridled45@abc.com or hottietottie4u@abc.com. It is always recommended that you create an e-mail account that can easily identify who you are. There are several variations; however, typically an e-mail address that includes your first, last name, or a variation of the two is best. For instance, Jessica George may choose an address such as jgeorge@abc.com, or jessicageorge@abc.com or jessicag@abc.com. Avoid the use of adjectives or other colorful words that will cause others to perceive you as unprofessional. One bonus of having this account is it already exists when you are ready to submit applications for internships and future employment.

Earlier, we discussed the fact that your instructors may be responsible for several courses in one semester. To facilitate a timely response to your e-mails, it is recommended that you append a signature to your e-mails that identifies the course you are enrolled in, your student ID, and other pertinent information. One example is a signature that includes

Your first and last name; University Student ID # (NOT your social security number)

Student, M.A. in Mental Health Counseling Program

Your university e-mail address

Your alternative, nonuniversity e-mail (optional)

Example:

Jane Doe, L#1234567

Student, M.Ed. in CMHC

Jdoe@abc.edu

Jane.doe123@abc.com

Instructors may also rely heavily on communicating via phone for students enrolled in online programs. Ensure that the voicemail recording attached to your contact phone number is also professional in nature. It would be extremely inappropriate to provide your instructors with a contact number that has the following voice message "Hi you've reached hot sugar . . ." or an inappropriate song, music, or other unprofessional messages. It may sound funny or far-fetched, but sadly, these are all examples that I've heard. When you provide your instructors with your contact information, ensure that the number provided leads to a professional voice message in the event you are unable to answer the call. In conclusion, if you want to be taken seriously as a professional, your contact information also needs to exude professionalism. Keep the personal you separate from the professional you in regard to all phone numbers and e-mail address provided.

Seeking Support From Faculty Members

Instructors are assigned to not only facilitate the course and grade your work, but they are also available for support and to assist with maximizing your success in your courses. However, students must be proactive in identifying the help that they need and communicating this need to their instructors. Many students are of the inaccurate perception that they may be a bother if they were to contact their instructors for assistance. The opposite is true. Instructors admire and welcome students who are willing to keep improving.

In an online course, there are various avenues for seeking support from faculty members. The most common method is by reaching out via timely e-mails. There are instances when faculty members would have loved to assist; however, a student contacts them hours before an assignment is due or worse, after the deadline has passed. Respecting the time of your instructors and providing them with adequate time to respond is highly recommended. Remember faculty members also teach several other courses, they also have deadlines to meet, they attend meetings, travel to conferences, devote family time on weekends, etc.

Another method of receiving support from faculty is via videoconferencing. Many academic institutions use Adobe Connect, which is a web-conferencing platform that enhances collaboration. Others utilize Skype and other conferencing options. These provide a sense of connection, as you're able to both see and hear each other. Contact your instructor ahead of time to schedule a web-conferencing appointment at a time that works for both of you. Many instructors also reserve scheduled office hours and others allow for individual appointments outside of these hours. Students may also receive support via phone, or if they reside within the vicinity of the campus, they may opt to meet faculty members on-campus.

Support may come in various forms including providing additional resources, individual consultations on course content and directing to you more appropriate forms of assistance based on the need. Familiarize yourself with the resources and types of support available to you as a student. These forms of support are available to both campus-based students and students enrolled in online programs. Students in online programs who need accommodations such as captioning services for webinars, alternative test formats or extended testing times, need to become familiar with the procedures for doing so. Often you are required to first register with the Office of Disability Services who will then certify and provide you with an Accommodation Letter outlining the types of accommodations for which you've been approved, to present to your instructor. Instructors are not required to provide any accommodations in their classroom unless this letter is received, so it is wise to be proactive at the beginning of the course. The procedures differ based on the academic institution so research what is required of you before formally beginning your courses.

There are times when students overestimate their understanding of course materials and their ability. It is always great practice to thoroughly review the feedback received from your instructors and contact them early on if you need further clarification. Waiting until the final week of the course, or after you receive your final grade for the course is usually too late to effect any real change.

Instructors recognize that life happens and that students may experience illness and/or other life situations that may impair the ability to complete assignments on time or to complete the course. It is recommended that you contact your instructor as soon as possible to determine what types of support and options may be available to you. Waiting until after you've missed a deadline and earned an F, or worse, not communicating with your instructor at all, does not help the situation.

At times, students fail to reach out for support from faculty due to a lack of awareness that additional support exists, or their personalities or cultural backgrounds may inhibit them from help-seeking behaviors. When these reasons exist, remember that your instructors are very often student centered and culturally sensitive, and account for these differences in their techniques and approaches.

Summary

The number of fully online academic programs continues to steadily increase in the United States as well as in other countries. Researchers have demonstrated that online learning is just as effective and in some cases, more effective than traditional face-to-face classrooms. With an increasing number of students opting for online programs due to the conveniences and flexibility they provide, it becomes crucial that students are equipped with the knowledge, skills, and resources needed to successfully navigate these programs. Many students in online programs are in danger of feeling isolated, disenfranchised, and unsupported in their learning. An active online learning community is one way to counteract this; however, the instructor cannot achieve this alone. The success of online programs also depends on the efforts of its student participants (West, 2010). This chapter presented students with pertinent information aimed at assisting with maximizing satisfaction and success with the online learning experience.

About the Author

Wendy L. Greenidge is an assistant professor in the Department of Counseling and Special Populations at Lamar University with over 15 years of experience in the field of mental health counseling. She is a Licensed Mental Health Counselor (LMHC) and holds several certifications in many subfields of counseling. Wendy is a Fulbright Scholar Alumna with a strong interest in improving online counseling programs as well as establishing and improving international mental health programs. Her research interests primarily focus on increasing utilization of professional counseling services through culturally appropriate interventions. More specifically, her work examines the psycho-cultural correlates of help-seeking in international populations and develops strategies for reducing the barriers to help-seeking.

Wendy is also interested in counselor wellness, play therapy, family counseling, and infusing technology and expressive therapies in counselor education programs and counseling practice. She has published numerous articles on her interests, presents at the local, national, and international level and facilitates mental health workshops internationally. Wendy also serves on several committees with international counseling associations and journals such as the *Caribbean Journal for Psychology*. She has worked in various professional counseling settings including inpatient, partial hospitalization, outpatient programs, in-home counseling, K–12, and college counseling settings, substance abuse, and marriage and family agencies. She enjoys working with children and families.

Additional Resources

4 ways to make a good impression in online classes. (n.d.). *US News*. Retrieved from http://www/usnews.com/education/online-education

15 rules of netiquette for online discussion boards. (n.d.). *Online Education for Higher Education.* Retrieved from http://blogs.onlineeducation.touro.edu/15-rules-netiquette-online-discussion-boards/

Bures, E., Schmid, R., & Abrami, P. (2009). Developing a perspective, inter-connecting, and bringing it together: Who chooses to use a labeling feature in online conversations in a graduate course? *Educational Media International, 46*(4), 317–334.

Canada, M. (2000). Students as seekers in online courses. In R. E. Weiss, D. S. Knowlton, & B. W. Speck (Eds.), *Principles of effective teaching in the online classroom* (Vol. 84, pp. 35–40). San Francisco: Jossey-Bass.

Chen, G., & Chiu, M. M. (2008). Online discussion processes: Effects of earlier messages' evaluations, knowledge content, social cues and personal information on later messages. *Computers & Education, 50*, 678–692.

Dalley-Hewer, J., Clouder, D., Jackson, A., Goodman, S., Bluteau, P., & Davies, B. (2012). Facilitating critical discourse through "meaningful disagreement" online. *Journal of Interprofessional Care, 26,* 472–478.

Gabriel, M. A. (2004). Learning together: Exploring group interactions online. *Journal of Distance Education, 19*(1), 54–72.

Gilbert, P. K., & Dabbagh, N. (2005). How to structure online discussions for meaningful discourse: A case study. *British Journal of Educational Technology, 36*(1), 5–18.

Mastering online discussion board facilitation. (n.d.). *Edutopia.* Retrieved from http://www.edutopia.org/stw-online-learning-downloads

Merrill, M. D., & Gilbert, C. G. (2008). Effective peer interaction in a problem-centered instructional strategy. *Distance Education, 29*(2), 199–207.

Online etiquette guide. (n.d.). Good practices for communicating and participating online. *Madison College.* Retrieved from http://madisoncollege.edu/online-etiquette-guide

Palloff, R., & Pratt, K. (2003). *The virtual student: A profile and guide to working with online learners.* San Francisco: Jossey-Bass.

Participating in online discussions. *Academic Success Center.* Retrieved from http://www2.swccd.edu/~asc/lrnglinks/olddiscbd.html

Weiss, R. E. (2000). Humanizing the online classroom. In R. E. Weiss, D. S. Knowlton, & B. W. Speck (Eds.), *Principles of effective teaching in the online classroom* (Vol. 84, 47–51). San Francisco: Jossey-Bass.

Writing with classmates. (n.d.). *The etiquette around discussion forums.* Retrieved from http://onlinelearningtips.com

References

Palloff, R., & Pratt, K. (2001). *Lessons from the cyberspace classroom.* San Francisco: Jossey-Bass.

West, R. (2010). A student's guide to strengthening an online community. *TechTrends, 54*(5), 69–75.

PART II

Nuts and Bolts of Counselor Preparation

8

Respecting Diversity in an Online Environment

Robyn Trippany Simmons, Tiffany Rush-Wilson, and Breyan Haizlip

Chapter Overview

This chapter is designed to raise your awareness of diversity and the expectations related to respecting diversity during your graduate education. Understanding elements of diversity and how they may impact interaction in the online environment is critical to your success. This chapter will guide you in developing a sense of self-awareness around diversity issues and will assist you in becoming more aware of the role that diversity plays in human interactions.

Learning Outcomes

Upon completion of this chapter, students will

1. Explore the appropriate ethical mandates for sensitivity to diversity

2. Increase awareness of their own use of language and potential microaggressions when engaging with peers in the online environment

3. Become familiar with parameters for difficult discussions, as well as the purpose in developing a high degree of respect and sensitivity in the online environment and its potential impact on work with clients

4. Consider the influence of social media and current events as factors for the experiences and influences of communication within the online classroom

Introduction

Counseling is a profession steeped in relationship nuances and communication. As such, much of your graduate education will focus on relationships and communication even when the content is not skill-based. Communication is more than just words—it includes the context of those words, body language, vocal tones, and eye contact. Respecting diversity and being culturally affirming are certainly based in communication and relationships, as well. The question is, then, how do you begin to develop your knowledge and skills related to diversity in an online learning environment? How do we both demonstrate sensitivity to differences in peers when we are unable to hear tone of voice, see facial expression, and be in the physical space of others? Essentially, words on a computer screen need to become a practice, a philosophy, an action that moves beyond content knowledge without having the opportunity to demonstrate the skills associated with these words in a face-to-face environment.

Challenges that exist with regard to respecting diversity in the online environment include the balancing act of respecting the individual, appropriate boundaries, and limit-setting when needed. Your professor will often set the tone for interaction and also demonstrate transparency and vulnerability to assist in your development of these skills. It is important for you to recognize the learning process and to allow yourself to recognize your knowledge limits, to allow for mistakes to be made, to take responsibility for those mistakes, to be open to feedback, and to ask yourself some tough questions like "Did you intentionally mean to cause conflict around a discussion because of unresolved issues?" "Do you exist in the space of privilege?" "Do you feel powerless?" These may not be the types of questions you will be able to ask yourself at the beginning of graduate school, but embracing vulnerability and being open to discussions regarding privilege and oppression will have a positive impact on your counseling practice. The focus of this chapter is to help you manage these challenges and provide some best practices for respecting diversity in the online classroom.

Ethics and Diversity

The pinnacle ethical standard for counselors, A.1.a of the American Counseling Association *Code of Ethics* (ACA, 2014) maintains that counselors "respect the dignity and promote the welfare of clients" (p. 4). As future members of the profession, you will need to embrace this as a guiding principle for work with clients and strive to be culturally sensitive counselors.

A particular challenge that we have seen in the online classroom is the perceived anonymity that exists when students are not face-to-face with each other. Additionally, without context and other communication cues (e.g., facial expression, tone of voice) messages may be misunderstood. Thus, it is important to consider the parameters for these types of conversations (see Table 8.1).

Table 8.1   Ground Rules for Online Conversations

Principle	Ground Rule
Respect	• Ask questions, but do so respectfully.
Flexibility	• Offer opinions, but do so flexibly.
Honor	• Share thoughts, but do so honorably.
Communication	• If there is a concern, set up a time with your professor to talk through those concerns.
Sensitivity	• Consider editing or removing any discussion board or online post if you think that it has the potential to be offensive or hurtful.
Courage	• Be willing to engage in difficult conversations but do so in a healthy rather than destructive manner.
Goal Orientation	• Remember that the goal is to build upon your skills, so you can work with clients in a culturally affirming manner.

Although you are likely just beginning your counseling degree, we strongly encourage you to review the *Code of Ethics* (see, www.counseling .org/resources/aca-code-of-ethics.pdf). The review will allow you to identify both the standards for engaging with clients and the principles behind the standards that you will need to internalize. For example, standard A.4.b of the ACA *Code of Ethics* (2014) indicates that counselors do not impose "values, attitudes, beliefs, and behaviors" (p. 5) on clients. Further, this standard indicates that counselors should seek training in areas for which they may be at risk. One way for you to begin this process as you delve into your online training is to inventory your own values, attitudes, beliefs, and behaviors. Doing so may help you to increase awareness of your beliefs and values; to recognize that others may have different values; and to avoid imposing your beliefs on your peers. Even when you do take these steps, your peers may struggle to provide discussions and responses in a respectful manner. We recommend taking a higher road in these instances and allowing your professor to address any concerns with a peer's behavior. While having an open discussion about difficult issues is important, it is the professor's responsibility to provide guidance regarding the balance of personal values and professional responsibility. The professor may also help facilitate an open forum discussion that assists in developing relationships and modeling elements of communication that facilitate understanding beyond what can be read on the computer screen.

Attending to modeling from your professor is important because you will be expected to emulate the principles and characteristics of what is being taught as noted in ethical code F.7.b (ACA, 2014). The online classroom introduces a healthy initial challenge for practicing within the constraints of asynchronous, non–face-to-face learning. Your professors have the responsibility to serve as gatekeepers for the profession and evaluate your ability as well as your peers' abilities to emulate the principles required. Hopefully this will not be an issue for you. However, when a student does struggle with these (or any other) ethical principles, your professors are required to evaluate the potential for professional impairment that may harm clients. As a whole, your professors will likely work with students to remediate deficits but the end result may be that some students are not a good fit for a counseling graduate program. It is important for you to recognize that the online classroom discussions are a place where faculty members have the opportunity to monitor and evaluate your ability to interact effectively with others. What you post in an online environment can become part of the evaluation process that leads to remediation and/or dismissal.

"No offense, but . . ."

When a phrase begins with "No offense, but . . ." there is often something unpleasant on the other side. To open this section of the chapter, let's look at an anecdote told by one of this chapter's authors.

While I was studying for my doctoral level clinical boards, a friend of mine took and passed the bar exam. To celebrate her accomplishment, and my accomplishments-in-progress, we went to have hot chocolate at a local coffee shop. While having our hot chocolate in the suburban neighborhood where I lived at the time, a man approached us and said he'd overheard our conversation. He congratulated us on our accomplishments and then went on to tell us that we "weren't really black." He went on to say "no offense, but, you may look like black women on the outside, but clearly you work out, and I heard you talking about your professional achievements. That's not what you people do." We were both insulted and disgusted by his comments and found them to be incredibly offensive despite the fact that he made an attempt to provide a neutralizer prior to making his subversive, racist, sexist, and classist comments. I was taught as a child to beware anything that follows the phrase "no offense, but . . ." and despite my preparation from my parents, and my friends preparation from her family, these comments were still angering and hurtful.

It can be very offensive and condescending to be on the receiving end of comments like the ones mentioned in the previous paragraph. To be identified as an *exception* to a group with which a person self-identifies, and therefore to be *acceptable* because the person believes you defy the group's stereotypes can be hurtful and insulting. Statements like "you're a good athlete, for a girl" or "you're really polite for a Northerner" or "I'm surprised you're so sensitive, since you are a man" are examples of these types of phrases.

In many cases, the issue is not as obvious as the examples above. Sometimes people speak or behave in a manner that is not blatantly offensive, but clearly is intended to be hurtful and dismissive. This type of behavior is called a *microaggression*, a term identified by Dr. Chester Pierce in 1970. There are several specific examples of such backhanded engagements that fall in this category in which the perception of one's group membership is thought to be an accurate predictor of another person's character or behavior. Can you think of any that you have experienced or maybe taken part in? It is important that you have a familiarity with these concepts that can leave the recipient of such words and actions feeling as if they are aberrant and not part of the group (DeAngelis, 2009). Having an understanding of the impact these types of actions and words may foster an ability for you to build stronger therapeutic alliance with clients, increase empathy, and facilitate therapeutic value.

During your course of graduate study, you will spend a great deal of time learning about multicultural issues, terms, and competencies. We think it is important for you to have a good foundation from the start. As you engage in your online classrooms, it is important to recognize that there are several subtypes of microaggressions (see Table 8.2: "Behaviors of Concern") related to race, culture, sexist behaviors, religious intolerance, and other discrimination (Sue et al., 2007). The first of these is *microassaults*. These are conscious and intentional actions or slurs, such as using racial epithets, displaying offensive symbols, or deliberately serving a person belonging to the dominant group before serving someone from another group. For example, Jane Doe, a practicum student in a class of six, made a post in the online classroom. She addressed four fellow students (all of whom had previously noted that they belong to the same religious group) in three different discussion board posts; excluding the single, "different" person. The instructor, in response, addressed all six students in the post and reiterated the importance of ethical, mature, counselor-like behavior in all postings in the classroom. Next are *microinsults*. Microinsults are verbal and nonverbal communications that subtly convey rudeness and insensitivity and demean a person's racial heritage or identity, sex, or religious affiliation. For example, in an ethics classroom a student we will call John Doe confronted another student about his ability to truly grasp a concept related to being a mandated reporter. John responded to his classmate, who had a question about when to contact authorities, "Well of course you don't understand and that makes sense, given how *you all* 'discipline.'" The instructor consulted with a colleague prior to responding and ultimately chose to not only directly address "John" but also to take another step. The instructor contacted John to discuss the comment and then addressed the entire class about appropriate responses, differences in opinions, and how to ethically engage in the classroom. Finally, there are *microinvalidations*. These are communications that subtly exclude, negate, or nullify the thoughts, feelings, or experiential reality of a person from a marginalized group. For example, during a

Table 8.2   Behaviors of Concern

Microaggressions	Speaking or behaving in a manner that is not blatantly offensive, but clearly is intended to be hurtful and dismissive
Microinvalidations	Communications that subtly exclude, negate, or nullify the thoughts, feelings, or experiential reality of a person from a marginalized group
Microassaults	Conscious and intentional actions or slurs, such as using racial epithets, displaying offensive symbols or deliberately serving a person belonging to the dominant group before serving someone from another group

videoconference meeting of an online theories class one student struggled to grasp a concept. Another student, who had some previous experience with the intervention in question, said to the confused student, "I used to specialize in that treatment. Don't worry about it. It's a complicated procedure." The instructor commended the student for sharing with the class a little about their level of expertise, commended the other student for inquiring about the concept, reiterated the value of both past experience and inquiry, and then proceeded to provide the requested information. In each example, note how the professor modeled the appropriate intervention. As a student, what would you do if you were on the receiving end of the microaggression?

Of the aforementioned concepts, Sue et al. (2007) primarily focused on microinsults and microinvalidations. Due to their insidious nature, these microaggressions put disenfranchised people in a psychological bind. Sue noted that a person may feel insulted, but he or she may not really be able to voice exactly why. Their perpetrator will likely not acknowledge that anything has happened because they are oblivious to the notion that they have been offensive. Individuals may also be concerned about a concept called stereotype threat. This is a situation in which a person is afraid to behave in a given way because they believe that they may reinforce negative stereotypes already believed to be true about a group with which they self-identify. Originally introduced in 1995 by Steele and Aronson, stereotype threat can be a very powerful factor in how a person chooses to behave in social situations even when that behavior is different than what they would ideally choose. Stereotype threat often leads the recipient of social aggression to wonder if they are making a mountain out of a molehill. Internalizing stereotype threat can lead to internalized oppression. This occurs when oppressed or marginalized people internalize the prejudices of the oppressor, begin to believe them, and create introjections for their own children and their fellow oppressed. It differs from self-hatred in that it is derived from societal oppression. The student who self-identifies as a member of an oppressed group and refuses to give peers reasonable extensions on assignments because she is concerned about maintaining the stereotypes of women in her group as *weak* may be evidencing signs of stereotype threat.

Additional stressors can come by way of *model minority* status. It is often stressful when someone tries to live up to the seemingly positive stereotypes attributed to one's group. Being a studious Asian person, a maternal female, an athletic man, a polite southerner, etc. may add undue stress to a person who wants to nullify the effects of subversive speech and negative stereotypes. Research shows that uncertainty is very distressing to people and can be damaging in a variety of settings including the workplace, educational settings, in daily life, and even in therapy (DeAngelis, 2009). As an example, the student "Tonya" is a member of a group that promotes the superiority of men over women and generally does not support women being formally educated. In the online classroom she demonstrates an exemplary work ethic, submits all assignments early, completes all extra credit assignments, and submits work beyond what is required to the instructor. She wants the instructor to believe she is worthy, especially since the instructor is male. The instructor notices signs of distress in the student, has seen her submit video-recorded assignments in which the student looks close to tears and is aware that the student has gone "beyond the call of duty." The instructor chooses to support the student by contacting her and reiterating the requirements of the course identified in the syllabus and gently informed her that her extra submissions to the course are inconsistent with the rules of the course and create extra work for the instructor. While the instructor had some concerns about the mental well-being of this student, he remained in the role of instructor despite being a licensed counselor. He submitted his concerns about the student's anxiety to the appropriate office based on the university's student concern protocol.

Respecting Different Beliefs

The world is comprised of many different types of people who have varying viewpoints and beliefs. As counselors and counselors-in-training, we are ethically obligated with making an attempt to understand the worth of these differences and the importance to our clients and communities. Because counselors are human, there may be times, however, when we face dissonance and conflicts between our personal beliefs and professional dictates. This concept is illustrated by the experiences of a counseling doctoral candidate. "Nate" was a fellow counseling student who had a background in mental health research from a different university. In sharing information about his master's degree thesis, he noted that his thesis was based on interviews of members and the guiding text of a religious group thought by many to be controversial and evil. He described his experiences of interacting with the group and shared that people from his religious group seemed to be unaccepting of his research efforts. He reported having some surprise about their reactions and the lack of tolerance for a group they did not truly understand. There were quite a few erroneous assumptions his group held about the other group. People, according to him, were unwilling to listen to his arguments or even accept the organization as a "real religion." He said he learned quite a bit about respecting differences of other groups and learned a lot about acceptance from members of a group he had been taught to not accept.

Humans are very diverse. This is part of what makes us interesting. In instructional and supervision experiences, you will learn that there are many correct ways to engage in . . . and some to be avoided. There are many healthy, functional, and interesting ways in which people engage in daily life yet they may differ significantly from the choices other people may make. In counseling and coursework activities, it may be useful for you to consider your own problem-solving and thinking processes and how you critique the answers of others. While not a scientific exercise, this is a way for you to understand how differences may be received. Consider the following scenario: You are standing in New York City and are told that you have to be in San Francisco within a week. How would you get there? Some of you might say that you would fly across the United States. Some would drive. Some would take a train. If you are an outside-the-box thinker, you might try to circumnavigate the world through Europe and Asia back over to North America. The overall point of the example is to illustrate the idea that there are many different paths one can take to end up in the exact same destination that can be equally important, valuable, and respectable.

Unfortunately, not everyone believes that different paths are valuable. For example, a very well-known celebrity was being interviewed on a local morning radio station. During the interview, this particular artist identified several actors that she would never date if she were single again because these men weren't spiritual. When probed more about this, the singer was able to confirm that she had not based her assumptions about these men's spirituality on anything that they said. In fact, some of the aforementioned men described themselves as being very spiritual people. She based her assumptions of their spirituality on how she conceptualizes spirituality in her own life. She identified the types of work projects that they accepted as being indicative of those that a nonspiritual man would take. The interviewers found this to be interesting because the types of things this singer disliked about the roles these actors chose were very similar to the subject matter in her own songs. Further, she seemed to be unwilling to accept people who lived their lives differently than she lived her own. As an individual person, this may be something that we don't find unusual. As a public figure who entertains everyone, her position seemed to be closed, exclusive, and a little disturbing. At times, in the online environment, instructors and students express positions that may be based largely on personal experience and anecdote. One writer (student or instructor) may consider his or her post to be a satirical commentary about the proposed mental health policy of a particular senator, while another may receive it as a political, and very personal, attack by another student. The mood and tone of the online classroom may be affected and possibly damaged by perceived attacks and negativity or dissention in the classroom.

As a counselor-in-training, you must be aware of how differences between lifestyles do not invalidate the worth of a person. Carl Rogers (1961) identified unconditional positive regard as something that counselors internalize about the being of the person sitting in the office with them. While it may be difficult to accept specific actions committed by a person, questioning the ultimate value of the overall person is inappropriate, and inconsistent with the dictates of our profession. Clients often present with challenging concerns; but do such concerns invalidate the being, and value, of the client? In the online classroom your professors can approach invalidation in three manners: preventative (primary), secondary, and tertiary. A preventative approach would be instructors posting the expectations and rules for the classroom at the beginning of the course with consequences for violations of the rules and policies explained. If there is a teleconference or videoconference option for the course these issues can be reiterated with students. Secondary and tertiary approaches require instructor intervention during, or after, the infraction of classroom netiquette. Incorporating department policy, guidelines, and classroom management strategies (such as gentle, yet timely redirection and confrontation) are necessary techniques for the online instructor.

As a student, you should consider what might be at the root of this type of behavior. Engaging in this process will improve your ability to understand the root of client issues. Fear of the unknown, prior negative experiences, shared erroneous information, and other factors contribute to intolerance (Takaki, 2008). Xenophobia contributes strongly to abhorrent reactions and a lack of understanding of people from other countries. Consider the following exercise to help you identify personal biases and perceptions. First, take some time to examine ways in which you may be viewed as an oppressor by people who do not self identify as being members of your same group. This may be hard to imagine, but try to put yourself in the shoes of someone who might take that perspective. Next, consider how it feels to recognize the impact that this perception can have on someone with that perspective. It can be surprising to see yourself through another's lens as someone whose existence may be disliked, feared, or unwanted by others based on their perception of you or the group to which you belong.

Raising Consciousness

Not long ago, my daughter, who is in the fifth grade, came home from school and shared that one of her classmates called her a "slave." Immediately, my mind needed to know the cultural demographics of this classmate. I needed to know if the classmate was Black or White or Latino perhaps; I needed to know if her classmate was a male or female. For some reason, my mind was not able to reconcile any strong parental advice without these variables. So in my best counselor voice, I asked my daughter to share the race and/or ethnicity of the accused classmate.

"He's White," she shared pensively, "Why?"

Driven unconsciously by my own internalized racial discourse, I replied, "Well, tomorrow . . . you go to school and tell that White boy . . ." —my daughter swiftly interjected and confidently asserted, "Mom! I'm not racist." Taken aback by her budding cultural intuitiveness, I asked, ". . . well what did you do?" Her response, "I told him that it makes sense that he's not doing well in Social Studies; slavery was abolished in 1865."

I am grateful to my daughter for this lesson. It has allowed me to become more aware of how my own culturally informed biases impact my perceptions of others every day. This awareness is the vehicle by which consciousness is raised. When our consciousness evolves, we begin to develop the tools to more critically examine other aspects of our cultural worldview.

Fortunately, this experience is commonplace for many people. We are all afforded opportunities in our daily lives to take note of how culture (i.e., race, gender, sexual expression, religion, varying abilities, etc.) influences our experiences with others. Consequently, counseling researchers have formed consensus around the proposition that awareness is the foundation upon which multicultural counseling competency (MCC) is built (Cates, Schaefle, Smaby, Maddux, & Beauf, 2007; Mollen, Ridley, & Hill, 2003; Ponterotto, Gretchen, Utsey, Rieger, & Austin, 2002; Spanierman et al., 2010). As empathy is the heart of the counseling relationship, awareness is the soul of empathy that allows our relationship with clients to deepen in meaningful ways.

Yet still, the question remains, "How can you make a focused effort toward cultivating cultural awareness in your graduate program? How can you translate these experiences into consciousness-raising for your counseling practice? Your professors are tasked with utilizing the virtual platform as a vehicle for eliciting the critical dialogue and internal vigilance that fuels MCC. The goal for online counseling instructors then is to leverage the distinct benefits of the virtual environment to engage counseling trainees in consciousness raising learning activities. While it may seem that traditional face-to-face classrooms are exclusively ideal for these experiences, virtual classrooms offer a sense of anonymity that can serve as a "safety net" for you. Similar to being able to say something in a text message that would be almost impossible to say in person, consider how you can use your online environment to develop meaningful expressions and explorations that might be difficult to initiate otherwise. While your online classroom will have your name and may even have a picture associated with your participation, there is still a sense of anonymity that offers an advantage unique to online instruction that can help challenge you to develop personally. You shouldn't avoid joining the discourse—no matter how challenging to you. These strategies can support your development of culturally affirming virtual classrooms. Additionally, we as gatekeepers possess increased insight of student blind spots, stereotypes, and cultural biases which we can address in the online classroom.

Focus on awareness. Training virtual counseling students toward MCC is an ongoing process that we embrace as counselor educators with a goal of initiating your cultural awareness. It is through awareness that raised consciousness emerges. Our efforts as professors toward raising consciousness help you to gradually integrate more multidimensional paradigms into all areas of your clinical practice. While setting your learning goals toward raising awareness and consciousness may seem rudimentary, taking the time to build a strong and resilient MCC foundation is the key to being a competent and caring counselor across differences—and over time.

Balance your approach. As a student, you are encouraged to engage in academic debate and to engage online with your learning resources, peers, and the instructor. Because of the nature of our profession, we are constantly balancing our *altruistic* (i.e., "I do this to help people!") and *narcissistic natures* (i.e., "I am the one who can help people!"). Both archetypes are necessary for counselors to possess, but any strength in excess becomes a weakness. When counselors find themselves overemphasizing one aspect of culture (i.e., racism, sexual expression, religion, etc.), it may be an indication of one-sidedness. Balance is the key. As you go through your graduate program, keep this idea of balance in mind.

Setting reasonable expectations. With virtual courses occurring over a matter of weeks, you must set reasonable expectations for yourself for what can be achieved in this time. Counselors are often passionate about MCC and are fully vested in developing this vital aspect of counseling skill. Remember that you have to develop your multicultural competence over time and to use all of your learning experiences to develop your ability to become a change agent. You are capable of positively impacting the world one client at a time.

Begin with the basics. Once you have completed a self-assessment and set reasonable expectations, we suggest that you seek out learning resources that will help develop your empathy for diverse populations. Many of us have experienced being "the other" or "one of them" in some form—just as many of us have experienced being "part of the group." Taking a deep exploration of your learning resources that operationalize and examine the terms *privilege* and *oppression* will help you to normalize typical challenges of introspection regarding worldview. Keep it simple, but anticipate that with every resource (i.e., journal articles, textbooks, research, etc.), a new lens begins to develop. As you begin your journey toward becoming a professional counselor, we encourage you to explore how your personal identity is connected to a larger social context (i.e., marital/relational status, appearance, education level, learning disability, address, use of language, etc.) that may situate you from a different vantage point. This allows you to begin building a communal contextual consciousness in the virtual setting by which you become gradually more aware of: (a) your own power and privilege within varying social contexts; (b) the client's experience within these contexts; and (c) the intersection that exists in the client/counselor dyad.

Cultivating internal vigilance. *Internal Vigilance* is the willingness to interrogate one's own thoughts, feelings, and behaviors in an effort to dismantle faulty thinking patterns that perpetuate marginalization in real time. We are all guilty of deferring to the reality of a broader systemic social issue as opposed to looking within. We gravitate in excess toward our altruistic nature to avoid conflict, misunderstandings, and mischaracterizations. At times, adult learners who have learned how to navigate the politically correct terrain of the real world will also attempt this avoidance behavior in the online forum. We invite you to consider this as you engage in discussions throughout your graduate program. Remember that internal vigilance is how the goal of awareness is achieved. Some of my favorite redirecting questions include:

1. How do you see yourself as an individual impacted by and/or impacting this broader social issue?

2. What experiences have you had personally that shape your perspective on this topic?

3. How can you personally relate to the perspectives of your clients?

4. What are some reasons that members of your cultural group might prefer a less directive counseling approach?

5. Research suggests that racial/ethnic minorities may have a great level of mistrust regarding participation in research opportunities. What are some characteristics of your personality that might support developing a stronger sense of trust between you, the researcher, and your ethnic/racial minority participants?

As you begin employing these strategies and engaging in consciousness-raising discourse, you will also notice the emergence of more meaningful dialogue among your peers. As you and your peers become more engaged in your own personal and professional growth, you may find an interesting desire to engage others offline as well. Remember that the lens you are developing as a professional counselor will help you to see the world from a social learning framework. Keep in mind that consciousness raising is a natural progression and that you should start with achievable goals toward advocacy.

Social Justice and Counselors

As our consciousness evolves through awareness, so does the need to do something. At some point, engaging in critical dialogue plateaus and ideas of social justice advocacy begin to emerge. Arguably, advocacy is the natural evolution of MCC. As you begin to develop a deeper and broader sense of empathy for each client and the social contexts in which they live, you will begin to want to use your own privilege to empower others. Here are some insights that we believe will help to foster a social justice advocacy orientation among virtual counseling students.

#Social justice advocacy. One of the many advantages to online learning is that both the students and the instructor have to embrace technology. We live in an era in which technology has made many in the world feel more connected. We are able to find and interact with more people virtually; those that share our views—and many who see the world differently. Technology also allows us to be more aware of the experiences and stories of others. As a generation Facebook educator, I am often informed of world-shifting events via social media. Current counseling students are at the nexus of this evolution and carry the responsibility of using technology (i.e., social media, Web pages, blogs, etc.) as a catalyst for positive social change. Consider how you can work with your peers to develop the technical acumen for advancing social change on behalf of your future clients.

Advocating for underrepresented students. At the age of 62, my mother was laid off, and the company that she gave two decades of her life to closed its doors. I don't know that I will ever be able to fully understand what that was like for her—yet I lend her my empathy. Also at the age of 62, my mother found a way back to school to pursue the dream she had deferred to be a mother. I don't know that I will ever be able to fully understand what that was like for her—yet I am able to lend her my empathy. I became an online instructor for many reasons, but mostly because I know that without virtual learning environments, many exceptional individuals that have real-life responsibilities would not be able to pursue a counseling degree otherwise. Professors in the online environment are keenly aware of these student needs and take pride in advocating for the needs of adult learners by empathizing with the broader social context that is a part of their identity as online students. As professors, we hope this model will inspire you to do the same with your clients. Although we may never be able to fully understand another person's journey, we can lend them our empathy. We hope that you see the importance of advocating for the needs of historically marginalized clients (i.e., people of color, women, individuals with few economic resources, people with disabilities). Part of your training will be focused on methods of broaching these conversations with colleagues, work administration, and other entities that are the key to the social change efforts we want to accomplish.

Summary

How does discussion about acceptance and tolerance relate to respecting diversity in the online counselor education environment? Intolerance for differences, the idea of a single individual having multiple differences, and moving "beyond toleration" are contemporary challenges that face our profession (Dobbernack & Modood, 2013). Information gathered from news outlets and social media support the current trend toward mistrust, exploitation of social ills, and sociopolitical relations. Counseling professionals (both future clinicians and counselors) are charged with supporting clients, counselors-in-training, and supervisees as they navigate a tense social environment, introspect about their roles, their impact on the community, their communication, and their engagement in relationships. Such a willingness for self-examination is necessary to further the development and maintenance of a healthy profession.

And, ultimately, it is often your professor who will invite you into this place of examination—whether in a brick-and-mortar or virtual counselor training environment. When invited, take the opportunity to grow and begin development of your new lens.

About the Authors

Robyn Trippany Simmons received her EdD in Counselor Education in May 2001, as well as a BA in Psychology (1994) and MA in Community Counseling (1996) from the University of Alabama. She serves as Residency Director for the School of Counseling at Walden University. She has taught a variety of courses including diagnosis and assessment, internship, professional orientation, among others. Dr. Trippany Simmons's research and clinical interests include sexual trauma, vicarious trauma, play therapy, and professional identity issues. She has presented locally, regionally, and nationally and has several publications related to these topics. Further, she is a Licensed Professional Counselor in Alabama and is a Registered Play Therapist. Dr. Trippany Simmons lives in Alabama with her husband and two children.

Tiffany Rush-Wilson received her PhD in Counseling at the University of Akron in 2003. She currently serves as the Skill Development Coordinator for Counseling Unit at Walden University with a focus on both the online classrooms and in-person residencies. She has taught a variety of courses in the Mental Health Counseling and Psychology programs. Professionally, Dr. Rush-Wilson is independently, and dually, licensed and certified as a counselor in the United States and Canada. She is interested in the impact of language and communication on mental health, body image, and has worked in community mental health, children's services, and extensively in private practice. She is a member of both American and Canadian Counseling Associations and the Academy for Eating Disorders and has participated in community outreach and presented on Women's Issues, scope of practice and eating disorders at local, national, and international venues.

Breyan Haizlip received her PhD in Counselor Education and Supervision from Old Dominion University in Norfolk, Virginia, in 2009. She currently serves as Core Faculty at Walden University. She has taught a variety of courses in the Mental Health Counseling and Psychology programs.

Professionally, Dr. Haizlip is a Licensed Professional Counselor (LPC) and a Licensed Mental Health Counselor (LMHC). Her research interests are focused broadly on multicultural counseling, with particular interests in sexual expression, identity development, and the intersections of gender and race/ethnicity. She is a member of the American Counseling Association. She maintains an international and national presentation profile, presenting on issues of culturally responsive education, women's empowerment, and inclusionary education.

References

American Counseling Association. (2014). *Code of Ethics*. Alexandria, VA: Author.

Cates, J. T., Schaefle, S. E., Smaby, M. H., Maddux, C. D., & Beauf, I. (2007). Comparing multicultural with general counseling knowledge and skill competency for students who completed counselor training. *Journal of Multicultural Counseling and Development*, 35(1), 26–39.

DeAngelis, T. (2009). Unmasking "racial microaggressions." *Monitor on Psychology*, 40(2), 42–45.

Dobbernack, J., & Modood, T. (2013). *Tolerance, intolerance and respect: Hard to accept?* Basingstoke: Palgrave Macmillan.

Mollen, D. E. B. R. A., Ridley, C. R., & Hill, C. L. (2003). Models of multicultural counseling competence. *Handbook of multicultural competencies in counseling and psychology*, 21–37.

Ponterotto, J. G., Gretchen, D., Utsey, S. O., Rieger, B. P., & Austin, R. (2002). A revision of the multicultural counseling awareness scale. *Journal of Multicultural Counseling and Development*, 30(3), 153–180.

Rogers, C. R. (1961). *On becoming a person*. Boston, MA: Houghton Mifflin.

Spanierman, L. B., Oh, E., Heppner, P. P., Neville, H. A., Mobley, M., Wright, C. V. , . . . Navarro, R. (2010). The multicultural teaching competency scale: Development and initial validation. *Urban Education, 46*, 440–464.

Steele, C., & Aronson, J. (1995). Stereotype threat and the intellectual test performance of African Americans. *Journal of Personality and Social Psychology, 69*, 797–811.

Sue, D., Capolilupo, C., Torino, G., Bucceri, J., Holder, A., Nadal, K., & Esquilin, M. (2007). Racial microagressions in everyday life: Implications for clinical practice. *American Psychologist, 62*(4), 271–286.

Takaki, Ronald I. (2008). *A different mirror: A history of multicultural America*. Boston: Little, Brown and Company.

9

Academic Integrity

Carolyn Berger and Ruth Ouzts Moore

Chapter Overview

This chapter will identify and describe different types of academic dishonesty, some of which are specific to online programs. First, we will cover integrity in academic writing. A full understanding of plagiarism is essential for understanding ways to avoid behaving dishonestly in academic writing. To best understand how to prevent dishonesty in writing, we will address ethical writing styles, specifically American Psychological Association (APA) style, and how students can use APA style to write with integrity. Due to the complexity of integrity in online education, the final section will address some of the ethical concerns specific to distance learning.

Learning Outcomes

Upon completion of this chapter, students will

1. Define the different types of academic dishonesty that can occur in online counseling programs

2. Analyze steps to access resources that will help them prevent academic dishonesty

3. Distinguish how to behave using academic integrity in many different ways throughout their counseling preparation program

4. Describe why it is crucial for counselors-in-training to apply principles of academic integrity in their counseling preparation program

Introduction

Integrity in academia is a multifaceted topic and online education adds greater complexity to this issue. It is crucial that graduate students understand the different ways to behave with academic integrity as well as ways to prevent academic dishonesty. Behaving with integrity is of utmost importance for counseling students since ultimately the skills obtained in graduate school will be necessary to best meet the needs of clients.

Definition and Intentionality

Integrity is defined as "the quality of being honest and having strong moral principles" ("integrity," n.d.). Academic integrity is therefore the quality of being honest in all work pertaining to one's education. Academic integrity applies to coursework, such as tests, papers, projects, and presentations that are required to obtain credit in a class. Academic work also applies to scholarly activities outside of actual coursework, such as research projects, presentations at conferences, and writing for a publication.

There are instances when students are clearly being dishonest in their academics. Some students intentionally behave dishonestly, such as students who buy papers online or those who purposefully copy someone else's work and present it as their own. Intentional cheating is considered an intolerable offense at the university level and often results in expulsion. However, some students may behave dishonestly, but they then claim that their academic dishonesty was not intentional. For example, two students may decide to work together on an assignment and turn in the same work. While the professor did not clearly state that the students cannot work together, students must understand that they are always expected to do their own work. The only exception to this rule is when students are explicitly told they can work as a team and hand in the same work, such as with group projects.

While certain types of academic dishonesty may be unintentional due to lack of knowledge, this offense may result in the same level of punishment as an intentional offense. It is the responsibility of the students to educate themselves and make sure they understand what constitutes academic dishonesty. Claiming ignorance is unacceptable, especially at the graduate student level. Graduate students must make sure they thoroughly review their university's policies regarding academic integrity and ask their professors if any questions surface regarding these policies. It is also important to pay attention to your own intuition and common sense. If you are working on an academic task and you have concerns about using a resource or obtaining assistance from someone, it is always a good idea to consult with a professor in your program to make sure that you are following the policies of your university and behaving with academic integrity.

Integrity and the Internet

The Internet is an extremely useful tool to people in academia. The pervasive use of the Internet and electronic resources makes it quite simple to access a wide variety of resources from all over the world. Fortunately, it is no longer necessary to physically go to a library to photocopy journal articles. Instead, now students can pull up a journal article or an e-book on a wide range of topics. To make things even easier, today it is unnecessary to be on a home computer to gain access to many of these resources. Many people have Internet access on their phones, laptops, or other personal devices such as iPads or tablets, and therefore can access online resources from any physical location. While the accessibility of online resources is a huge benefit to graduate students, these resources can be severely misused if students lack awareness of how to behave with academic integrity.

It does not take a skilled computer expert to figure out how to use electronic resources and the Internet as a means of academic dishonesty. In addition to accessing professional resources (e.g., journal articles, textbooks), students can also access resources such as PowerPoint presentations, term papers, and websites on a wide variety of topics. Copying and pasting sections from these resources may be a temptation; however, copying and pasting from resources without properly referencing the material is clearly a case of academic dishonesty. Some unscrupulous students could even use the Internet to hire a "shadow writer" to do their online work for them. The temptations are more profound than ever because access is at anyone's fingertips. While graduate students should already understand these blatant cases of academic dishonesty, it is important to mention a few of these obvious abuses of resources as severe cases of academic dishonesty do occur, even in graduate school.

There are a few questions you should always ask yourself if considering utilizing an online resource. First of all, is this a professional resource that your professor will allow you to use? If the resource is an unpublished paper that you came across online, and it is not an article from a refereed journal or another reputable organization, it is not a highly respected piece of writing. If you ever have any doubt on the professionalism of a resource, you should ask yourself, "Who wrote the article/piece? How do I know that the authors have the credentials they claim?" Another question you should ask is, "Do I know how to properly cite and reference this resource?" As always, whenever you are in doubt about a potential issue with professionalism or plagiarism, consult with your professor. Later in this chapter, we will cover APA style methods of citing and referencing since it is crucial to professionally reference a resource if you do decide to use it in your writing.

Integrity in Academic Writing

As mentioned above, it is always essential to cite and reference resources where you obtain your information. You want to make it clear when you are using someone else's ideas. If you do not cite resources when stating an idea, you are essentially telling your reader that what you are writing is your own original idea. There are multiple ways students can inaccurately represent their ideas in academic writing. These methods of misrepresentation are outlined in this section to ensure that you understand the depth and breadth of ways academic dishonesty in writing can occur. The primary way students can misuse other's work is through plagiarism. The Oxford Dictionaries define plagiarism as "the practice of taking someone else's work or ideas and passing them off as one's own" ("plagiarism," n.d.).

Considering that students can "take someone else's work or ideas" in many ways, the definition of plagiarism is quite broad, and so are the policies as outlined by professional associations. The American Counseling

Association (ACA) includes plagiarism within the *Code of Ethics* (ACA, 2005) for counselors. ACA code G.5.b. states, "Counselors do not plagiarize, that is, they do not present another person's work as their own work" (ACA, 2005, p. 18). The 6th edition of the APA publication manual states that plagiarism occurs when people "claim the words and ideas of another as their own" (APA, 2010, p. 15).

It is essential that students clearly read and understand their university's policies as they relate to plagiarism. Universities often have severe repercussions for students who plagiarize. Many universities consider any (or all) of the following as forms of plagiarism, and therefore punishable offenses:

1. Traditional plagiarism: Using another person's words as your own without giving proper credit. This can be in the form of blatant cheating (e.g., buying papers off the Internet or having someone write a paper for you), or it can be in the form of copying and pasting sections of someone else's writing into your own work.

2. Self-plagiarism: Reusing your own work to obtain credit in two different courses or for two different assignments.

3. Patchwriting: Failure to properly summarize someone else's work (Howard & Robilliard, 2008). For example, if a student copies a sentence from another source and replaces a few words with synonyms, this would be considered patchwriting.

The APA manual stresses that writers must give credit to the "individuals whose ideas, theories, or research may have directly influenced your work" (APA, 2010, p. 169). Resources containing ideas from other individuals can take on many forms. Examples of resources include books, articles, movies, websites, presentations, or even individuals (via personal communication). Keep in mind that your instructor may only allow the use of professional resources (e.g., professional books, refereed journal articles). The methods of properly citing and referencing will be explained further in a subsequent section.

Self-Plagiarism

As outlined in the previous section, self-plagiarism is generally considered a form of plagiarizing. However, self-plagiarism is still a somewhat nebulous topic. The APA (2010) publication manual states, "Just as researchers do not present the work of others as their own (plagiarism), they do not present their own previously published work as new scholarship (self-plagiarism)" (p. 16). This statement is directed more toward researchers who publish their writing; however, the concepts can be applied to students as well. The concept is that students must not reuse formerly submitted writings as new scholarship. Students must quote themselves when using portions from a past paper, just as they would quote another author's work. However, you should always consult with your professor if you are planning to cite a previous paper you wrote.

It can be tempting in online counseling programs to self-plagiarize. Discussion boards are often used in online courses in lieu of in-class discussions, and rather than typing up an original thought for the discussion board, a student could recycle past work. For example, a student may be given a discussion board assignment that closely aligns with a research paper that was done in a previous class. The student previously wrote a paper on Gestalt therapy techniques for a theories class. Then a few semesters later, the same student is now in internship and is asked to write a discussion board post where they are required to include information about a specific technique implemented with a client. The student may be tempted to copy and paste sections from the original Gestalt paper into the discussion board post. However, this would be considered self-plagiarism. If you find yourself in this type of situation, the best thing to do is to write the new assignment completely separate from the original assignment. If you do decide to reuse portions of a past assignment, plan to cite yourself but also consult with the professor to make sure that this is allowable.

Some universities outline a clear policy on self-plagiarism, but other universities do not. Therefore, it may be up to your professor to determine a policy on self-plagiarism in each specific class. In cases where the university does not have a clear policy, it is always better to err on the side of caution and not reuse past writings. One study sought out professors' opinions on academic integrity issues such as self-plagiarism (Halupa & Bollinger, 2013). The results of the study demonstrated that most faculty (54%) believed students who recycled any portion of their past writing were self-plagiarizing. The majority of faculty surveyed (80%) also reported that students who reused an entire paper they wrote for another class were self-plagiarizing. While these percentages are not at 100%, it does demonstrate that many professors consider recycling old papers or projects used in past classes to be problematic. Therefore, if you ever plan to reuse a portion of an old assignment, it is best to consult with the instructor and determine the best method of citing and referencing the past paper.

Patchwriting

In addition to self-plagiarism, it is important that students understand the concept of patchwriting. Patchwriting is defined as: "writing passages that are not copied exactly but that have nevertheless been borrowed from another source, with some changes" (Elder, Pflugfelder, & Angeli, 2010, para. 4). Patchwriting is an offense even if the student cites the original work. Students who use patchwriting in their work often do so because they do not fully understand the work that they are citing (Howard & Robilliard, 2008). Therefore, they copy and paste portions of the original work to try to cover the topic adequately. Oftentimes students who patchwrite may copy a sentence directly from a source and then look for synonyms to replace a few of the words. While this may not be blatant plagiarism, it is a form of academic dishonesty nonetheless, and it must be recognized and corrected.

Howard and Robilliard (2008) give recommendations for helping students avoid patchwriting. To effectively summarize someone else's work, she recommends several steps. First, you can skim the resource and read topic sentences and headings to get the general idea. Next, read the resource again, but this time, read each sentence and take your time trying to understand it. Now, read the resource a third time and take notes. Give yourself a short break (30 minutes should be sufficient), then write your own summary without looking at the original resource. Compare your summary with the original source to make sure that you did not unintentionally repeat phrases. If you did, use direct quotes and make sure to insert page numbers. Recommendations for using APA style to properly cite and reference will be covered in a subsequent section.

Turnitin and Other Plagiarism Detection Packages

While the definition of forms of plagiarism is complex, university faculty do have tools to help them identify the different forms of plagiarism when they occur. There are now a variety of tools to help detect plagiarism. Therefore, it is less complicated to verify whether or not a student has plagiarized in comparison to 5–10 years ago. Websites such as Turnitin, Viper, and iThenticate are used by many professors to scan papers for potential plagiarism. Professors can use these websites as they deem necessary. Some professors may use the plagiarism detection software for every paper handed in by every student, while others may only scan papers that seem suspicious.

Plagiarism detection websites often have enormous content databases where they index content. Turnitin advertises a database of over 40 billion current and archived websites as well as over 300 million student papers (Turnitin, n.d.). Turnitin also has partnerships with publishing companies and library databases where they obtain other sources such as textbooks and journals. When a paper is submitted for a plagiarism check on Turnitin, the paper is compared to billions of resources. The "originality check" is then performed, and the instructor is given a percentage that measures how much of the paper is the student's original words versus someone else's. For example, a score of 30% indicates that approximately 30% of the paper may have come from another source. The instructor can then see the sections of the paper that the Turnitin detection tool measured that the student may have been plagiarizing. Turnitin highlights this portion of the paper and identifies the original source that contained the specified wording. The instructor can then refer to the university's plagiarism policy in order to make an informed judgment call on whether or not this student truly "plagiarized" his or her paper.

It may be helpful for students to inquire about which plagiarism detection software is used in their counseling programs. Students can even scan their own work to see what the software detects. This is useful in cases where students are still working on developing a writing style. If students are concerned about whether or not their writing would be considered patchwriting, they can always show the instructor in advance of the project deadline, but students can also see if it is possible to run their paper through plagiarism detection software to do a self-check.

Preventing Plagiarism

Citing other people's work is essential to avoid plagiarism. There are two primary ways to give credit to others' ideas. If you are copying word-for-word from another resource, you must use a direct quotation. If you are not using a direct quotation, but are putting the idea into your own words (i.e., summarizing), you must still cite using APA style. Keep in mind that regardless of the type of citation you are using, citation "implies that you have personally read the cited work" (APA, 2010, p. 169). All references cited in the paper must be included in a reference list at the end of the paper, and if a reference is included in the references list, it must be cited within the body of the paper.

Quotation marks must be used when citing a source directly (i.e., copying and pasting). APA style requires that you provide the author, year, and page number where you found the direct quote (APA, 2010). Direct quotes should be used sparingly, and only when a paraphrase of the information would not capture the essence of the message you are trying to deliver. In other words, make sure there is a good reason you are using a direct quote. Reference the current edition of your APA manual to learn the variety of ways you can use a direct quote. The specific method of using APA style for direct quotes varies depending on the length of the quote you are using.

If you are not using a direct quotation, but you are using a concept or idea from a resource, you still must use a citation. APA style requires that the writer include the author and year of publication of the resource. It is important to note that replacing one or two of the author's words is not sufficient if citing without quotations. Instead, you need to completely rephrase how the author stated it so that it truly is in your own words. This will help you avoid the academic error of patchwriting that was referenced in the earlier section.

As a student, you will learn a significant amount of information. However, just because this information has been acquired does not make it your original idea. Therefore, you need to reference the resources where you learned this information when using it in a paper. Then cite this resource appropriately according to APA style. For example, in your theories class, you will learn about Ellis' Rational Emotive Behavior (REBT) Therapy, the A-B-C model, and how it is important to help clients dispute their irrational thoughts (Ellis & Ellis, 2011). When writing about this technique, just because you know about this model, does not make it your idea. Therefore, when using ideas from Ellis' REBT model, you must always cite where you learned this information.

Why Do Counselors Use APA Style?

The APA writing style has already been referenced several times throughout this chapter (APA, 2010). It is important that graduate students in counseling recognize that APA style is the standard writing style for the profession of counseling. Different disciplines have their own preferred style of writing. For example, MLA (Modern Language Association) guidelines are typically used in the field of humanities (Yale College Writing Center, 2015). Chicago Style (University of Chicago) is primarily used with historical research (Yale College Writing Center, 2015). APA style, which is outlined by the American Psychological Association, is commonly used by psychologists and other professionals in the behavioral and social sciences (APA, 2010). To learn more about APA style, you will need to review *The Publication Manual of the American Psychological Association, 6th edition* (APA, 2010). The manual was first published in 1929 and has been revised several times over the years (APA, 2010). It includes information about ethics, word choice, language, graphics, and writing style (APA, 2010).

APA style addresses issues that are important for counselors to consider in their writing, such as the importance of using nonbiased language. When writing about people, it is important to consider the language used to avoid bias and stereotyping. APA recommends specific techniques in regard to writing about people of different disabilities, genders, and sexual orientations. For example, APA style recommends that when discussing people, avoid using *he, she,* or *he/she* because readers can get confused and only picture one specific gender when interpreting what you wrote. APA style recommends using plural pronouns so *they* and *their* can be used (APA, 2010; Paiz et al., 2010).

APA Style Resources

Using APA style in the beginning can be a challenge; however, fortunately there are a number of resources you can use to assist you in writing in APA format. In addition to the resources discussed in this chapter, it is strongly suggested that you research APA style guides available through your university. Many graduate programs offer their own APA style resources.

APA Style Manual

The APA style manual is very helpful, especially for students who would like an easy to access resource that can be pulled right off their own bookshelf. While the Internet is full of useful tools for using APA style, sometimes the answers are more easily found by referencing your own book. Students can bookmark their most frequently referenced pages of the APA manual and become familiar with the format so that it is more efficient to use the manual as opposed to searching online for a specific APA style question.

The most recent 6th edition of the APA manual has useful sample papers that you can refer to when writing APA style papers (APA, 2010). Keep in mind that the first printing of the 6th edition APA manual contained errors in the sample papers, so make sure that you have the second printing (APA, n.d.). It can be challenging to learn and remember all the different rules for writing a paper, and the sample papers highlight the most important formatting rules. The title page and headers have their own structure and formatting rules, and if you have a sample paper in front of you, it is easier to format the title page and headers appropriately.

The APA style manual also has useful chapters on how to write professionally (APA, 2010). One chapter focuses on grammar and usage, such as agreement of subjects and verbs and dangling modifiers. Another chapter focuses on writing style, including punctuation, capitalization, and the use of abbreviations. For students who need an overview of the best writing techniques, it would be helpful to buy the publication manual and read about the most effective writing methods according to APA style.

APA Templates

One confusing issue with using APA style can be the proper formatting of your word processing software document. APA style requires a different running head style on the title page than on subsequent pages. Therefore, students need to learn how to properly insert headers and footers using their word processing software. Students should also understand how to set up the format of the paper so that the first page has a separate header from the rest of the document. The formatting of the different levels of headings can also be confusing, and while many word processing software packages (e.g., Microsoft Word) offer suggested header levels for writing, these usually do not align with APA style.

Microsoft Office offers APA style templates that you can download online for free. If you do an Internet search for "Microsoft Word APA style template," you will find a number of different options. These templates are basically frameworks that are set up for you to type your own text into for proper APA style formatting. The templates generally have the title page, abstract, headers, subheaders, and reference pages set up for you in APA format. However, it is important that you ensure that the template is in the most up-to-date APA style format. Also, make sure to verify that the website you are using comes from a reputable source, such as the official Microsoft Office site (e.g., office.microsoft.com). This will help prevent downloading a virus onto your computer.

Bibliographic Software

There are a number of different types of bibliographic software programs (also called citation managers) that can assist you with formatting your citations and references according to APA style. Bibliographic software assists writers with using citations and references in a paper in a variety of professional writing formats, including APA style. If writing a short 3- to 5-page paper, you may not find the use of bibliographic software to be necessary since your reference list will likely be manageable. However, if writing a longer paper, such as a master's thesis or doctoral dissertation, the use of bibliographic software is valuable as it can help you write your paper much more efficiently.

Bibliographic software enables the writer to catalog references as they are found. Many university library online catalogs have the option to download references into a format that can be merged into the bibliographic manager. Writers can also manually enter references into the bibliographic manager. When it comes time to write the paper, there are plug-ins for Microsoft Word that enable the bibliographic software to "communicate with" the Microsoft Word document. While writing the paper, the author can insert citations from the bibliographic software. The reference will then automatically be added to the reference list in the writing style selected (i.e., APA style).

Some of the more common bibliographic software programs include EndNote, Zotero, and Mendeley. Choosing which software to use can be challenging, but comparison guides can assist you with this decision (Penn State University, 2012). One big difference between bibliographic software programs is that some can be accessed online on any computer, while others must only be used on one computer. If you use several different computers in your work, this is a function you would want to have online. In choosing a bibliographic software, it is also important to consider which one is most commonly used at your university. That way, if you run into questions, there is most likely someone at your university who can assist you.

While bibliographic software expedites the writing process, it takes time to train yourself and learn how to fluidly use one of these software programs. There is a learning curve and the first time the bibliographic software is used it will take longer since the writer is still adapting to the use of this new software. However, after using the software a few times, the process gets much easier and in the end can be an essential time-saving tool. This tool will help you cite and reference more easily in your academic writing, which is another useful way of preventing academic dishonesty.

Citing Sources

Now that you have a basic understanding of APA style and have found the resources you want to use in your paper, you need to be sure they are properly cited. Citing information ensures that you are giving proper credit to the author. So, how do you know when to cite? As a general rule of thumb, citations are used to reference the works of any individual whose ideas, theories, or research influenced your writing (APA, 2010).

There are many different writing styles that can be used when citing information. Perhaps you have come across articles that were published in APA, MLA, or Chicago style, or maybe you have used one of these writing styles in an earlier academic program. *Writing styles* are simply publishing standards and guidelines for authors to use when writing and/or citing information. In this section, you will learn more about citing information in APA style.

Citations in the Reference List

The first step in citing information involves knowing where to put the citation. Citations are included in the body of the text, as well as at the end of the paper. At the end of your paper, you will have a reference page containing a list of all of the resources you used when writing your paper. You must have personally read the work if you cite it in your reference page (Lambie, Sias, Davis, Lawson, & Akos, 2008). Earlier in the chapter, you learned the difference between primary and secondary sources. You would not include a secondary source in your reference page if you did not review that particular document (Lambie et al., 2008).

A reference cited in the reference page provides the reader with the author's last name and first initial, the year the document was published, the title of the document, and publishing information. For example, a journal article cited in your reference page would look similar to this:

Whitlock, J., Wyman, P. A., & Moore, S. R. (2014). Connectedness and suicide prevention in adolescents: Pathways and implications. *Suicide and Life-Threatening Behavior, 44*(3), 246–272. doi:10.1111/sltb.12071

Notice that along with the authors' names, the year of publication, and the title of the article, you also see the name of the journal. The first set of numerical digits indicates the volume and volume number, and the second set of digits is the page numbers. You will then see the doi number, which is an alphanumeric string assigned to an article when it is published and made available electronically (APA, 2010). If you know an article's doi number, you can use that number to locate the article.

There is a section of the APA manual that specifically addresses formatting references in the reference list. You can find this information on pages 180–192 (APA, 2010). You will notice that there are differences in the way that various publications are cited. For example, journal articles, books, and periodicals are all cited differently. In the paragraph above, we showed how to cite a journal article. See the example below related to citing a book.

Capuzzi, D. (2009). *Suicide prevention in the schools: Guidelines for middle and high school settings.* Alexandria, VA: The American Counseling Association.

This citation looks a little different than the previously listed citation for the journal article. The author's name is given, the title of the book, and the publisher. Chapter 7 of the APA manual contains reference examples (APA, 2010). Page numbers are given to help you find examples of the specific citations you need. It is always a good idea to keep your APA manual nearby when you are writing so that you access information quickly and easily.

In-Text Citations

The body of your paper should contain citations to direct the reader to the source of the information you are providing. These citations are known as *in-text citations.* An in-text citation lets the reader know that you have borrowed this information from another source and directs the reader to the source in the reference page (APA, 2010). Pages 174–179 of your APA manual address in-text citations. Remember the book and journal article we referenced earlier in this section? We showed how those citations would look in the reference list at the end of a paper. Now, let's see how those same sources would look as in-text citations in the paragraph below.

> Capuzzi (2009) discussed warning signs related to adolescent suicide. Adolescents who attempted suicide in the past were considered to be at higher risk for suicide (Capuzzi, 2009). It is important that counselors be aware of this risk factor, as well as other risk factors that may indicate that a suicide attempt is imminent. Whitlock, Wyman, and Moore (2014) reported how adolescents' feelings of connectedness are related to the presence of suicidal thoughts and behaviors. There is variation in the way that males and females experience connectedness (Whitlock et al., 2014). Therefore, more research is needed to explore the relationship between gender and connectedness in suicide prevention.

In the first sentence, the reader is directed to Capuzzi's book, which is listed in the reference page. Note that in the second sentence, the reader is directed to the same publication, but the citation is provided at the end of the sentence instead of at the beginning. Either way is appropriate. The third sentence includes a citation with three authors. All three authors' names are listed the first time, however the phrase *et al.* is used in the fourth sentence after the first author's name. Et al. is a Latin abbreviation that means "and others." When citing three to five authors, you list all three authors in the first citation; thereafter, you use et al.

By now, you may start feeling as though citing information can be rather tedious. Citing references in many cases can be pretty straightforward, but there may be times when you find it difficult to cite a particular source. For instance, how do you cite a document from a website? What if the author is unknown, or you can't find the date of the publication? First, take a deep breath and relax. Finding the information you need might take a little more time than you expected, but the information likely exists. Second, try not to feel discouraged. Scholarly writing is a developmental process, and it will take time and practice to become familiar with APA style. The good news is that there are a lot of resources available that can show you how to cite even the most challenging documents.

Clearly, it is important to keep your APA manual handy when you are writing so that you can quickly reference the sections that you need. Suppose you are using a direct quote from a website with no page numbers. How do you cite it? First, try looking in the index of your APA manual. If you look under "Online Material," you will see "Online material, direct quotation of." The page numbers (171–172) and the section number (6.05) are given. If you turn to that section of the manual, you will find the section "Direct Quotations of Online Material Without Pagination." Sometimes you have to do a little exploring of the index before you find what you need. But, you can trust with the thorough nature of the APA manual, you will be able find what you need.

There are also online resources available that can help. For example, Purdue Owl is on an online writing lab that can give you specific information about APA style (Paiz, J. M. & Spronk, C., 2015). You can conduct a search by entering your specific question pertinent to APA style, and the information will be presented. Purdue Owl is considered to be a reputable site and can be a good substitute for finding citation examples, particularly when you do not have your APA manual with you. In addition, APA workshops are available on this site.

You may also discover that there is software available (both for free and for purchase) that will format your paper and insert the citations for you. Use caution when using these types of software programs. Not all of them format the information correctly. If you choose to use existing software or templates, you should still use your APA manual as a reference. Be sure that the software uses proper formatting and citing.

Self plagiarism. The APA manual has reference examples for a wide variety of resources (APA, 2010). If your professor allows it, you can reference past papers that you wrote to avoid self-plagiarism (see examples in the APA manual for citing unpublished works). Citing previous papers you wrote will prevent ethical violations of self-plagiarism. Always consult with professors before citing yourself as they may not allow it. If your professor does allow you to cite yourself, do so sparingly.

Personal communication. In addition to providing a style for citing unpublished works, APA also has a method for referencing personal communications, messages in electronic mailing lists, and messages in discussion groups, just to name a few examples. If your professor allows you to cite these forms of resources, always do so in a professional manner as outlined in the APA style manual. It is more scholarly to reference professional resources (e.g., journal articles and professional texts) in comparison to those listed above (e.g., personal communications). However, if you need to cite informal resources it is important to understand that there are professional methods of citing and referencing these types of documents and communications.

Developing a Professional Writing Style

One of the reasons students may commit errors of plagiarism is that they have not developed a professional writing style. Therefore, rather than appearing incompetent, the students copy portions of other people's writing to make themselves sound more professional. It is crucial that graduate students develop a solid writing style to avoid errors such as plagiarism and patchwriting. This section will offer recommendations for developing your own professional writing style.

Some people may wonder why counselors must use APA style and learn to write professionally. While most of counselors' time is spent as a practitioner, counselors must have solid writing skills. Counselors must write numerous reports, including intake assessments, treatment plans, progress notes, and other important paperwork. These reports may be read by a number of professionals including, but not limited to, physicians, lawyers, insurance company professionals, social workers, psychologists, and other mental health–related professionals. Counselors' credibility and professionalism will diminish significantly if they cannot communicate professionally in writing. Clients will also see your writing style, and if they cannot understand your writing or see that there are many writing mistakes, clients will be less likely to respect and trust your professional judgment.

It is important, therefore, to consider how to hone your writing skills while in graduate school. Hopefully you came into your graduate program already possessing the basics of writing while in your undergraduate program. However, regardless of the status of your writing skills when you entered your graduate program, it is important to refine these skills as they relate to the profession of counseling.

In the beginning of your counseling program, it is essential that your professor assess your writing skills. You will write a number of papers throughout your graduate program, and it is important that you obtain feedback from your professors regarding your writing style. You need to be open to hearing professors' feedback so you can then use this feedback to hone your writing skills. If you know that your writing style needs significant work, it is crucial that you consult with your professor to find ways to improve. Many universities offer writing assistance through the form of writing labs and other tutoring resources. While it can be humbling to recognize that your writing is lacking, the only way to get help is to first acknowledge that you need to improve. Then seek help to improve, whether it be through an additional writing course or through the assistance of a developmental editor at your university.

Ethical Functioning Within an Online Arena

Ethical, competent counselors all possess professional judgment and solid decision-making abilities. Practicing ethical behavior in graduate school is a good way to prepare for a career in the counseling field. There will be many times as a counselor that you come across ethical dilemmas and one key step in resolving a dilemma is to consult. As a graduate student, if you feel hesitancy or uncertainty regarding whether or not an action is acceptable and professional, it is crucial that you consult with your instructor. Asking another student is not sufficient as the student is not the person who will make the decision as to whether or not you behaved with integrity. Therefore if you have questions about ethical behavior in your online class, always ask your instructor. The next section goes into more detail regarding how to properly give credit to another person's work.

Test-taking

Online instructors are completely aware that they have no control over what students can and will do during a test-taking session. Expecting students to take an online quiz or exam in their own home without consulting books, notes, or the Internet is unrealistic. However, that is not to say that students will never encounter an online test where they cannot access the Internet or other resources. It is important that you clarify with the instructor what is acceptable in his or her class in relation to what can be accessed during tests. Instructors often make online quizzes and tests timed. That way, even though students have access to resources, if they do not know the material as a result of studying, time works against them in the test-taking environment. Students who spend too much time searching for information will most likely run out of time and their grade may suffer.

Online learning platforms (e.g., BlackBoard, Moodle, Edmodo) offer tools to instructors to prevent cheating on tests. Instructors are aware that students may attempt to share test questions with fellow students. Randomizing the questions, as well as the responses, is one way instructors prevent cheating in classes. The instructor may also use a bank of test questions that are randomized to ensure that each student receives a different set of questions. Instructors may also opt to use essay questions that assess students' learning. These types of questions are more difficult to cheat on as the student needs to come up with an original answer. Instructors should also wait until after the test period has closed prior to sharing student feedback on exams. This helps prevent students who finished the exam from sharing feedback on answers with other students who have not yet taken the exam.

Fraud in Online Courses

Online students have more opportunities to behave dishonestly than face-to-face students. It would be much more challenging for a face-to-face student to have someone else attend class in his or her place. However, in an online environment where cameras are not always used, this temptation may be stronger. In fact, there are online services where you can pay someone to take a class for you. Some universities are requiring students to use a website to tape themselves at their computers while taking an exam to prevent this type of fraud. In addition, some universities have an on-campus residency requirement for online programs; however, not all universities do. Some students may complete their entire degree without setting foot on a college campus.

While it is not acceptable for a student in any educational program to fraudulently complete a degree, for counseling students this offense is especially egregious. Counseling programs are designed to prepare students to work with a variety of populations who suffer from moderate to severe mental illnesses. Without the proper training, a counselor working with these populations could do severe harm to an individual. ACA (2005) code C.2.a. states, "Counselors practice only within the boundaries of their competence, based on their education, training, supervised experience, state and national professional credentials, and appropriate professional experience." Counseling students who fraudulently

Table 9.1   Guide to Success in Academic Integrity

Goals/Challenges	Strategies for Success
Integrity in the Internet	
	• Understand the definition of academic integrity. • Avoid using papers written by others. • Do your own work.
Integrity in Academic Writing	
	• Understand the definition of plagiarism. • Cite and reference where you get your information. • Avoid patchwriting. • Know the codes of ethics related to plagiarism. • Know university policies related to plagiarism and self-plagiarism.
APA Style	
	• Purchase an APA manual and use it. • Avail yourself of other APA style resources. • Make sure every reference is cited in-text and vice-versa.
Online Ethical Functioning	
	• Follow the posted guidelines regarding online quizzes and tests. • Do your own work.

complete their degree are clearly in violation of this ethical code as they should not practice as a counselor until they obtain the appropriate education and training. Imagine if your physician or surgeon cheated his or her way through medical school. The same concept applies to counselors as we work with people in need of our assistance. Our clients may be suicidal or in danger of harming others, and we must have the expertise and competency to best meet their needs or we are putting people in danger.

Summary

There are many angles to take into account when considering academic integrity, and even more when examining integrity in online counseling programs. It is crucial that counselors-in-training understand how to prevent errors pertaining to academic dishonesty. A primary way to behave with academic integrity is to rely on APA style as a guide for writing. Learning how to cite and reference properly is essential for implementing standards of academic integrity. This chapter presented a number of recommendations and tools for future counselors to use, both while in graduate school, and in the future as a practicing counselor.

About the Authors

Carolyn Berger, PhD, is an assistant professor at Nova Southeastern University. She obtained her master's and doctorate degrees in counseling from University of Florida. Dr. Berger has taught both fully online and hybrid counseling courses. She has developed numerous templates for online courses and also serves on the professional standings committee for the psychology and counseling programs at her university.

Dr. Ruth Ouzts Moore is a Distance Clinical Professor at Lamar University in the Masters of Clinical Mental Health Counseling Program. She has presented nationally and internationally in the areas of abuse/trauma, play therapy, high-conflict divorce/parental alienation, and creative counseling techniques. Dr. Moore is the president of the South Georgia Association for Play Therapy and the secretary of the Association for Creativity in Counseling. Dr. Moore has published in peer-reviewed journals and scholarly resources. She is frequently called to serve as an expert witness in criminal, chancery, and youth court for her involvement in child abuse and child custody cases.

References

American Counseling Association. (2005). *ACA Code of Ethics*. Alexandria, VA: Author.

American Psychological Association. (2010). *Publication manual of the American Psychological Association* (6th ed.). Washington, DC: Author.

American Psychological Association. (n.d.). *Corrections of the first printing of the Publication Manual of the American Psychological Association, Sixth edition (2009)*. Retrieved from http://supp.apa.org/style/pubman-reprint-corrections-for-2e.pdf

Capuzzi, D. (2009). *Suicide prevention in the schools: Guidelines for middle and high school settings*. Alexandria, VA: The American Counseling Association.

Elder, C., Pflugfelder, C., & Angeli, E. (2010). *Handout: Comparing policies*. Retrieved from https://owl.english.purdue.edu/owl/resource/929/15/

Ellis, A., & Ellis, D. J. (2011). *Rational emotive behavior therapy*. American Psychological Association: Washington, DC.

Halupa, C., & Bollinger, D. U. (2013). Faculty perceptions of student self plagiarism: An exploratory multi-university study. *Journal of Academic Ethics, 11*, 297–310. doi: 10.1007/s10805-013-9195-6

Howard, R. M., & Robilliard, A. E. (2008). (Eds). *Pluralizing plagiarism: Identities, contexts, pedagogies*. Portsmouth, NH: Heinemann Boynton/Cook.

Integrity. (n.d.). In *Oxford Dictionaries online*. Retrieved from http://www.oxford-dictionaries.com/us/definition/american_english/integrity

Lambie, G. W., Sias, S. M., Davis, K. M., Lawson, G., & Akos, P. (2008). A scholarly writing resource for counselor educators and their students. *Journal of Counseling & Development, 86*(1), 18–25. doi:10.1002/j.1556-6678.2008.tb00621.x

Paiz, J. M., Angeli, E., Wagner, J., Lawrick, E., Moore, K., Anderson, M., Soderlund, L., . . . Keck, R. (2010). *APA stylistics: Avoiding bias*. Retrieved from https://owl.english.purdue.edu/owl/resource/560/14/

Paiz, J. M., & Spronk, C. (2015). Purdue writing lab. Retrieved from https://owl.english.purdue.edu/writinglab

Penn State University (2012, August). *Choosing a citation manager*. Retrieved from http://www.libraries.psu.edu/psul/lls/choose_citation_mgr.html

Plagiarism. (n.d.). In *Oxford Dictionaries online*. Retrieved from http://www.oxford-dictionaries.com/us/definition/american_english/plagiarism

Turnitin. (n.d.). *Content*. Retrieved from http://turnitin.com/en_us/features/orig-inalitycheck/content

Whitlock, J., Wyman, P. A. and Moore, S. R. (2014). Connectedness and Suicide Prevention in Adolescents: Pathways and Implications. Suicide and Life-Threating Behavior, 44: 246–272. doi: 10.1111/sltb.12071

Yale College Writing Center. (2015). *Why are there different citation styles?* Retrieved from http://writing.yalecollege.yale.edu/advice-students/using-sources/principles-citing-sources/why-are-there-different-citation-styles

10

Online Research

Michelle Perepiczka, Donna Sheperis, and Ruth Ouzts Moore

Chapter Overview

This chapter will provide you with some guidance on conducting and using research in an online program. Specifically, this chapter tries to demystify the process of accessing, using, and understanding counseling research from the comfort of your home rather than the confines of a campus library. We address how to identify and narrow a research topic, navigate databases, and cite your sources. Finally, writing tips for the online learner are offered.

Learning Outcomes

After reading this chapter, you will be able to

- Analyze the quality of counseling-related databases
- Analyze the quality of materials found in counseling-related databases
- Search counseling-related databases
- Identify time-saving shortcuts for searching for counseling-related materials needed for research projects

- Search for scholarly information outside of the library
- Determine if a website is credible
- Paraphrase material from a source
- Cite material from a source both in-text and in the reference page
- Distinguish paraphrasing from plagiarism
- Define elements of research questions necessary for research writing
- Identify listservs that provide support to counseling graduate students
- Narrow research topics using a standard process
- Describe ways to organize the writing process

Introduction

This chapter will serve as a helpful guide for the very start of the research process including discussions on how to identify a research topic, finding and evaluating databases, navigating through a database to identify needed resources, and searching for materials outside your university library. This chapter will also review some helpful tips for citing sources in your paper and evolving your initial notes into a fully developed written piece.

It is very common and perhaps expected to be overwhelmed or nervous about conducting research. The process can seem foreign. However, some aspects of research are commonplace in our society today with our use of smartphones, tablets, and user-friendly programs. You are most likely engaging in the steps similar to an academic research project a few times a week! Let's consider an example to try to calm some of these nerves.

Imagine you would like to find a restaurant for dinner. You may pull up a search bar such as Google or Yahoo to research restaurants. You may condense your search using key terms that fall into the categories of a particular zip code, type of food, level of stars, ambiance, or price point. By continuing to narrow your search, you will identify places that fit your craving. You may also do a complementary search via Yelp, Urbanspoon, or Menupages to supplement your original search or find additional details. The process to find where to go to dinner is similar to finding journal articles you need. Not so intimidating when you think of it this way!

Before we launch into the chapter, remember you are not alone in your research endeavors. A large support system is available to help you with your projects. Faculty, teaching assistants, reference librarians, and peers can all assist you with this process. You do not have to research alone.

Identifying a Research Topic

Throughout your experience as an online student, you will be required to write research papers on topics of interest to you. While this may sound like a straightforward request, deciding what to write about and how to write about it can be challenging. Adding in the isolation of working on your own in an online format complicates the process further. Because you don't have the luxury of hanging out in the student union talking with your classmates about a paper for class, we hope to provide you with some methods to make the process easier for you.

What Is a Research Topic?

A research topic is really just something you intend to write about. For most projects, even at the graduate level, conducting original research involving data collection is not the purpose of these papers. A research paper is the product of a targeted effort at gathering, critically analyzing, organizing, and presenting the scholarly material available on the subject (de Figueiredo, 2010). A research paper should not just better inform you, but should make a contribution to the existing body of literature. Because of this, the topic is a critical component.

Clearly, you will want to write about something of interest to you. While you may be given a broad range of topic areas (e.g., substance abuse counseling), you will have the power to choose within that range to find something that speaks to you and you want to know more about. Thinking about what interests you is the beginning of developing a research topic. Then the honing process begins! Think of finding a research topic like a spiral (see Figure 10.1); we start on the edge of the subject and work our way into the center until we land on the actual topic that is meaningful to the project.

Using the assignment to guide you. In most school-based situations, you are writing for an assignment that has some instructions to guide you. As students, you may feel like those guidelines are not specific enough, but chances are they are set up to allow the most flexibility, autonomy, and creativity for students to showcase their understanding of the topic. Clearly, if you are given some parameters related to topic, you want to stay within those. If, for example, you are preparing to write a paper on clinical interventions to use with a particular population and you choose to write a historical overview of Castro's Cuba, you are off the mark. However, within the parameters you can find your niche.

Figure 10. 1   The Research Topic Spiral

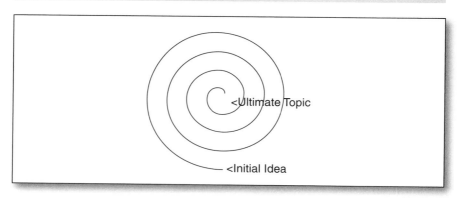

In addition to topic parameters, assignments often have particular elements you will need to address. These elements will help define your research topic. Using the example of the paper on clinical interventions, you may be asked to speak to interventions that come from the humanistic theories, cognitive theories, and solution-focused theories. As such, you would not choose to write exclusively about cognitive work with a particular population. You will likely even use some of these points from the instructions as section headers in your paper to keep you on track. Another guideline that may be present in the instructions is a page limit. Some assignments have them, some do not. But if you are writing a short paper, your topic will necessarily be constrained.

Elements of research questions. How can we go about deciding on that ultimate topic? One way is to consider research questions. Research questions often begin with one of the Five W's: *who, what, when, where,* or *why.* The word *how* can also be used but is often covered within the Five W's. Using these interrogatories helps you decide what you want to write about. For example, let's say you are interested in domestic violence. Clearly, this is too large of a topic to write about with any real depth. Instead, you will use one of the Five W's to define the topic.

- Who is most likely to seek help for domestic violence?
- What symptoms are common in children living in domestically violent situations?
- When do women who are in domestically violent relationships leave?
- Where do perpetrators of domestic violence seek treatment?
- Why do people stay with their domestically violent partner?

Inspirations for Research Topics

Chances are, if you are enrolled in a counseling program, you have already defined some client populations that are of interest to you. However, many students feel unsure about what topic they should be writing about. Since hanging out at the student union and chatting with classmates is not possible, how does the online student get inspiration?

Engage your classmates. One way is through virtual conversations with classmates (Dixson, 2010). Either in the class itself, or in another platform, there are often ways for online students to connect virtually. Perhaps your cohort or class has a Facebook page. Maybe your online course has a Class Café section. If your instructor holds webinars, there may even be a live chat feature that would allow you to connect with your peers. Reach out! Pose questions about topics. Share what you are reading about and ask others to do so as well. Get creative to find ways to brainstorm with the people who are in your same boat.

Join professional organizations and listservs. We hope that you also belong as a student member to the American Counseling Association, the American Mental Health Counselors Association, and/or the American School Counselor Association. Attending conferences and networking with other like-minded professionals can really be inspiring! Also, becoming a member means you will receive the publications, including newsletters and scholarly journals, published by the organization. The articles in these publications are also a source of good ideas.

Another resource for all students that is particularly useful to online students is a listserv. A listserv is an e-mail distribution list where one person sends a message and it "posts" to all members of the listserv. Most listservs allow you the option of receiving individual e-mails as they are submitted or a digest version, which is a single e-mail every few days or once a week containing all messages in a thread. Given the nature of online education, having messages in your e-mail that you can retrieve at your leisure is helpful.

The American Counseling Association does not provide a listserv but does make note of two on its website that are useful to graduate counseling students (ACA, 2015). Counsgrads is a listserv operated by faculty at The Ohio State University (n.d.) since 1997. Currently, over 1,000 students are members of the listserv. This unmoderated forum exists for counseling graduate students to have a place to engage in dialogue about all manner of professional issues, including research topics.

The discussions can get quite lively with this many members, and active participation is encouraged. Many students find this listserv to be a great place to get and strengthen research topics and ideas. Students interested in Counsgrads can visit http://go.osu.edu/COUNSGRADS.

A second listserv of interest to many counseling students is specific to multicultural issues and is called Diversegrad-L (ACA, 2015). This list is comprised of students, counselors, counselor educators, and others across the United States and Canada interested in discussing topics related to cross-cultural and diversity considerations. Diversegrad-L has over 500 members offering counseling students a rich, interactive, environment. To subscribe to this list, students need to send the message "SUBSCRIBE DIVERSEGRAD-L" by e-mail to Listserv@listserv.AMERICAN.EDU.

Work smarter, not harder. Another source of inspiration can be research you have already done in past courses. For example, a student recently called one of the chapter authors to talk about narrowing down a research topic (wait—call your professors for a consultation? That is another great way to start to narrow down your topic!). The student, Sierra, indicated that she was interested in studying forces that shape how adults feel about themselves; specifically, how their experiences in life contributed to their sense of self-worth and satisfaction with who they are. Wow, that is a lot to try to study! Can you see some of the challenges in this research topic? First of all, "experiences in life" can mean anything from school sports to the presence of a grandparent in the home. Then, self-worth is another huge topic. It turns out that Sierra had written a paper in undergraduate courses about how the types of toys they played with as a kid influenced their sense of gender. As we talked, we were able to discover that she was still interested in the same sorts of things but wanted to broaden her knowledge base with her next study. Her undergraduate paper serves as a source of inspiration.

Test Out Your Topic

How will you know if you have found a good topic? More importantly, how can you decide if the subject area is too big or too narrow to study? A very common way to organize your thoughts is to use a triangle to begin to narrow your topic choices. Consider the first thoughts you have as the very general topic. Then take it one step further and narrow that topic. Chances are, the topic is still too broad. Try narrowing it even further. Finally, using the Five *W*'s, narrow it still further to a specific idea (See Figure 10.2).

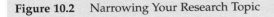

Figure 10.2   Narrowing Your Research Topic

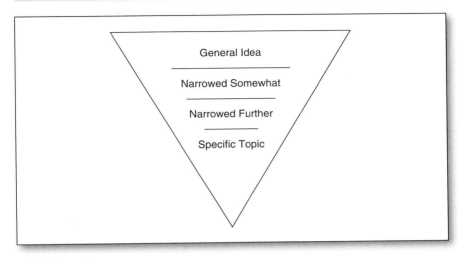

General Idea

Narrowed Somewhat

Narrowed Further

Specific Topic

What might this look like in practice? Perhaps you are interested in substance abuse counseling. Clearly that is a topic that is too broad to research for a single assignment? Now think further, what element of substance abuse counseling is of interest to you? Perhaps you discover that you are interested in alcohol use in college students. Again, a large topic! Think further and narrow that topic down. Your next step might be to consider prevention of alcohol use in college students. Finally, you will apply the Five W's to discover some potential research questions. You may be curious about "What factors prevent alcohol use in college students?" or "When are college students most likely to binge drink?" Your final topic may be defined as prevention of binge drinking in college students. Your research topic process would look like the one shown in Figure 10.3.

A benefit of the research triangle is the fact that you can engage in this process alone. However, it is our hope that you will reach out for help as you begin to make these decisions. Let's go back to the example about Sierra. She initially wanted to research influences on self-worth. However, we quickly learned that this topic is entirely too broad. She began talking with others in her life about this interest and asking what contributed to their self-worth. Taking this action helped her to determine some suitable search terms to take to the library databases for further exploration.

Figure 10.3   Narrowing the Research Topic: Example

When reviewing current literature on the topic, you should be able to narrow your search even further (Boudah, 2011). You will want to read what other scholars have written on the subject. In fact, you will want to do a lot of reading. The more reading of existing literature you do, the better a writer you will become (Doloughan, 2012). As you read, one area of interest will be to discover if the subject has been so exhaustively researched that further research would not really add to the existing body of literature. For example, one thing Sierra was considering was whether a positive support system of friends and family influenced a person's sense of self-worth. This idea has been well-researched and the answer is a resounding yes. As such, further research along this same vein may not be very productive. In research, we call this the "so what?" factor. When you decide what you want to study, you need to be able to answer, "So what makes this unique/important/needed?"

Conversely, there may be a large "so what?" factor, but the phenomenon is too new to have much research yet (Cornell University Digital Library Resource, 2015a). For example, something likely happened in the news this week. An election, a plane crash, a change in the stock market, or a celebrity split. You might be interested in how this event impacted a certain population. Unfortunately, the event is still too new to study. You will be better off studying the impact of an event that happened some time ago so that you have some literature to cite in your paper. Remember that getting a manuscript to publication can take a year or more. The most recent articles likely use data from two years prior. Getting sufficient literature on a new phenomenon takes time.

Finding and Evaluating Database Resources

What Are Databases?

Let's start at square one with learning what it means when we refer to a database. A database is an electronic warehouse of journal articles, book reviews, psychological instrument reviews, dissertations and master's theses, government documents, news articles, and conference papers or presentations. Imagine a keeper of all of the information who contracts with various professional organizations and owners of journals to obtain the resources to fill up the warehouse. The keeper then organizes the various materials in a way that is searchable based on key phrases. Amazon and Youtube are great examples in everyday life of databases we use. See, this is not such a foreign or difficult topic!

We can compare an online database to how libraries operated in the past. Librarians would work to collect as many books as possible within a particular scope. The librarians would then organize the books based on the Dewey decimal system. The readers would physically go to the library, search for books within available categories with the help of the card catalogue, and then walk over to the bookshelves to locate the book. We are doing the same thing with databases; however, we open a website to complete the process instead of driving to the library.

Professional databases are unique in that they are not free to the public like community libraries or many websites such as EBay or Wayfair. Professional database access is purchased by universities or other institutions; access to databases is made available to individual users by the larger organizations. To access available databases through your university, you will want to connect with a reference librarian. Be sure to ask for the university webpage to log in to the databases as well as your username and password.

Getting to Know Specific Databases

Different databases are available to you. Try to not get confused or overwhelmed about which one to use. We will categorize these and make them simple to understand based on what you are looking for. Think of it like we are going fishing in various waters looking for certain fish! Really just the type of information the databases contain makes them differ from each other much like different bodies of water are home to various fish. Some databases contain a wide variety of materials (ocean contains diverse fish), while other databases are narrower and focus on a particular professional field (ponds are home to limited types of fish).

First, we will review the databases that contain a wide variety of information. This category includes Academic Search Premier, Dissertation Abstracts Online, EBSCOhost, and Educational Resources Information Center (ERIC) databases. These are considered scholarly databases, meaning the articles found here were assessed for quality prior to being published by the journal editors (aka the articles are subjected to peer review). They are also multidisciplinary, which means they contain information from diverse professions such as the following: social sciences, education, humanities, engineering, language and linguistics, computer sciences, arts and literature, medical sciences, and ethnic studies. Academic Search Premier, ERIC, and EBSCOhost will provide access to journal articles, while Dissertation Abstracts Online will link you to master's theses or dissertations.

You might be asking, when would I use these particular databases? These databases can be used to see what you might discover across disciplines on a topic. For example, counselors are not the only ones interested in the outcomes of counseling interventions for the elderly. Many times government agencies, health care companies, medical providers, public policy makers, and even educators are interested in the impact of counseling for persons 65 years of age and older. The outcomes can inform best practices, needed policy decisions, where to invest resources, and more. A search in these databases is much like casting a wide net to see what you find out in the entire ocean!

Let's transition our focus to the databases related to counseling journal articles specifically. This is much like casting a net in just one body of water. PsychInfo and PsychArticles are examples of counseling specific databases. Both are coordinated by the American Psychological Association (APA). You may find resources from other disciplines in this database such as neuroscience or nursing; however, the topics will all be related to the helping professions. These are great to use when wanting to find resources on mental health topics as it may be related to the helping professions.

We can take our open water exploration into databases even narrower by discussing databases specific to counseling assessments! This is like casting a net in one particular pond where a certain type of fish lives. PsycTESTS, Health and Psychosocial Instruments (HaPI), and Mental Measurements Yearbook all contain information related to instruments to measure various aspects like dimensions or characteristics of personality, academic or educational abilities and interest, vocational skills or interests, psychology, and other related areas. These databases contain information about test authors, test purpose, scoring information, psychometric properties of the assessment, and/or test reviews for published or unpublished instruments.

Evaluating Databases

Being a researcher means you are a consumer of information. You have a responsibility to analyze the information you find to determine if it makes the cut! In essence, you have a duty to determine if the resources fit the criteria for relevance to the project. Databases can provide you with a plethora of reliable information; however, you determine if it is valid for what you are exploring. For instance, suppose you are researching for a paper on historical post-traumatic stress disorder (PTSD) treatment outcomes for soldiers who served during the Vietnam War. A recent article focused on PTSD outcomes of military soldiers who recently returned home from the War on Terror would not be the best overall fit. However, this may come up as it would fit related search terms. It will be up to you to determine what part of the article, if any, would fit your population and their struggles. It can be tricky, but you just have to consider what you really want to find.

Materials. You can start your evaluation by looking at the databases themselves to see if these will contain resources that will fit your needs. You could consider the types of materials covered in the database such as journals, books, newspaper articles, or conference resources. In the case of historical PTSD treatment outcomes for Vietnam veterans, a researcher may want to find a database that includes newspaper articles as there may be relevant information from the news and books that may compile historical treatment protocols or outcome reports in addition to journals.

Source of Information. Another evaluation point would be assessing if the database includes information about the source of the information.

Some journals, news articles, or books may be commercial or academic publishers. If a researcher wants to focus on all opinions on mental health treatment for war veterans, then having representation from various publishers may be needed. Or, if a researcher wants to look specifically at a right- or left-wing perspective, then knowing the source of the data might come in handy.

Date range available. Timeliness of database records plays a role here too. In many cases, students will be looking for articles published within the last 10 years; however, this is not always the case. Seminal research from the great thinkers of our time such as Freud, Adler, or Pavlov are not within the last decade but their work is still relevant as it laid the foundation for future research in some cases. In addition, some topics are based in the past such as Vietnam veteran PTSD treatment outcomes. Access to older articles in addition to newer ones may be necessary.

Updating frequency. How often a database is updated might be helpful to know if you are researching a very timely topic such as preventative violence interventions with veterans suffering with PTSD returning home from the War on Terror. You may want a database that updates daily or monthly to ensure the latest information is accessible instead of updated quarterly or less frequently. When searching for information on the Vietnam veterans, the frequency of updates may be less of a focal point.

Evaluating Respective Items

Now that you evaluated the databases and selected the search criteria you want to use, your next step will be to evaluate the materials you find. The areas to evaluate are if the article is peer reviewed or comes from a primary or secondary source. Each of these is relevant in the literature. However, as mentioned before, it is up to you to determine what is most appropriate for your research.

Peer reviewed. You will hear the concept peer reviewed frequently. The term *peer review* refers to the checks-and-balances process the article went through to ensure the content is of high quality. The peer review process includes an editorial board reviewing the article, critiquing it, having the authors make updates or corrections, and then deciding whether or not the work is quality. The process can be blind, which means the reviewers do not know the names of the authors. The most common type of resource you may find in databases will be published journal articles that are peer reviewed.

Many projects require articles that are peer reviewed; however, some research topics that focus on analyzing opinions of others would not necessarily need articles that underwent the peer reviewed process. One example would be a research project to identify themes within "Letters From the Editors" contained inside counseling journals. Letters from the editors are commonly not peer reviewed, so you would not be looking for any articles that fall under that umbrella.

Primary versus secondary source. Information can come from either a primary or secondary source. Again, both play a role in literature, but it is up to you to decide what best suits your needs. A primary source is firsthand information about a phenomenon or topic of focus (VanderMey, Meyers, Van Rys, Kemper, & Sebrank, 2011). In general terms, the person providing the information was actually present for an event. An example of a primary source is an American Red Cross Disaster Health Team Responder who worked to support a community that was destroyed by a natural disaster and was interviewed to learn about the support efforts. Primary resources are commonly academic journal articles (Galvan, 2006), and the information in them may have been obtained through interviews, surveys, experiments, empirical research articles, or observations of the primary resources.

A secondary source is secondhand account of an event (VanderMey et al., 2011). An example of a secondary source is a news reporter who gathers, analyzes, and relays information from the American Red Cross Disaster Health Team Responder to provide his or her interpretation of the support efforts. Secondary sources come in many forms such as journal articles, textbooks, news articles, radio or television, documentaries, or even encyclopedias (Galvan, 2006).

Navigating Through Databases

Maneuvering your way through a database to find materials on a topic is a lot like shopping at a grocery store to find a specific item. You need to know the following: (a) the type of store such as a general or specialty store (like a general database or a focused one); (b) the various categories of foods sold such as fresh produce, canned or boxed goods, frozen foods (like articles, assessment tools, book reviews); and (c) how the aisles or products are organized (like key words to search in a database). When you know your way around, then you can go right to what you are looking for. If you do not know the store very well, it might take a while or you could become frustrated. Let's try to avoid the pain and agony of searching for resources by giving you a map to guide the way!

This section will address various steps to consider when conducting a search for materials. We will use the example of investigating ways to reduce graduate student anxiety about conducting research using peer-reviewed articles to walk through this.

Logging in. Beginning with first things first, open your browser to your university's library login webpage for databases. This is where you will enter your username and password provided to you by your school. Once this is open, you are ready to get started.

Database selection. Next, you will need to select the database you would like to use to conduct your search. You will probably have a few options available from your university. Try to familiarize yourself with the options. Many main pages will provide a description of the various types of databases. Select the one (or multiple if available) that best fits your needs. For our example, we could choose PsychInfo because it is likely to have information related to education, counseling interventions, graduate students, and more based on the description of the database we learned earlier.

Full text or not. Third, consider the amount of time you have to complete your project. If you need articles to complete a project quickly, then you can limit your search to Full Text only. This will ensure all the listings will have either a pdf or html copy of the article you can read on demand. However, if you have a few extra weeks to request articles through interlibrary loan, then you could leave that search option open to all abstracts.

Peer review. Be sure to read the instructions closely for your project. Are you required to have all peer-reviewed articles? Also, consider your topic. Does your topic seem to rely only on empirical articles? If the answer is yes to either or both of these, then you will want to click the box to have all articles collected be peer reviewed. If you have some wiggle room or your topic necessitates non-peer-reviewed articles, then leave this unselected. For our example of anxious graduate students, we would want to find peer-reviewed journals so we would select the box.

Key terms. The next step will be to brainstorm key words or descriptors related to your topic. The database will use these words to generate a list of related articles. You will want to be as accurate and specific as possible to filter out unrelated articles. Whatever words you put into the database will be directly tied to what you get out. Thus, if irrelevant words are put in, then irrelevant articles will pop up!

When you generate a list, you will want to be creative. For our example of investigating ways to reduce graduate student anxiety about conducting research, we can focus on a few elements for search terms. First, we could focus on the population. Common terms to use would be *graduate students, college students, adults,* or *learners.* Another area to focus would be on the problem we are interested in which is anxiety. Terms for that could be *anxiety, nervous, worry,* or *fear.* We could develop this further to a phrase like *fear of research* or *research anxiety.* A final point to look at is the impact of treatment. These words could be *intervention, therapy, counseling, treatment,* or *coping.* This is a great list to get started.

Here is a hint about finding descriptive terms to use. If you find an article that perfectly matches what you are looking for, then refer to the key word list the author may have included under the abstract. You can incorporate any of those terms as well as the author's name in a more specific search too!

Consider the appropriateness of the terms you use if you discover you are not finding what you need. Remember, putting irrelevant terms into the database will yield irrelevant articles. If you want to look at medication to treat graduate student anxiety about research and used the word *drug* in your search, then you may find a good amount on illegal drugs with college students that may not be relevant. You will want to be specific and as accurate as possible.

As you conduct your search and experiment with various terms, you will want to start with general terms to see the amount of results you get, then get more specific to find articles that are more on target with what you are looking for. To narrow your search or even to expand it some, you could use Boolean operators, which are words that connect search terms. These words include *and, or,* and *not.* For the example project, we could use these in the following way: graduate student and research anxiety and clinical treatment or medication not illicit.

Refine search. If you come across the problem that you have too many articles to review and are unsure how to change your key words, then you can rely on the refine search options too. The refine search control panels usually have forced choices for you to narrow the playing field. You can reduce the original list by source type (e.g., book, article, news article, instrument review), age of your preferred sample (usually grouped by decade), gender of participants (male and female), date of publication, or methodology (quantitative, qualitative, or mixed methods). This can be a great way to filter through a large number of articles.

Invest time and patience. The final element to take under consideration when conducting a search for materials is time and patience. You might not find what you are looking for in the first attempt. At times you might feel overwhelmed with the number of articles to sift through and other times you might be afraid that nothing exists on your topic. Remember, help is available to you. If you get stuck, then please turn to a peer, faculty member, or reference librarian to get you unstuck and back on your way.

Outside of the Library: Website Resources

There are many websites available outside of the library that can provide invaluable information about a given topic. The benefit of using outside website resources is that they are easily accessible. For example, do you want to know more about life on Mars? Open a browser, pick a search engine, type in *life on Mars*, and you can quickly get a variety of websites from which to choose. There are certainly advantages to using website resources outside of the library, however there can also be disadvantages. How do you know if the information you find on the Internet is accurate? Conducting a search on the Internet can be tricky. You not only have to know where to find the information, but you also have to evaluate the websites to determine if the material is credible and trustworthy.

Searching the Web

The first step in obtaining information from the Internet about your research topic is selecting your browser and search engine. You might be wondering what the difference is between the two? A *browser* is computer software that retrieves and displays websites. Think of it as an infrastructure that puts pictures, images, and information together in the form of websites. Google Chrome, Mozilla Firefox, Internet Explorer, and Safari are some of the most frequently used browsers. A *search engine* is a website that looks for other websites based on your key word search. Google, Bing, Yahoo, Ask, and AOL are common search engines. Selecting a browser and a search engine is really just a matter of preference. You may like the way one search engine organizes information over another. You may also find that some browsers work faster on your computer than others. Once you have selected your browser and search engine, you are that much closer to getting the information you want about your research topic.

Wikipedia

You might notice when you conduct various key word searches that the *Wikipedia* website is retrieved quite often. Wikipedia is an online encyclopedia, and it may contain some good information about a topic. Wikipedia is a great place to get general information about a topic and find references that can lead you to additional information. For example, if you search *cognitive behavioral therapy* (CBT) on the Wikipedia website, you will find a basic definition of CBT, a description of how it is used, and references at the bottom of the page. Wikipedia can be a great place to get started, particularly when you need more information about a topic and are not sure where to look. However, it is important to note that the information retrieved from Wikipedia is not peer-reviewed nor is it considered to be scholarly material. Anyone can publish an article on Wikipedia when registered on the site. Therefore, it is possible that you may find information that is not accurate. Consider using Wikipedia as a place for fundamental information, but use other websites for scholarly information.

Finding Scholarly Websites

Finding scholarly information on the Internet is often just a matter of knowing where to look. Some resources are available for free, and others are available for a fee. You might be curious about why all resources are not free. As we mentioned earlier in the chapter, if you join professional organizations such as the American Counseling Association, you receive a subscription to *The Journal of Counseling and Development* as one of the benefits of your membership. Most professional organizations offer the same courtesy. But, suppose you find a journal article on line published by an organization with which you are not a member. Many of those articles are available for a fee if you access them outside of the library. These charges are to offset publishing expenses. If you find an article on the Internet that is available for a fee, you might try searching an online library for the article. Many times you can obtain the same article free of charge through a library, and if it is not available, you can get it via interlibrary loan. There are also plenty of websites that contain scholarly information that you can access free of charge.

Google Scholar. Google Scholar is a free search engine that retrieves information from academic publishers, universities, and professional organizations. You are more likely to find peer-reviewed journal articles, conference papers, technical reports, and other scholarly works using Google Scholar than you will with other search engines (Brown, 2013). For example, if you conduct a search on Google Scholar using the key words *humanistic counseling*, a variety of websites are listed. These websites lead you to a number of scholarly works. Google Scholar can be a great resource when searching for a research topic, particularly if you use the *Advanced Search* option (Brown, 2013). To access this search option, click on the arrow on the right in the single search box. You can search by author, publication dates, and journal titles. Many full-text articles and PDF files are available. Another advantage of using Google Scholar is that you can create an e-mail alert allowing Google Search to notify you when any new items are added that match your search (Brown, 2013). Simply click the *Create Alert* envelope on the left side of your search results.

Government websites and organizations. Government websites, organizations, and research centers can be a great place to find statistics and other scholarly information (University of Western Sydney Library, 2015). Simply type your key words into a search engine along with *.gov, .org,* or *research center,* and you will find numerous sites (University of Western Sydney Library, 2015). For example, suppose you are writing a research paper on counseling children in foster care who are awaiting adoption. You are interested in knowing the statistics related to the number of children in the United States who are in foster care and the percentage of those cases who are awaiting adoption. If you type in the key words *children in foster care awaiting adoption* and *.gov,* you will see a variety of child welfare and government websites identified in the results list. These websites are likely to contain credible information.

Smithsonian Research Online. The Smithsonian Museum houses nine research centers (Brown, 2013). Smithsonian Research Online (SRO) is a portal that is managed by the Smithsonian Institution Libraries. There is a box that allows you to search your topic by key words, or you can access full text versions of articles using their digital repository. Using SRO is a great way to keep up with current scientific research. You can find more information about SRO at http://research.si.edu/.

Mendeley. Mendeley is a free on-line library that contains millions of research articles and papers (Brown, 2013). Think of Mendeley as a reference manager and an academic social network. You can use Mendeley to organize the information you retrieve by saving websites and papers in your own online library which can later be used with in-text citations and in your reference page (Brown, 2013). You can cite as you write using any device. There is a key word search available, or you can use the *Advance Search* option and search by author, publication date, or document type (Brown, 2013). Go to www.mendeley.com for more information.

Journal TOCS. JournalTOCS is a free collection of the tables of contents for over 21,000 journals. You can conduct a keyword search and browse journals by topic or you can enter your keywords to search within specific journals. Using JournalTOCS is easy. You simply set up a free account, and then you can follow particular journals of interest. You can request that future tables of contents from those specific journals be e-mailed to you. For more information about JournalTOCS, go to http://www.journaltocs .hw.ac.uk/.

Evaluating the Website for Credibility

Now that we have discussed how to find information online, we should mention the importance of analyzing the information to determine credibility. Such a task may seem fairly simple; however, determining a website's credibility can be an arduous task, in that it requires advanced skills and competencies (Ivanitskaya, O'Boyle, & Casey, 2006). Ivanitskaya et al. (2006) found that many students have difficulty judging the trustworthiness of Internet sites and documents. Students were often more interested in finding information quickly rather than verifying the integrity of the site. You may retrieve a variety of websites when searching the Internet, but it is important to remember that you must analyze the website and its content thoroughly (University of Western Sydney Library, 2015). Cornell University Digital Library Resource (2015b) recommends evaluating the website's purpose, authority, reliability, currency, and coverage before using the information in your research paper.

Purpose. When reviewing a website, you must first consider the purpose. Is it there to sell you something, or does it seem genuine in its intent to deliver information? Some websites provide information, but they have a hidden agenda and are often trying to sell you something (Cornell University Digital Library Resource, 2015b). The information on the website should seem to be more factual in nature than opinion-based. Otherwise, you might need to question the integrity of the site.

Authority. You will want to know about the author of the site; this information should be easily attainable. For example, you might see a section that says *Who We Are* or *About Us* (Cornell University Digital Library Resource, 2015b). Once you find the author information, consider whether or not this is an author with whom you are familiar. If not, look at the author's credentials. Does the author seem to be an expert in this area? We also mentioned earlier in the chapter that *.gov, .com, and .org* websites often contain scholarly information. To whom does the domain belong?

Reliability. If you are going to cite a website as a reference, then you need to know that the site will still be there in the future. A good starting place when making this determination is to see if the links on the page work (Cornell University Digital Library Resource, 2015b). If not, you might question the site's dependability.

Currency. Currency is related to reliability in the sense that not only do you need to know that site will continue to exist, you also want to be sure that the information is not outdated. Take a look at when the site was last revised (Cornell University Digital Library Resource, 2015b). How often do they update the site? If you are unable to find a date displayed on the webpage, type the phrase *javascript:alert(document.lastModified)* in the address bar and hit *Enter.* A window will open and show the date and time when the page was last updated (Cornell University Digital Library Resource, 2015b).

Coverage. When reviewing the information on the website, it is important to assess the thoroughness of the content. Is there sufficient information on the site, or has important information been omitted? You may also want to consider whether the website is completed versus being under construction (Cornell University Digital Library Resource, 2015b). Be hesitant to use information from incomplete websites. Barker (2002) created a document titled *Web Page Evaluation Checklist* that will help you in determining the credibility of websites. It is available through the University of California, Berkeley. For more information, go to http:// www.lib.berkeley.edu/TeachingLib/Guides/Internet/EvalForm.pdf.

Tricks to Finding Supplemental Resources

After you do all the hard work using traditional methods of finding helpful resources, now it is time to let those resources do some of the work for you. Let us share a few tricks of the research trade to help you find even more resources based off of the goldmine you already have in your hands.

Usually, when you are researching a topic, key players or authors will appear over and over again when you are searching in databases. These researchers are the experts in the field in your topic. You want to uncover all the stones they laid during their research expedition. You can achieve this by doing a little investigation into these particular people. For instance, Dr. Richard S. Balkin is the expert in adolescent counseling. If you found a few articles with his name, then you are bound to find more as he has over 50 publications and counting! You can search for his name in library databases or even in a general search engine. You just might uncover his professional website and/or his university webpage that posts a list of his publications and presentations online. These treasure boxes of webpages are available for many scholars who are also faculty members. Jackpot!

Another way to find more articles is to identify a specific journal that seems to publish articles on your topic. Review the bundle of articles you found to see if you find a theme. For instance, if you are investigating empirically supported counseling interventions for preschool children, then you might have come across articles from the *International Journal of Play Therapy*. You can search for articles in this journal in library databases or even online via their website. Some journals such as *The Professional Counselor* and the *Journal of School Counseling* have the articles available on their website.

A third way to find diamonds in the rough is to take a peek at the reference list for the articles you already gathered. The articles the author cited are already known to be valuable resources that have noteworthy content. Try to find these articles to expand your search. Think of the reference page like a web of available information. The best reference lists are in recently published dissertations. These authors are charged to incorporate all relevant information available on the topic of their dissertations. If you find a dissertation on your topic in the Dissertation Abstracts International database, then you just struck oil! That reference list will point you in the direction of all of the resources available on your topic.

Paraphrasing and Quoting

As you begin to think about writing your paper, consider the words you want to use. How will you say what you want to say? Hopefully, you have taken good notes from each resource along the way. But now, how will you put everything together? You might start by *paraphrasing* the information you have read. *Paraphrasing* refers to summarizing a portion of another author's work or rearranging the order of words in a sentence (APA, 2010). Each time you paraphrase an author, you need to provide a citation. *Direct quotations* involve using the exact words from a source (APA, 2010). Quotation marks are used around the author's words to indicate to the reader that the material is a direct quote. When citing quoted material, you must include the author's last name, the year the document was published, and the page number (APA, 2010). You must also present the words *exactly* as they are written in the source. Be mindful of the fact that direct quotes should be used sparingly (Lambie, Sias, Davis, Lawson, & Akos, 2008). When you overuse quoted material, you are simply showing the reader where you found the information. However, you do not demonstrate your ability to synthesize or apply those concepts. Thus, it is best to paraphrase as much as possible. Direct quotes should only be used when you want to have a strong impact on the reader or when the information is succinctly stated or presented in a manner that cannot be easily paraphrased. The use of paraphrasing allows you to give credit to the author, while at the same time, provide you with the opportunity to relate new concepts to your topic of interest.

Plagiarism

As discussed in Chapter 9, you should not present information in your paper as being your own if another source impacted you in some way (APA, 2010). Failing to give credit to an author and claiming unoriginal work as your own is called *plagiarism* (APA, 2010) and is a violation of the American Counseling Association (ACA) *Code of Ethics* (ACA, G.5.b., 2014). Many students struggle with paraphrasing, which leads to their inadvertently plagiarizing. Lambie et al. (2008) indicated that the best way for students to learn how to paraphrase is to become educated about how to properly cite information as well as to practice paraphrasing. Consider the passage below from Moore and Ordway (2013). Thereafter, you will find three student attempts at paraphrasing the information. As you are reading the students' responses, think about whether each student demonstrated acceptable paraphrasing skills:

Original Material

While interviews and observations can provide valuable information for a counselor who is trying to get an accurate picture of an alienated child's emotional difficulties, there are also limitations. In cases where severe parental alienation has occurred, a child may be resistant to making disclosures, or the child may mirror the parent's emotions and give disclosures that are verbatim to the parent's (Fidler et al., 2013; Gardner, 1985; Gardner, 1989). A counselor may also observe what seems to be a strained relationship between a targeted parent and an alienated child. However, the counselor may not realize that the child could really want a relationship with the targeted parent but is too afraid to express such desires due to strong feelings of loyalty toward the alienating parent (Baker, 2010). Moreover, in cases where mild or moderate parental alienation is occurring, the emotional effects on children can be less obvious. In either case, counselors may be working with children and not have a thorough understanding of how deeply those children are being affected by their parents' divorces. An untrained counselor might have the best intentions, but by providing support and validating the child's feelings of animosity toward the targeted parent, the counselor could unintentionally cause the child to become more entrenched in the alienation (Moore & Ordway et al., 2013). Therefore, when counselors have suspicions or have identified that a high-conflict divorce case is occurring and there is the possibility of parental alienation, more formal assessment measures may be needed to gain an accurate picture of the child's emotional difficulties and determine the best course of action for the child.

Student A's Paraphrased Material

Interviews and observations are great ways for counselors to get an honest picture of an alienated child's emotional problems, but there can be limitations. In situations where severe parental alienation has occurred, a child may be hesitant to share information, or the child may mirror the parent's emotions and make disclosures that are exactly the same as the parent's (Fidler, et al., 2013; Gardner, 1985; Gardner, 1989). In cases where mild or moderate parental alienation has occurred, children's emotional issues may be less apparent. In either case, counselors may be working with children and not have a thorough understanding of how deeply those children are being affected by their parents' divorces. An untrained counselor might have the best intentions, but by providing support and validating the child's feelings of animosity toward the targeted parent, the counselor could unintentionally cause the child to become more entrenched in the alienation. Thus, when counselors have suspicions that parental alienation is occurring, more formal assessment measures may be needed to determine the best course of action for the child (Moore & Ordway, 2013).

Student B's Paraphrased Material

When working with alienated children, interviews and observations can provide counselors with important information. Children who have experienced severe parental alienation may be reluctant to make disclosures in counseling. In cases where a child is experiencing mild or moderate parental alienation, their emotional symptoms may be less obvious. Formal assessment measures may be beneficial in the counseling environment to gain a more comprehensive understanding of the nature and intensity of the child's symptoms.

Student C's Paraphrase

The family dynamics associated with high conflict divorces can be rather complex. Conducting interviews with children and their family members, as well as observing their interactions with one another can provide counselors with vital information (Moore & Ordway, 2013). However, counselors working with this population should possess a certain level of knowledge and skill. For example, many children who experience mild to moderate levels of alienation from a parent may show few emotional symptoms, whereas those children who have experienced severe parental alienation may appear to have anger toward the targeted parent, when they really desire to have a closer relationship with that parent (Baker, as cited in Moore & Ordway, 2013). Counselors who are unfamiliar with these dynamics may inadvertently do harm to the families (Moore & Ordway, 2013). Thus, when working with families involved in divorce, it is imperative that counselors conduct comprehensive assessments that include formal assessment instruments to ensure that they do not further perpetuate the cycle of alienation (Moore & Ordway, 2013).

Let's begin by evaluating Student A's paragraph. What did you notice about the student's response? Although the student provided in-text citations, there was little variation from the original authors' work and Student A's paragraph. Student A changed several words and rearranged some of the sentences. However, Student A's paragraph was too similar to the original passage to be considered original work. Therefore, Student A committed plagiarism.

Student B's paragraph was somewhat similar to the original work; however, there were places where the student attempted to paraphrase the information appropriately. What was your biggest concern with Student B's paragraph? Did you notice that Student B did not have any citations in the paragraph? As we discussed earlier in the chapter, all works that influence your writing should be cited. Even if Student B paraphrased the information correctly, failing to provide in-text citations is a form of plagiarism.

Now let's review Student C's paragraph. Student C kept the original meaning of the paragraph but was able to reword the article and make it original. Student C provided in-text citations, including citing a secondary source. Of the three students, Student C seemed to have the most significant level of understanding, as the student was able capture the essence of the original paragraph but expressed that understanding in his or her own words.

Writing Tips

While reading this chapter, you have taken in a lot of information about how to prepare to write your research paper. You have learned about finding research topics and narrowing them down to something manageable *and* interesting. You have learned a lot about databases: how to find them, search within them, and not become overwhelmed by them. Finally, you have read about (yawn) writing in APA format and avoiding plagiarizing the work of others. Some of these topics may not seem very exciting but, frankly, they are all necessary to crafting that wonderful paper that is going to educate you about a topic, showcase that knowledge to you faculty or to a reviewer, and earn you excellent grades in your graduate program! All of these elements focused on the *why* and the *what* behind your writing. Now, let's talk about the how.

Organizing Your Writing

As with any project, taking on a research paper requires good organizational skills. As much as we like to think we can keep up with the readings and retain all that good information, it is easy to get lost in the search. Think about the last time you shopped for that perfect pair of shoes on the Internet (or something you like to comparison shop for). Typically, you look at a website, then try to find a better deal, then you might look at a slightly different style, which takes you to an even better deal, but then you decide those aren't the ones you want so you try to figure out where you were when you found that perfect pair, and . . . whew! To avoid this information overload that requires you to have perfect recall, we recommend that you take notes while reading the articles you have found. You might even make index cards or notes on your computer of the key elements contained in a particular resource so that you can quickly find it when you prepare to write (Roberts, 2010).

A second recommendation is to start your writing with an outline. That outline may shift and change as you delve deeper into the literature but having a sense of the flow of your paper, from broadest topic to the most narrow, can really help you organize your thoughts. Inserting ideas, topic sentences, and reference suggestions into the outline is a further step in organizing the paper and may make it easier to go back into the document and flesh out the content (Creme & Lea, 2008).

As much as most of us hate to acknowledge it, we probably need a schedule for writing. When will you be able to do the research, or pre-work, of writing? When can you spend time on an outline? When can you begin to flesh out the content? Finally, when will you be able to actually write the paper once all of this organizational time is spent toward the project? Having a due date is one thing but understanding that there needs to be a due date for each element is what keeps good writers on task. In undergraduate programs, we often hear students say that they wrote their papers by pulling an all-nighter. It has been our experience that the all-nighter approach doesn't work when it comes to research papers. Rather, a systematic method with a defined time frame will produce your best results.

Supporting Your Writing

Organizing your writing is essential, but garnering support for the work is helpful as well. You have already learned about plagiarism checkers such as Grammerly and Paperrater. Did you know that these systems also help check grammar, spelling, syntax, and composition? It is common even among seasoned writers to need help with clarity. What makes sense to the writer does not always make sense to the reader. These programs help spot areas for improvement.

Perhaps the best support for your writing is other writers. Network with people in your courses and offer to share resources and edit for one another. Good writers become good writers because they do more than just write: They also read. Reading the writing of a peer or serving as a peer editor actually makes you a better writer. So, make a deal with a classmate and trade papers a few days before it is due. Give each other time to make revisions after the peer edits. You will be amazed at the difference it can make in your own writing!

Summary

Scholarly writing, initially, may seem overwhelming and intimidating. It is important to realize that having such feelings is a normal part of the writing process. Luckily, there are resources available that can make the writing process less daunting. A carpenter cannot build a house without the necessary tools, just as an individual cannot write a research paper without the needed resources. Our goal in this chapter was to guide you from the start of the research process to the beginning of writing your paper. You now know how to develop a research topic, locate websites and databases, and evaluate websites to find credible, scholarly information. You also have been provided with helpful writing tips and sources that can assist you when citing information along the way. Hopefully, this chapter has helped dismantle your writing fears and given you new writing tools for your toolbox. One of the most important tools in that toolbox should be positive thinking. Scholarly writing gets easier the more you do it. So, keep writing!

About the Authors

Dr. Michelle Perepiczka, PhD, LMHC, RPTS, NCC, is Core Faculty at Walden University. Her clinical areas of specialization are play therapy, sexual assault, anxiety, and child and adolescent counseling. She actively serves as the Governing Council Representative for the Association for Humanistic Counseling and is on the Association for Assessment in Research and Counseling research committee. She also serves on the editorial board for the *Journal of Counseling and Development* as well as the *Journal of Humanistic Counseling*. Her research focus is in counselor wellness and outcome-based research.

Dr. Ruth Ouzts Moore, PhD, LPC, NCC, is a Distance Clinical Professor at Lamar University in the Masters of Clinical Mental Health Counseling Program. She has presented nationally and internationally in the areas of abuse/trauma, play therapy, high-conflict divorce/parental alienation, and creative counseling techniques. Dr. Moore is the president of the South Georgia Association for Play Therapy and the secretary of the Association for Creativity in Counseling. Dr. Moore has published in peer-reviewed journals and scholarly resources. She is frequently called to serve as an expert witness in criminal, chancery, and youth court for her involvement in child abuse and child custody cases.

Donna Sheperis, PhD, LPC, NCC, ACS, is an associate professor in the Department of Counseling and Special Populations at Lamar University. She earned her PhD in Counselor Education from the University of Mississippi. Dr. Sheperis has taught in land-based and fully online programs since 2000. She is a Licensed Professional Counselor in Mississippi and Texas; a National Certified Counselor; a Certified Clinical Mental Health Counselor; and an Approved Clinical Supervisor with over 20 years of experience in clinical mental health counseling settings.

Donna Sheperis is active in the counseling profession holding leadership positions in the Association for Assessment and Research in Counseling and the Association for Humanistic Counseling. She is active in scholarship and research as well with multiple articles in peer-reviewed journals. In addition, she has 10 book chapters, an instructor's manual, and a textbook in print. She is the coeditor of *Clinical Mental Health Counseling: Fundamentals of Applied Practice* for Pearson Publishing and *Ethical Decision Making for the 21st Century Counselor* for SAGE Publications.

References

American Counseling Association. (2014). *Code of Ethics*. Alexandria, VA: Author.
American Counseling Association. (2015). *Listservs*. Retrieved from http://www.counseling.org/aca-community/listservs

American Psychological Association. (2010). *Publication manual of the American Psychological Association* (6th ed.). Washington, DC: Author.

Baker, A. (2010). "Adult recall of parental alienation in a community sample: Prevalence and associations with psychological maltreatment." *Journal of Divorce and Remarriage*, 51, 16-35.

Barker, J. (2002). *Web page evaluation checklist*. The Teaching Library, University of California, Berkeley. Retrieved from http://www.lib.berkeley.edu/TeachingLib/Guides/Internet/EvalForm.pdf

Boudah, D. J. (2011). *Conducting educational research*. Thousand Oaks, CA: Sage.

Brown, T. (2013, March 27). Finding current research using free online resources. [Web log comment]. Retrieved from http://blog.library.si.edu/2013/03/finding-current-research-online/

Cornell University Digital Library Resource. (2015a). Identifying a research topic. Retrieved from http://digitalliteracy.cornell.edu/tutorial/dpl3100.html

Cornell University Digital Library Resource (2015b). *Evaluating resources.* Retrieved from https://www.library.cornell.edu/research/introduction

Creme, P., & Lea, M. (2008). *Writing at university: A guide for students*. McGraw-Hill International.

de Figueiredo, A. D. (2010). Writing a research paper: From the parts to the whole. *International Journal of Research & Review*, 423–427.

Dixson, M. D. (2010). Creating effective student engagement in online courses: What do students find engaging? *Journal of the Scholarship of Teaching and Learning, 10*(2), 1–13.

Doloughan, F. (2012). Transforming texts: Learning to become a (creative) writer through reading. *New Writing: The International Journal for the Practice & Theory of Creative Writing, 9*(2), 182–203. doi:10.1080/14790726.2012.658066

Fidler, J. B., Bala, N., & Saini, A. M. (2013). *Children who resist post-separation parental contact: A differential approach for legal and mental health professionals*. New York, NY: Oxford University Press.

Galvan, J. L. (2006). *Writing literature reviews: A guide for students of the social and behavioral sciences* (3rd ed.). Los Angeles, CA: Pyrczak Publishing.

Gardner, R. A. (1985). Recent trends in divorce and custody litigation. *The Academy Forum*, 29(2) 3–7.

Gardner, R. A. (1989). *Family evaluation in child custody mediation, arbitration, and litigation*, Cresskill, NJ: Creative Therapeutics.

Ivanitskaya, L., O'Boyle, I., & Casey, A. M. (2006). Health information literacy and competencies of information age students: Results from the interactive online research readiness self-assessment (RRSA). *Journal of Medical Internet Research, 8*(2): e6.

Lambie, G. W., Sias, S. M., Davis, K. M., Lawson, G., & Akos, P. (2008). A scholarly writing resource for counselor educators and their students. *Journal of Counseling & Development, 86*(1), 18–25. doi:10.1002/j.1556-6678.2008.tb00621.x

Moore, R. O., & Ordway, A. (2013). The mirror without a face: The assessment of parental alienation among children of high-conflict divorces. In *Ideas and research you can use: VISTAS Fall 2013*. Retrieved from http://www.counseling.org/knowledge-center/vistas/vistas-2013/

Purdue Owl Online Writing Lab. (2015). APA formatting and style guide. Retrieved from https://owl.english.purdue.edu/owl/resource/560/01/

Roberts, C. M. (2010). *The dissertation journey: A practical and comprehensive guide to planning, writing, and defending your dissertation*. Thousand Oaks, CA: Corwin.

The Ohio State University (n.d.). *Counsgrads*. Retrieved from https://lists.osu.edu/mailman/listinfo/COUNSGRADS

University of Western Sydney Library (2015). *What is a scholarly website and how do I find one?* Retrieved from http://uws.au.libanswers.com/faq/40115

VanderMey, R., Meyers, V., Van Rys, J., Kemper, D., & Sebrank, P. (2011). *The college writer: A guide to thinking, writing, and researching* (4th ed.). Boston, MA: Houghton Mifflin.

11

Academic Residencies

Joffrey S. Suprina and Jeremiah T. Stokes

Chapter Overview

This chapter will prepare you to better understand the residency component of coursework and how to maximize the benefit of such experiences in your program. The topics discussed in this section will prepare you for planning and participating in academic residencies. The sections explored are as follows: the importance of academic residency; different types of residencies; financial aspects of residency; international versus domestic residency; preparing for and getting the most out of your residency experience; the role of gatekeeping at residency; fostering a collaborative attitude; professional behavior and disposition; understanding the faculty review process; and understanding and preparing to attend professional conferences.

Learning Outcomes

Upon completion of this chapter, the student will

- Understand the importance of a residency to counselor education
- Differentiate the types and formats of residencies

- Understand the financial aspects of residency to make cost-effective choices
- Distinguish between international versus domestic residencies
- Apply guidelines for getting the most out of a residency experience
- Address the role of gatekeeping at residence
- Facilitate a collaborative attitude
- Emulate professional behavior and disposition
- Understand the faculty review process
- Apply strategies to prepare for participation at professional conferences

Introduction

Successful counseling is facilitated through a quality therapeutic relationship that requires effective interpersonal skills. Due to distance learning being an increasingly prevalent educational format in counseling programs across the world, students find that pursuing their degrees from the convenience of their own home is an advantageous and practical endeavor (Quinn, 2001). This is considered to be an extremely valuable resource for individuals that do not have the luxury of attending traditional counseling programs. However, due to the interactional nature of the counseling process, students are expected to be proficient in face-to-face communication (Quinn, 2001). As such, counseling programs usually include some sort of residency component that facilitates face-to-face interaction to refine and apply knowledge learned, develop counseling skills, network with peers and professors, and develop professionally. Such a face-to-face interaction may be facilitated in a variety of ways from the traditional classroom experience where all the instruction takes place live within the classroom to a combination of online instruction, webinars, and residencies that vary in length and focus.

The Importance of Residency

Why are academic residencies an important component for online and blended counseling programs? An academic residency can provide beneficial opportunities to counseling students. The four main concepts of academic residency are refining and applying knowledge previously learned, skill development, networking with peers and professors, and professional development. These areas are by no means exhaustive, but can be viewed as some of the foundational pieces comprising your residency experience.

Refining and Applying Knowledge Previously Learned

Academic residencies are an important time where students can develop a richer understanding of the counseling process by viewing and participating in various learning formats and activities. Although academic residencies are different in format and design, they all seek to help students further develop their knowledge of the counseling process (Sells, Tan, Brogan, Dahlen, & Stupart, 2012). The residencies are infused with the curriculum to build upon material learned in your course work. Thus, the professors in your counseling program will have expectations of your ability to discuss, refine, and apply previously learned material. The goal is that the residency will advance you to the next level of your development as a counselor or counselor educator. Aligned with that goal, the residency will also focus on furthering the development of your skills. The next section will discuss exercises that enhance skill development while attending residency.

Skill Development Exercises

Your skill set as a counselor in training or counselor educator should be a focal point while attending residency. It will be to your advantage to participate as much as possible in all of the activities designed to build and enhance your skills as an emerging counselor or counselor educator. The exercises will depend greatly upon your university, the program, and the type of residency. Some of the exercises may entail mock counseling sessions with individuals or groups, application and interpretation of assessments, practice with intakes, designing research projects, teaching your peers, and collaborative discussions with peers and professors on mental health topics. Counseling is an interpersonal process, so the time for live interaction in residencies is invaluable in developing those important interpersonal skills. Equally important for your future in the profession are the networking opportunities that residencies provide.

Networking With Peers and Professors

Although online interaction allows you to interact with your peers and professors through discussion boards and other means, nothing can replace face-to-face live interactions. The residency is an ideal platform for you to interact more closely with both your peers and professors. As such, this experience is designed to be collaborative in nature; providing students the opportunity to develop a rapport with each other, as well as with faculty members (Sells et al., 2012). We will discuss collaboration and networking in greater detail later in the chapter.

Professional Development

First, let's talk about professional development. As you can imagine, residencies are tremendous opportunities to develop your professional identity and other professional skills that will benefit you throughout your career. Often your interaction with others in your field helps you refine your professional identity and area of specialization. Through lively discourse and debate you discover your values, beliefs, passions, strengths, and weaknesses that will guide you in your continued professional development and refinement.

Furthermore, the residencies often emulate what a counseling professional gets to experience when attending a professional conference. The experiences you have planning, arranging, preparing, and actively participating in the residency will mirror your future professional endeavors. Remember that you are not only learning valuable content but also process. Pay attention to what works and build upon those successes for future residencies and professional conferences.

Different Types of Residencies

It is important for us to understand the different types of academic residencies in counseling programs. Your academic program may entail certain residency requirements that are specific to that university. You should possess the foreknowledge of what type of residencies you will be participating in prior to starting the academic program. Although most counselor educators recognize the benefit of face-to-face interactions, different programs will utilize varying processes to facilitate that interaction. In general, residencies fall into two primary categories: course based or program based.

Course-Based Residencies

Course-based residencies (CBR) align with the individual course and focus on achieving the objectives related to that individual course. The residency component may be spread out throughout the course such as one evening a week, or it may take the form of weekend workshops between 1 and 4 days in length. There may be one or more sessions such as meeting for two different weekends within the length of the course. The residency may be a combination of activities such as lectures, experiential activities, presentations, and role-play. Whatever format or activities are used, they will align with the objectives of the individual course being taken. For example, a course in counseling theories will focus on learning the theories and applying the theories in case conceptualizations or in practice.

Program-Based Residencies

Program-based residencies (PBR) are usually of longer duration and less frequency than CBR's. PBR's are often once a year and can be from 5 to 7 days in length. Unlike CBR's, they will usually focus on a variety of topics and multiple program objectives. So you may spend part of the residency on skill development and another on research knowledge. Earlier residencies may focus more on orientation and early developmental topics while later residencies may prepare you for practicum or dissertation.

Web-Based Residencies or the Virtual Classroom

The newest form of face-to-face instruction is the use of webinars. Some programs are beginning to use webinars as a replacement for an on-ground residency. They may be used in lieu of or to augment on-ground residencies. They may be used for both course-based and program-based residencies. These interactions use technology such as GoToMeeting, Adobe Connect, and Watchitoo to provide real-time interaction between students and faculty. The technology allows the professor to share PowerPoint presentations and other documents or media via the Web in real time with the students. Depending on which technology is used, the professor and students can share webcams of themselves to augment the experience. Some professors may even be presenting from a real or mock classroom with other students live in the class along with a blackboard and other interaction. These "residencies" can provide the convenience of being at home, with the benefit of live interaction with faculty and peers. Another benefit of such an interaction is that the session can be recorded to allow students to revisit the content as needed. Whether a CBR, PBR, or virtual residency, each comes with unique costs.

Financial Aspects of Residency

Academic residencies, whether course based, program based, or virtual, have financial considerations. In this section, we will review the different types of residencies and the expenses related to them. It is wise to have an understanding of the monetary needs that will be required of you for residencies before you are enrolled in your counseling program. Depending on the individual, the program, and the academic institution, costs will vary. As a student, you should prepare to allocate funds for tuition, transportation, accommodations, food, and equipment.

Tuition Expenses

One of the first costs to consider is tuition. For most CBRs, there is no additional tuition fee for the residency, while some PBRs may have an additional fee to cover the costs of the instructors, space, equipment, and materials. It is essential to allocate specific funds for the residency tuition, just as you will for any other course in which you are enrolled. Students who are receiving financial aid may be able to include any tuition costs as qualifying expenses covered by their financial aid. If the student does not use financial aid or assistance for the residency, the tuition costs will be the responsibility of the student. Planning ahead is always the best strategy.

Transportation/Travel Expenses

Transportation and travel fees will be a necessity for most students, unless students are in a close proximity to the university or residency site. In this section, we will explore three different types of travel expense based on the distance of the residency: within 100 miles, within a day's drive, and beyond one day's drive. In addition, this section will cover transportation during the residency.

For those within a 100-mile radius of the residency site, you may consider commuting to and from the residency. Such a strategy can be more cost effective for shorter duration residencies such as an evening residency or 2-day weekend residency. Before deciding to commute longer than 2 hours, however; consider how you handle the stress of traffic or a long drive and if that will inhibit your ability to participate and learn in the residency. If it will potentially diminish the impact of the residency, then seek another student attending the same residency for a ride share companion or consider finding housing nearby. Sharing the driving can diminish the negative consequences of a commute. If no one is available for a rideshare, then consider local housing. Although it will cost a little more, if it increases your learning of knowledge and skills, it is worth it.

For those within a day's drive, driving to the residency site is an option. However, you will again want to explore the stress of the driving experience and its impact on your ability to learn. Drive sharing is again a good option if you can locate a fellow student within reasonable distance of you. Driving for a day or more may also require a longer leave from your employment, which can diminish your income. For some, a plane or a train may prove the better value, if you do not need a car when you get to the residency site.

For those traveling from more than a day's distance or internationally, you will likely need to fly. Preplanning and purchasing tickets as soon as possible is often advantageous for the best rates on airfare. Additionally, packaging airfare, hotel, and rental car needs may provide additional discounts. Most universities that require residencies make efforts to host them in cities with large airport options that allow students the most flexible, and economical, means of travel.

Regardless of how you will arrive, make sure to figure in a reasonable travel time that allows for traffic or delayed flights. It can be terribly stressful to be running late for a residency. Additionally, some programs only allow limited tardiness before the residency needs to be retaken. Plan ahead.

Once you reach your destination, you will need to consider how you get from the airport to the hotel, from the hotel to the campus or classroom site, and how you will access restaurants or other areas of interest. Many airports have inexpensive shuttles to specific hotels, and you can check to see if your hotel is on the list. Some programs will arrange a shuttle to and from the campus or classroom site as well. Gather that information before making your final arrangements. What you save on a discounted hotel reservation may cost you in transportation to the campus. You should also develop friendships with your fellow students as you can rideshare at the residency with those who have a car or even split a taxi for savings. Gather as much information as possible, consider all your needs, and then find the best combination that addresses them efficiently and frugally.

Hotel/Food/Essentials Expenses

In selecting your lodging consider your specific needs: How far is it from the airport; what type of facility do you seek (hotel, motel, suite, efficiency, etc.); what amenities do you seek (gym, spa, restaurant, etc.); how far is it from the classroom; and how far is it from restaurants or entertainment. Although they often cost a little more, a small efficiency that has a small kitchenette can help you save some money on food if you are going to use it. Start by requesting hotel information from the university. The information regarding hotel stay may be found on the academic program websites and will usually give suggestions for hotels nearby with which they have a discount agreement. The particular locations suggested may provide student discounts and other accommodations for students such as a shuttle to the campus or a happy hour reception. Although another hotel may be cheaper, consider transportation and other amenities in your comparison costs. Staying where other students are staying is also beneficial as it provides opportunities for study partners, ride shares, and pleasant exchanges.

Students should also keep in mind that food will rarely be provided by the universities or hotels during their attendance of residency. Therefore, arrangements should be made to pay for food and basic necessities while attending residency. Communicate with fellow students to creatively address food needs, such as going to a grocery store and cooking if someone has a kitchen available. Ask the local students for recommendations of good places to eat at a reasonable price. It can also be good to pack some snacks to help you through. For example, a good cheap breakfast is a packet of instant oatmeal that can be easily carried in your luggage and made with the coffee maker in your hotel room. In addition to transportation, lodging, and food, you will want to consider your equipment needs.

Equipment

As an online or blended program student, you likely already have a computer and some basic software. However, to be more effective in a residency, you may need a laptop, tablet, or other portable devices to help you in taking notes, accessing your papers and materials, searching the Web, or presenting your topics in a class. Additionally, if you are participating in a virtual Web experience, you will want a webcam and headset that has both ear pads and a microphone. The virtual experience is enhanced with the headset and webcam as it allows each student to participate visually and verbally while diminishing the chances of feedback and extraneous sounds. Except for the laptop and some brands of tablets, most of these items are relatively inexpensive and can be purchased online or on sale with time to search. It is cheaper to plan ahead and not wait until the last moment to purchase the items you need.

International Residencies

In addition to the reflections listed above for both domestic and international residencies, you will have some additional considerations when preparing for an international residency such as money exchange, a passport, electricity, and cellphone. Many universities offer destination residencies for US students, which allows them to travel overseas. You will need to research the currency that is used where your residency will be held. Although many countries will accept American dollars, some will give more value for the local currency. Websites like X-Rates.com can provide current rates and calculators for figuring values of purchases. Although some hotels will exchange your currency, you will often get a better rate from other exchange options. Some research could save you some significant expense.

International travel usually requires a current passport. It is important to remember that it can take as much as 3 months to get a passport and that is if no significant problems arise. It is never too soon to start the process for a passport. Once you get it, keep it in a safe place for easy access.

Much of our equipment, laptops, cellphones, tablets, hair dryers, etc. require electricity. Power sockets are not universal. Do some research on what specific power adaptors you need for where you will be traveling. You usually only need one adapter, but may want to bring a small multi-plug or power strip to enable you to plug in more than one item at a time.

Finally, that cellphone on which you rely may not be usable overseas. Check with your provider to see if you can get service where you are going. Most plans allow for a short-term international access with an add-on fee for the traveler. Another option is to buy a disposable phone while in the country of residence, but then you will still need access to all of your phone numbers and data. Plan accordingly. Once you have coordinated all of the logistical matters of travel, lodging, and equipment, it will be time to focus on preparation for the residency itself.

Preparing for and Getting the Most out of Residency

As if the travel logistics weren't enough, we also need to consider other preparations for residencies. How should students prepare for residencies? Preparation for residency will depend greatly upon the university and type of residency. However, students should make careful plans nonetheless. This section will discuss: the preparation process of the residency prior to enrolling in a program; residency frequency and duration; residency locations and environment; and general expectations while attending residency. As you navigate through this section, try to see how the residency can best benefit your learning experience as a counseling student.

Preprogram Residency Preparation

Students pursuing a distance learning education in counseling should have a thorough understanding of all requirements of their respective programs. This knowledge should include the residency requirements in order for students to graduate from the program. The information regarding residencies should be conveyed through the program website, admission's materials, and during pre-enrollment academic advisement. If a prospective student cannot commit to that program's specified residency requirements, he or she should reconsider the decision to enroll in such a program. This is because residencies are not optional, but rather a requirement for satisfactory academic progress and degree completion. After you have committed to a counseling program and are fully aware of the residency requirement, you will need to begin to allocate time and resources to attend.

Frequency and Duration

Learners should know how many residencies are required for completion of the program, attendance dates and durations that are usually posted for students along with the course schedule, and the program outline (Sells et al., 2012). Students should allocate time for residencies, as well as transportation time to and from them, within their work schedules and family obligations. Although some programs have more flexibility than others, residency options for dates and location are usually limited. It often requires the student to adjust to the residency schedule. The frequencies of the residencies vary depending upon the demands of the program itself; however, most programs require students to attend several residencies before the completion of the program.

Many of the online counseling programs will hold residencies any-where from 2 to 7 days in duration. Residencies usually start in the morning and can last the entire day. Students are expected to attend each day and fully engage with other students and faculty. As you can imagine, it is an intense process that is exhausting to all involved. However, if students do not fully participate, schools will generally not pass the student for that academic residency. In the event that a student cannot attend a residency, he or she must consult with their respective professor and academic advisor for direction in handling the matter. Consequences of illness or other circumstances that delay or inhibit full participation can result in a lower grade, added assignments, or failure that requires that the residency be retaken. If anything should arise that will impact your full participation in a residency, contact your instructor and advisor immediately. There are more options to address challenges prior to the residency than after a day is missed. Upon developing a schedule for the time needed for your residency attendance, it would be good to begin conceptualizing the type of environment in which the residency will be held.

Locations and Environment

Residency locations also vary depending upon the university. Some institutions will conduct residencies on the specified campus; others may have multiple site options such as branch campuses, hotels, convention centers, and other general locations. The location of the residencies will be that of a professional and academic environment with areas designed to accommodate students for class lectures, presentations, group exchange, faculty and student interaction, academic advisement, assessment, and various other activities. It may take some planning to best prepare you for acclimation to the location and environment. For location, it is good to keep in mind any time difference as a result of a time zone change. A west coast student taking an east coast residency may be required to start residency at 8 am daily. That is 5 am west coast time!

Remember that it can take up to a day of adjustment for each time zone crossed. Additionally, you will want to research the facilities to get the "lay of the land" prior to the residency or after arrival but prior to class. Researching how you will get to the classroom location, room names or numbers, transportation options, etc. will help make the experience less stressful so that you can concentrate your energy and mental focus on learning. Preparing effectively will help you to better address the academic expectations of residency. The next section will discuss a general theme of what is expected of you while you attend the residency.

General Expectations While Attending

Residencies are formulated for students to enhance their critical thinking skills and further develop their knowledge of the theoretical constructs learned in their coursework (Sells et al., 2012). There will be specific activities that engage the students in pursuing a deeper knowledge of the material taught in the virtual classrooms. There are activities designed to further develop an understanding of counseling literature, research, and theory. These areas of the residencies may be conducted in the form of classroom discussions, presentations on specific counseling related topics, practicing skills, and assessment. Students will be expected to participate in the activities presented. To fully participate and get the most from the experience, you should thoroughly review the activities and specific goals of the residency and make sure that you have fulfilled prerequisite homework and preparation (reading book chapters or articles, completing any preresidency assignments) as well as have access to any equipment or materials necessary (books, laptops, tablets, digital recorders, etc.).

The academic residencies in counseling related programs will also require students to be proficient in their ability to apply theory into practice (Sells et al., 2012). It is important to distinguish some of the differences between master's and doctoral level counseling residencies. During the beginning stages of residencies within master's level counseling programs, students will receive more of an introductory format of theoretical and applicative learning. The student will have the opportunity to further conceptualize the scientific nature of counseling through: observational learning, presentations by experts on early stages of professional counseling development, group discussions and activities, faculty evaluations, "mock" individual and group counseling sessions, supervision from doctoral students and faculty, assessments, etc.

Counseling students in doctoral programs will have different expectations placed upon them while attending residency. Doctoral students in counselor education and supervision and related programs will be expected to possess a thorough understanding of the counseling profession. Thus, the residency experience will be designed to prepare students for leadership positions in the counseling field. The activities and learning formats of these residencies may engage doctoral students in providing supervision to master's level students. Also, because doctoral programs prepare students for teaching in higher education, many of the activities will have students present lectures, as well as develop a teaching pedagogy.

As students, it is advisable that the residency experience be perceived as a learning resource designed to develop and enhance your skills as a scholar-practitioner. Upon the completion of an academic residency, students should return to their coursework with more knowledge and a better understanding of academic and professional goals.

The Role of Gate Keeping at Residency

In addition to providing opportunities for you to enhance your knowledge and skills, residencies provide opportunities for your instructors to do valuable gate keeping. Counselor educators are mandated to identify deficiencies in counseling students that may hinder their ability to be effective in the field. Your instructors will be observing your interpersonal interactions and application of skills to assess your ability to be effective, ethical, and multiculturally competent. Even in classes that are not skill based such as a research course, the instructors will be observing how you interact with your peers and the instructor. It is important to note that even outside the classroom, instructors will observe your interactions. It will not benefit you to be mindful of your interactions in class and then to be disrespectful or express bias in the hallway or at a restaurant. Your instructors will be looking to see that you are consistent in your interactions as a large contrast between your counselor identity and your outside identity may be difficult to uphold and could portray incongruence and insincerity to your future clients, students, or supervisees. Such inconsistency or incongruence can result in harm to the client and breach an ethical principle.

Fostering a Collaborative Attitude

Collaboration—The Professor's Perspective

Teamwork and collaboration are imperative within counseling. In the clinical setting, you may be required to work with clients, staff, other clinicians, insurance agents, and the public on a variety of endeavors including scheduling, treatment, case management, and billing. There may be a receptionist scheduling an intake, a clinician conducting the intake, a psychiatrist prescribing medications, a nurse dispensing medications, a case manager monitoring a case, a therapist providing individual sessions, another clinician leading a psychoeducational group, a resident aid assisting the patient to get from place to place and an administrator who handles the billing. Each member of the team is required to facilitate the efficient treatment of the client. Such teamwork and collaboration require specific knowledge and skills to facilitate effectively.

Counselor education also requires teamwork and collaboration. You may be required to work with a university president, vice president of Academic Affairs, college dean, program chair, professors of different ranks and specialties, staff, grants managers, teaching assistants, research assistants, and students. Residencies can help you to develop those skills by providing opportunities for you to do group projects with fellow students, and interact with professors, staff, and other personnel to facilitate an effective residency. Every interaction within your residency experience is an opportunity for learning and growth. Now that you have a professor's point of view, why don't we take a look at residency from the prospective of the student?

Collaboration—A Student's Perspective

From a student's perspective, it is essential to view the residency experience as an opportunity to collaborate with faculty and other students. Collaboration and cohesion should be an underlying student objective; interaction and engagement with others is an expectation. This time should be used to further develop the preexisting relationship you have with other students and professors. Communicating with others during residency will allow you to share your personal experiences, as well as gain insight into facets of your program where there are uncertainties. The residencies will generally be very team oriented in nature, and many of the students will find this dynamic enriching. Usually students will find that the groups grow stronger and bonds are formed as the residency progresses.

Students should also use this opportunity to meet and interact with faculty members. Keep in mind; these are the individuals who are usually communicated with technologically. They are there to answer all of your questions and concerns; it is advisable that students take advantage of that time. They also only know you by your name, and the quality of your work, due to the online format. It is important to put a "face" with your name, as well as identify yourself on a more personal level. Engaging with faculty and students alike can also be an opportunity to connect on a professional level. Students may also find it advantageous to seek out mentorships from their respective faculty members. While mentoring relationships are requirements for some counseling programs, they are recommended for all students, and the residencies are an excellent opportunity to establish or reinforce such a relationship.

Professional Behavior and Professional Disposition

In addition to your expectations to collaborate with others, you will also be expected to conduct yourself appropriately while attending your residency. Academic residencies facilitate an environment that is academically and professionally oriented. The atmosphere is created to capture the essence of the classroom, the counseling relationship, and the ethical constructs that govern the field of counseling. Therefore, students should conduct themselves with a demeanor that is reflective of the counseling program in which they are enrolled. The professional conduct while attending residency should mimic that of the school code of conduct, and behaviors should reflect such. If the residency is being held at an outside entity separate of the university, such as a hotel, students are expected to represent their respective university and the profession to which they are aspiring. As such, behavior that is ethical, multiculturally sensitive, respectful, and conducive to learning will be expected throughout the residency including interactions between classes, at meals, or even the hotel pool.

In the event that students do not conduct themselves in accordance with the university's expectations of the aforementioned academic and professional disposition, they may be subject to reprimand. Consequences could entail faculty intervention and evaluation, or in a worst case scenario, program termination. The counseling programs must ensure that the academic residencies not only coincide with the expectations of the university, but also meet guidelines of accrediting bodies in academia, professional associations in the counseling field, and academic and professional standards deemed necessary for counselors-in-training. The next section will discuss review processes utilized by faculty. It is crucial to understand what is expected of you while attending residency.

Understanding the Faculty Review Process

You may wonder: How will I be assessed within your residency? In this age of accountability, professors are looking for evidence that you are achieving the objectives outlined for the course or program. Additionally, if the program is CACREP (The Council for Accreditation of Counseling and Related Educational Programs) accredited, they will need to be able to document your achievement of the CACREP objectives that are usually integrated into course and program objectives. It is beneficial for you to review all the stated objectives for the courses and program and consider the grading rubrics for all assignments to make sure that you are addressing each objective thoroughly. If there is any doubt about the objectives, request clarification from the instructor prior to submitting an assignment. It is also helpful to remember that there are often objectives related to multiculturalism, ethics, technology, research and interpersonal effectiveness that cross all courses and program objectives. It is beneficial to keep those in mind in all your assignments and interactions.

Networking and Preparing to Attend Professional Conferences

In addition to developing good collaboration and teamwork skills, the residency will help you to build your professional network. Most counseling professionals start their professional network with students within their cohort or class and their professors. The cohort or group from residency is one that you will get to know more intimately than your online counterparts and become, in effect, your home group. The connections you build with your peers will serve as those consultants you seek when you need support for difficult ethical dilemmas. They will be collaborators when you propose a presentation for a professional conference or when you are conducting research or writing a manuscript for publication. Similarly, your professors can evolve into lifelong mentors who will continue to support your growth throughout your career.

Your residency may be a good introduction to what it is like to participate in a professional conference. There are many similarities, such as making travel arrangements, scheduling, and networking, etc. One thing that your future employers will look for is your participation in and contribution to the profession. Showing that you participate in continuing education by attending professional conferences and workshops will enhance your marketability as a committed professional. When you present at conferences, provide workshops, and serve on professional committees, you emulate a developing expertise and leadership within your profession.

Student Experiences

Included below are some examples of student experiences at residency:

Student 1: "The most positive experience I have gained in attending residencies at my university is the ability to do more hands-on work. Although my program is blended, much of the learning is done online. So, being able to apply theory into practice during my residency experience was a huge plus. Also, another experience I had while attending my residencies was how the daily schedules were designed. It seemed that every minute was accounted for, and I learned so much. My professors, and my peers, were very interactive."

Student 2: "My first residency experience was really poor. The reason being is that I was not prepared to face the logistical challenges that lay ahead. First, the hotel that I chose was 5 miles away from the residency location. I did not think this was going to be an issue, as the city where I attended my residency had plenty of public transportation. However, during the times I needed to travel, the city was extremely busy, so I had difficulties with the commute. Also, I was not financially prepared for the costs of residency in total. Hotel, food, and travel were not something I planned for financially when I enrolled in my counseling program. I took on too much by thinking the residency was manageable, both financially and time wise. Since that experience, I am more diligent in my planning and have cut costs through ride and room sharing."

Student 3: "My first experience with brainspotting, a psychotherapy technique, was first introduced to me in my second residency. I had the opportunity to experience how brainspotting works with the guidance of my on-site professor at residency. It was inspiring and gave me the perspective of how clients feel when they try new techniques. This experience helped me understand what I learned in my course work by being able to see it in live action. Another positive experience was building relationships with fellow classmates. We are coming together for the same purpose. The unique qualities of ourselves unite us and helped fortify classmate alliances. Residencies can be extremely beneficial to your learning experience as a counseling student."

Table 11.1 Guide to Success in Academic Residencies

Goals/Challenges	Strategies for Success
Enrolling in the Right Program	
	• Make sure that the program's accreditation aligns with your goals. • Review the residency format for compatibility with your learning style and schedule. • Review the program's ability to support your development within your area of specialization.
Managing Financial Demands	
	• Be proactive (do your research beforehand). • Plan ahead (purchase airline tickets and make hotel reservations early). • Explore packaging for greater savings (combine travel, hotel, and car from one provider). • Be creative (explore ride or lodging sharing, food preparation options, borrowing equipment, etc.). • Budget ahead (save financial aid disbursements to cover residencies, etc.).
Getting the Most Out of Residency	
	• Review the city, housing, transportation, facility layout, and food options early. • Complete any prerequisite assignments and be prepared for completion of any in-residence assignments (necessary literature, equipment, and tools). • Bring all the tools you will need such as laptops, digital recorders, or tablets. • Fully participate in all activities. • Take advantage of collaboration, networking, and mentoring opportunities. • Be respectful, professional, ethical, and multiculturally sensitive in all interactions.
Preparation	
	• Be proactive and do your thorough research (see above). • Get plenty of rest and be healthy prior to residency as it is demanding. • Be mindful in packing all that you will need.

Summary

Becoming an effective counselor requires application of face-to-face counseling skills in individual and group sessions. Developing such skills requires opportunities to come together with your peers and professors to refine your knowledge and skills. This chapter reviewed the various approaches to residencies, their benefits, and how you can get the most out of the experience. You learned to differentiate between course-based and program-based residencies, as well as domestic and international residencies. You were provided with guidelines for getting the most out of your residency experience while making cost effective choices. Additionally, you learned about the role of gatekeeping and how to exemplify the professionalism and attitudes that your professors are seeking. Finally, you learned how a residency can help prepare you for lifelong engagement in the counseling profession. One of the joys of the counseling profession is that many of the habits and skills you learn in the program will serve you well in many of your life activities and relationships throughout your career. Keep learning and growing.

About the Authors

Joffrey S. Suprina, PhD, is the dean and associate professor of the College of Behavioral Sciences at Argosy University. In addition to leadership positions within Argosy University, he has also held leadership positions in the field with Chi Sigma Iota and the Southeastern Association of Counselor Education and Supervision.

As a practitioner scholar, Dr. Suprina has been a licensed counselor working with a wide variety of clients in a myriad of settings. Dr. Suprina regularly presents at professional conferences and has published in a variety of professional journals as well as the American Counseling Association Encyclopedia of Counseling. He is the editor of *The Practitioner Scholar: Journal of Counseling and Professional Psychology* and contributing editor of the *Journal of Trauma Counseling, International.*

Dr. Suprina, received his BA from Rollins College, his MA in Professional Counseling, and PhD in Counselor Education and Practice from Georgia State University's CACREP accredited programs. When not working, his

242 ONLINE COUNSELOR EDUCATION

avocation is music. He has sung internationally, including Carnegie Hall, and currently directs a church choir. No matter what the field, Dr. Suprina is dedicated to promoting positive change.

Jeremiah T. Stokes is a doctoral student at Argosy University, Sarasota. He is a national certified counselor and Board Certified PTSD clinician. He specializes in the treatment of anxiety, relationship issues, and trauma. He also helps people explore issues associated with addiction and substance abuse.

References

Quinn, A. C. (2001). Utilization of technology in CACREP-approved counselor education programs. (Order No. 3022238, Virginia Polytechnic Institute and State University). *ProQuest Dissertations and Theses,* pp. 124–124. Retrieved from http://search.proquest.com/docview/304729953?accountid=34899
Sells, J., Tan, A., Brogan, J., Dahlen, U., & Stupart, Y. (2012). Preparing international counselor educators through online distance learning. *International Journal for the Advancement of Counselling, 34*(1), 39–54. doi:http://dx.doi.org/10.1007/s10447-011-9126-4
Programmatic information was obtained through the following universities: Argosy University, Capella University, Regents University, and Walden University.

12

Field Experience

Debra G. Leggett, Josh H. Strickland, and Elizabeth Krzewski

Chapter Overview

The field experience is where students have an opportunity to put into practice all of the hard work they have been doing in their program. This chapter will prepare you for planning, selecting, and completing practicum/internship. Specifically, this chapter covers the process of selecting a field experience site; the importance of accreditation; and how to make the most of your practicum and internship experience. You will learn what to expect when developing your counselor skills at your field placement; the benefits of supervision; how to log your direct versus indirect hours; professionalism and how to best represent your academic institution; advocacy; and competency within scope of practice. These topics will prepare you to step into the real world of client care.

Learning Outcomes

Upon completion of this chapter, the student will

- Understand the process of selecting a field experience for practicum/ internship

- Examine accreditation requirements for the profession
- Apply tips to make the most of practicum and internship
- Understand what to expect when developing counseling skills at a placement
- Distinguish the difference between distance and in-person supervision
- Differentiate between direct versus indirect hours
- Model professionalism as a reflection of self and academic institution
- Address the responsibility to advocate for oneself as a supervisee
- Understand importance of working within the appropriate scope of practice

Introduction

Congratulations! You are ready to begin seeing clients and initiate your experience as a clinician. Some of the most common feelings are excitement, curiosity, fear, anticipation, and apprehension. These feelings are normal and expected at this stage. Here is where practice begins and your growth as a counselor continues. Your thoughts begin to be more reflective and you sharpen your clinical skills. So how do you know you are ready? Often you are nearing the end of your coursework while other times you will have completed the minimum requirements to continue on to the next step: practicum and internship. There are a number of things you will want to do in order to find, secure, and succeed in field placement.

Selecting a Field Experience Site

Before you can select a field experience site, you must understand the process your academic institution uses for site placement. Some institutions are more directly involved in placement than others. Your school may place students without asking your preference. It may have a list of sites that have been previously used. You may also be completely responsible for finding a site. If that is the case, your school may need a business contract with the site, obligating it to be affiliated with the school for a set period of time. Understanding the process your institution uses will help you in the initial stages of site selection.

Next, you will want to take inventory of your own life with regard to the timing of your field placement. Ask yourself what works best for you; deciding whether to complete field placement while taking additional courses or wait until the end of the program when all coursework is complete is unique to each individual's situation. Knowing what you can realistically fit in your schedule regarding workload is key for your decision making.

After your personal inventory, you want to review what your academic institution requires (e.g., hours, length of semester, length of practicum and internship, supervision hours, supervisor requirements, qualifications/ education of the supervisor as well as required experience of supervisor for practicum and internship). Often this can be accomplished by making an appointment and discussing your plans with your academic advisor, the professor in charge of guiding students with field placement, your dean, or even the director of clinical training. Each academic institution is designed a little differently; you may need to pick the most qualified individual to answer your questions. CACREP (The Council for Accreditation of Counseling and Related Educational Programs) accredited institutions are required to have someone designated as practicum and internship coordinator. If you are in a CACREP accredited program, that person is likely the one to choose.

Academically, you want to review which classes are required before field experience and in what order these classes should be taken to be best prepared for field experience. You need to review expectations with your clinical director for field placements at your academic institution. You want to be clear on the expectations of your academic program, as well as your state requirements needed in order to obtain both preliminary and full licensure. In addition, you will have a supervisor at your site and at your institution. Be sure you understand the requirements for meeting with your professor designated at your school for faculty supervision. Some schools offer only in-class supervision, where it is one large class and everyone gets a few minutes of supervision, some offer individual supervision, while others have a combination of both. As an online student, this supervision will likely take place via a webinar. Do not be afraid to ask questions because all of this is important. See Table 12.1 for some suggestions on the questions you need to ask.

If you are attending a nonaccredited institution, you will want to find out what requirements are needed for licensure. Most states will only provide you with a license if you meet the state requirements, which usually align with the requirements of a nationally accredited school's requirements. *Remember the hours completed prior to graduation do not count toward licensure in most states, but proving that those hours occur in your field experience may be a component of licensure.*

One of the most important considerations for site selection is the schedule. A suitable site must have hours of operation that will accommodate your needs. Many in this field of study are already balancing school, work, and family. Internships are involved and include more than just seeing clients. In addition, you will need to obtain necessary supervision,

Table 12.1 Suggested Questions

Review Expectations for Practicum/ Internship	Suggested Questions
	• What coursework must be completed in order to move forward with practicum/internship? • How many hours will I need at my site? • How many supervision hours do I need? • What are the requirements for my on-site supervisor? • What supervision does my program provide? • How will this practicum/internship affect my future licensure?

attend staff meetings, and create/review notes. You will need a site that has a schedule opening that will allow you to fit all of this in without having to rush the process. Life gets hectic and figuring out the scheduling aspect first really contributes to your success. For example, one counseling student was driving to another state three days per week, attempting to fit in the placement and make it work; in the end she was exhausted, her personal life suffered, and she was unable to keep up the schedule of being on time for clients for the full 15-week experience. Her work suffered and that impacted furture employment options. As you can imagine, proactively finding a site that harmonizes with your schedule will allow you to experience better outcomes.

Another aspect to consider when selecting a site is an area of specialty. When looking for a site you may want to consider a specialty like substance abuse, trauma, eating disorders, or others. It will be important for you to research specialty trends in the field as well as what is most popular and what area is most research-focused. You will want to select something that will make you stand out from the rest. In some states, it is difficult to be recognized as a counselor who just focuses on general mental health. Having a niche makes you more marketable. Additionally, having a specialty will heighten your clinical skills when seeing clients.

Ultimately, site selection is much like job selection and should be approached in similar ways. Apply the same skills you would use to search for a job. Some of this will be discussed in greater detail in Chapter 13, "Preparing for Employment." In general, you should research the reputation of the site(s) because you want to be successful. Ask peers what their experience has been. Ask your professors if they could recommend any great sites. If you are searching for a site in your area and your school is in a different area or state, contact some local mental health clinicians and ask their opinions or inquire among your network of colleagues. Join counseling listservs that may allow you to get feedback from other professionals in your area. In other words, ask around!

In addition, it is important to have a resume or curriculum vitae prepared (your academic institution should be able to assist you at your career services center either in person or online if needed). Have letters of recommendation and a reference list prepared and ready to submit. When selecting a site, it is best to select about three sites in order to ensure you have at least one agreement. Your personal selection of a site is just as important as a site's selection of you. Both you and the site are assuming risk of time, energy, and resources, so do your best to ensure that you and the site will be a good fit. Check out Table 12.2 that will direct you further.

Table 12.2 Guide to Success in Finding a Field Placement

Steps to Placement Selection		Tips for Success
Preparation for Practicum/Internship		
	• Make sure you have completed the coursework needed in order to move forward with practicum/internship. • Develop questions you want to ask, to ensure success. • Meet with academic advisor. • Meet with director of clinical experience. • Research counseling agencies in your area.	
Site Selection		
	• Be proactive (do your research of population, clinical orientation, etc.). • Plan ahead (ask about orientation to the practice or agency). • Explore training opportunities to enhance competency. • Complete all necessary paperwork.	

(Continued)

Table 12.2 (Continued)

Supervisor Selection
• Review the supervisor's qualifications, make sure they align with academic institution requirements as well as state licensing requirements (does the supervisor have the proper supervision credentials and licensure).   • Ask about style of supervision at field placement.   • Ensure supervisor has permission and access to clinical files in order to review your work with you.   • Complete paperwork, including supervision agreement (ask when you will meet: daily, weekly, monthly, as well as individual or as a group).
Time Management
• Utilize a planner.   • Examine your own schedule and how practicum and internship will fit in.   • Plan for when you will meet for supervision at your site and at school.   • Develop an outline of meetings and trainings required.   • Schedule time to write notes, review files, consult with other clinicians.   • Make time for you to ensure work/life balance.

CACREP Standards for Fieldwork and State Licensure Requirements

State licensing boards look to CACREP standards when deciding educational requirements and license and certification qualifications. CACREP has set the gold standard in counselor education (Reiner, Dobmeier, & Hernandez, 2013); therefore, licensing organizations model their requirements after CACREP. It is important for you to enroll and complete a program that follows CACREP curriculum. This may allow reciprocity when applying for licensure in other states.

When seeking licensure in a state where you did not complete your program, it is your responsibility to locate the state licensing board. In your conversation with the licensing board, you will need to ask them to identify their licensure requirements. Each state has its own list of requirements. There will be differences in coursework needed and in the amount of time needed in your field placement.

For instance, the state of Florida requires an applicant to complete 3 credit hours of a human sexuality course. This course explores the dynamics and development of human sexuality. It also helps the student to gain insight into his or her own sexuality, while increasing theoretical awareness and acceptance of the client's sexuality. However, in the state of Arkansas this coursework is not required. Even a counselor licensed 20 years in Arkansas with a successful private practice would have to take a human sexuality course in order to be licensed in Florida.

Another thing that may vary from state to state is how many hours you will have to log throughout your field placement. CACREP (2009) standards report a counselor-in-training should log at least 700 clock hours throughout field placement with a minimum of 100 hours in practicum and 600 hours in internship. The state of Arkansas wrote their requirements for practicum and internship completion to mirror those of CACREP. The states of Tennessee and Florida, for instance, have different requirements. Applicants in Tennessee only have to acquire 500 clock hours of training in practicum and internship. On the other hand, an applicant in Florida must have completed 1000 clock hours of training in practicum and internship in order to fulfill the initial requirements for licensure. Again, it is the responsibility of the counselor in training to identify and satisfy the requirements of the state's licensure application. Even though there are slight variations from state to state, being enrolled in a CACREP accredited or written program identifies you as having the baseline qualifications needed to practice as a counselor (Myers, Sweeney, & White, 2002). Due to many states modeling their licensure requirements to echo those of CACREP, you should be able to transfer coursework from state to state providing you keep your syllabi and pass your classes. Because some licensure boards won't accept a grade of C in a core area, make sure you are an A/B student in graduate school!

Being aware of the courses you need to take and the amount of hours needed in your field placement is important, as is an awareness of the requirements of the individuals supervising you throughout your field placement. If you are in a CACREP accredited program, your faculty supervisor will outline for you the specific qualifications needed by your site supervisor in order to meet the parameters of a CACREP field experience. When selecting your site supervisor, it is important to keep these qualifications in mind. Your faculty supervisor should meet the qualifications, but many potential supervisors in the counseling profession do not meet the baseline that CACREP has established. CACREP keeps the qualifications broad enough that it does not automatically narrow the field too much. For instance, your potential supervisor will need to have a graduate degree and carry a license in the helping profession, but he or she does not have to have a master's degree in counseling or a license in counseling. Instead, your supervisor will have needed to complete a master's degree in a program comparable to counseling and have the appropriate licenses and certifications that match their coursework.

It also important to notice your potential site supervisor cannot be new to the field of counseling. CACREP expects site supervisors to have at least 2 years of experience of professional counseling. Along with those 2 years, the site supervisor should have had training in counseling supervision. This does not mean your site supervisor has to have his or her full clinical license. Many states issue an initial license, and award a full clinical license when the applicant has completed post master's supervised clinical hours. Having two years of experience will put the site supervisor at the end of the process. The site supervisor also does not have to have a specialty license in supervision. Instead, they will need to have received training either through professional development or through the faculty supervisor in supervision. Essentially, your site supervisor needs to be a more senior member of the profession than you are and have some training in supervision.

You should also ensure your site supervisor is aware of your program's expectations, requirements, and procedures for students. CACREP standards mandate that you and your site supervisor meet on a weekly basis for individual supervision (CACREP, 2009). Your site supervisor needs to be aware of this before he or she signs the supervision contract. Be sure that your site supervisor attends an orientation with your faculty supervisor and/or program to become knowledgeable of the policies and practices of your field placement. The supervision provided at your placement will need to be aligned with the expectations and policies of your program. If you find your site supervisor does not meet the qualifications laid out by CACREP, you will need to address this with your faculty supervisor and identify a new site supervisor.

Getting the Most Out of Your Practicum and Internship

Practicum and internship, or field experiences, are what you have trained for—the chance to work with real clients! Remember this is a unique experience where being open to change and adaptable to new experiences is in your best interest. Be mindful of this both when starting your placement and during your entire time there. The practicum and internship experience is a reciprocal experience; you want to be open to learning from your site experiences, and you want to keep a watchful eye on your colleagues and superiors to learn from them. It is important to use your observational skills during this time. Just as much as you are paying attention and evaluating the experience, those at your practicum and internship site are evaluating your work, demeanor, willingness to learn, and approachability.

Willingness to learn and remain teachable throughout your career will assist you in substantial ways. As a counselor-in-training, you will notice it is helpful to know the facts, protocol, and process of all the theories and techniques you have studied. However, it is at your practicum and internship sites where you get to put those theories and techniques to the test. Rarely will clinical scenarios present in a textbook format. Most cases will usually present in a way you have not encountered. Having a general understanding what to do and how to provide treatment is key. It will be helpful to sit in on therapy sessions, watch therapy protocol techniques, or ask your colleagues and supervisors about anything you are unsure about. The conversations and the things you will observe will provide you with an invaluable experience.

Your internship/practicum experience is your opportunity to demonstrate your learning and discover more about what you have yet to master. During this process, remember you are learning. Throughout the practicum and internship experience you are a learner; it is okay not to know what to do, what to say, or how to implement a technique. You are there to learn. Many students find themselves at a placement with other students who are striving to complete the same goal of becoming an effective clinician. Resist the urge to make this a competition. Resist the urge to try to impress by pretending to know what to do when you really do not (your superiors will be able to see this and may interpret it as a sign of insecurity or lack of willingness to learn). You are a student; you are there to practice and learn something. When you are able to demonstrate the skills that you are learning with a level of humility, you will find the process even more enjoyable.

As you are demonstrating the skills you are learning, you will begin to be able to gauge your mastery. One way to measure your skill level is to ask your supervisor for feedback. Study how to apply the theory you wish to employ during your sessions. Read, reread, and review treatment protocol as well as what the client is saying to you. Then, discuss your sessions with your supervisor and work on conceptualizing what has taken place. Remember that while this experience is an opportunity to practice the protocols you have studied, the session must remain focused on the client, both what and how they present. You may intend to try a technique based on what the client presented with in the last session; however, if she is in crisis during the current session this is not the time. Be prepared, but do not have an agenda. Be open to make improvements. Do not expect yourself to be perfect; instead, expect yourself to be willing to learn and improve. As your clients respond to the techniques you are implementing, you will be better able to evaluate how effectively you implement the skills you have been taught.

You will maximize your practicum and internship experience when you fully acknowledge your position and role as both a clinician and learner. You are accountable to your clients and to your peers. Taking this responsibility will enhance your clinical experience. Take the initiative to present all of your clients in supervision and discuss difficult cases with your supervisor. Bringing your knowledge to your classroom supervision extends the practicum/internship experience past the counseling session hour. Reading material on diagnosis, treatment, and other materials will contribute to your overall sense of ownership and investment in the process. Asking for assistance in this learning experience does not necessarily mean that you lack knowledge or understanding. If you need help, ask. Do not let fear or intimidation stifle your experience. Remember you really only get to do this once. Owning your position as a learner will help you as you invest your skills in your clients.

If during the process you realize that something does not seem quite right, seek the input of those who are in positions to help you. Discuss your concerns and findings with your faculty supervisor as well as your site supervisor. Sometimes you may come across placements, topics, and clients that trigger issues of which you were unaware. When these occur, remember to bring this up in supervision and be open to entering personal counseling. It can benefit you in the long run, as it can minimize the chance that your own agenda will impact your clients as well as confront you with anything that may be an issue for you in your counseling sessions. Being open to the process, going with the flow, and looking for an opportunity to learn something will truly add to your experience.

Outside of classes, counselors-in-training have limited opportunity to demonstrate counseling techniques. During the field placement experience, counselors-in-training are expected to perform several direct hours. These hours are comprised of face-to-face contact with clients. Working with your supervisor, you will learn the best way to tailor your abilities and techniques to meet the needs of your clients. You will learn how to appropriately diagnosis and assess the client's narrative. The supervisory relationship will teach you how best to respond to the needs of the client in a way that upholds ethical decision making and marries theory and techniques. In the following examples, you will hear firsthand accounts of how students managed these challenges in their fieldwork experiences.

Reported Student Experiences in Internship/Practicum

Student 1: "My practicum field experience was really terrible. The poor field experience was surprising because I interviewed the clinical site supervisor prior to beginning and all the answers provided seemed spot on. I made sure to provide my affiliation agreement to my school; during the interview I had with the clinical director, I clearly outlined what I needed to be successful. The main reasons that made this experience bad were: I had no orientation to the agency's policies and procedures, my supervisor canceled or did not show up to supervision; lastly, my supervisor left me on-site alone with clients on several occasions; one particular time a client was suicidal. As a practicum student, I was not prepared with the tools and resources needed to ensure my success. This was a letdown, especially after clearly communicating what was needed and having the site supervisor ensure the practicum agreement could be met."

Student 2: "I had a fantastic experience with my internship site. I had very little experience working with the trauma population before and this internship site provided several trainings, various resources, and plenty of consultation and supervision. I remained organized, participated, and made sure my hours were documented and approved every week. I finished my placement with great success and a job offer waiting for me upon graduation."

Student 3: "My internship experience was not the best. In the beginning, I did not want to admit it, but I did not allocate enough time for me to be at my internship site to complete my hours. Instead, I complained my site was not giving me enough clients. I also was not accountable for my duties as an intern as well as not having a positive attitude resulted in my site supervisor releasing me from my site. I realize now, I was not conducting myself professionally and I am the only one to blame for how that experience turned out."

Developing Counseling Skills at a Distance

While much of the learning from an internship or a practicum occurs at the site, much will also occur at a distance. Practicum is when you, the counselor-in-training, can begin to make connections between what you know, how you know it, and how and when to implement it. You will sharpen your clinical skills by being familiar with your own learning style. For example, if you are a visual person, accessing the academic library and watching videos may be more helpful and suitable to your needs than listening to a lecture or reading about techniques. Knowing how you best learn will help you maximize your time as you choose activities that will improve your counseling skills.

One way to hone your counseling skills is through writing process notes. This involves recording sessions, with client consent, and creating a spreadsheet documenting your entire interaction with the client during the session. This is more than a transcript of the session, but also includes your interventions, observations, intentions, and reactions as well as the client's responses to your interventions. These can be examined while not with the client so further learning can occur. Reviewing your recorded sessions will allow you to practice looking for signs such as rate of speech, pitch, breathing, interruptions, and avoidance. Examine the session to make sure your approach best meets your client's needs and not your own agenda. Let's face it, no one enjoys watching their recorded sessions, but it is certainly helpful when learning how to build a solid set of counseling skills.

Another way practicum and internship help develop your counseling skills at a distance is through the requirement to keep records and review session notes. Increasingly, agencies and individuals are moving to electronic record keeping. First, please be sure to check with your ethical guidelines as well as state laws when adapting to this style of record keeping. Next, follow a style of note keeping which will allow you to follow the client's presenting issue, the interventions, progress, treatment protocol, and other things. Presenting these notes during supervision will help you learn how to write notes concisely while thoroughly capturing the session in its entirety. As you demonstrate your willingness to learn outside of your counseling sessions, your supervisors will be able to gauge your abilities and performance.

Multicultural/Diversity Issues Within Your Placement

Another opportunity to learn in practicum and internship is through the individuals who will contribute to those experiences from either similar and or different backgrounds. Integrating awareness and open discussion about how the particular differences add to the counseling dynamic is vital. During the process of developing as a counselor-in-training, some of the issues that arise can bring up some strong feelings or concerns within you. Paying attention to these feelings, concerns, and differences can be difficult; however, working through the differences and adding to your own competency can be the most rewarding and teachable moments you experience.

You can learn from the diversity of those influencing your practicum or internship experience only after you relate to who they are as people. It may be important to consider how similar and different you may be from your site supervisor as well as your faculty supervisor. Next, examine the similarities and differences among your peers. Then note which populations your peers are working with; look at similarities and differences compared to your own population. Once you have taken notice of the above mentioned similarities and differences, begin asking for a different perspective. Asking questions because you are interested in the meaning in the different scenarios to the different cultures, genders, or populations will yield a rich learning experience.

The knowledge and insight you will gain by investigating diversity issues will continue to provide you with tools to help heal others. At your site for field placement, you may want to ask about diversity training. If a training session is offered, attend it, take notes, and bring it to supervision. Look within your community, neighborhood, state, and professional associations for diversity training; the knowledge you can gain while distant from your site will greatly aid in your ability to help your clients.

Establish a collaborative working relationship with your supervisors, peers, and colleagues. Acknowledge the differences and allow yourself to be taught different possibilities. The personal growth of understanding yourself and others could end up surprising you and lead to opportunities and challenges you never knew existed.

Distance Supervision

In conjunction with developing your skills, supervision will be taking place during your internship or practicum. Supervision traditionally has been conducted face-to-face; however, with education embracing techno-logical developments, we are now able to conduct supervision at a distance. Many allow for distance supervision using such platforms as Adobe Connect, GoToMeeting, and Zoom. These electronic advancements allow us to connect, discuss, and meet in ways as if we were directly in front of one another, thus we are able to conduct distance supervision. Recorded sessions can be shown as if everyone were present in a classroom. The use of a video conferencing platform allows the supervisor to communicate directly, observe reactions, and provide support to the students as needed. This support can be provided to you as you participate from the comfort of your own home or office.

Whether face-to-face or distance, supervision can be an experience that will stretch and challenge each student to explore their potential. Meeting individually each week as well as in a group format will assist with assessing, conceptualizing, diagnosing, and providing treatment for all clients involved. During this process, your discussion with your instructor will assist with exploring thoughts, emotions, and actions. The process of providing and receiving peer feedback will be both encouraging and challenging as you grow together with peers. Instructors can provide constructive feedback, which will help students to examine their actions as well as guide students to gather and utilize the appropriate resources needed to benefit clients.

Aside from meeting weekly, you will be expected to complete assignments to fulfill your supervision experience. Supervision typically requires students to complete a weekly narrative describing what their experience has been, something they have learned, and how they have spent their time. This often includes a reflective section where students can journal their experience to a certain degree as an exercise that can be used to enhance reflection and discussion. Distance supervision should also include a platform for students to formulate questions that they have for the online supervisor as well as the site supervisor. Students submit this assignment weekly often in an online forum and respond to one another in order to generate additional communication outside of the group supervision setting. This also fosters professional network and growth among students. Supervision also requires assignments like case presentations, which have proved to be beneficial to tie in factual with practical knowledge. You will pick either one client or all your clients to complete this task in order to heighten your clinical skill. Presenting cases will build your confidence as well as indicate your ability to apply your knowledge to the clinical field.

While distance supervision can fulfill the requirements for your program, there are some disadvantages. Distance supervision is in real time, but only when it is scheduled; you cannot walk into your supervisor's office at school whenever you wish. While this is a disadvantage, you can benefit from it as distance supervision causes the supervisee to reflect more and find other resources which will benefit you professionally. Distance supervisors can provide a telephone number with a schedule of what other times the supervisor is available which is like office hours. Furthermore, meeting with the on-site supervisor, with the distance supervisor, and coming up with a supportive plan of available hours and open communication can also assist the supervisee with the understanding of when another supervisor would be available in case of an emergency.

Even though being able to log on remotely is a positive factor, the distraction inherent in an online environment may be challenging. Many things come up and can make it difficult to participate in distance supervision. While logging on to the home computer, family or household members may think you are available to address their wants and needs. Logging onto the computer instead of going to a physical classroom presents its own challenges; you will be responsible for keeping your attention on your meeting and not indulging in convenient distractions. Face-to-face, in-person supervision can present the same challenges; however, individuals tend to be more respectful and accountable in person since such behaviors may be obvious and immediately acknowledged.

Direct Versus Indirect Hours

Part of the accountability of field placement is documenting your hours. When you begin practicum or internship, you agree to complete your requirement of hours. This all needs to be documented clearly. To be clear in your documentation, you must understand the difference between direct and indirect hours.

Direct hours are all the hours you spend in session and group with the client(s). Loosely stating anything face-to-face with a client as direct hours would be incorrect. For instance, you may see the client in the waiting room or parking lot and be approached for conversation. This is not the place for therapy and does not count toward your counseling hours. You want to make sure the client's file refers to time spent in a session with you either individually or in a group setting. Some supervisors define direct hours as anything a counselor can bill for and be reimbursed.

Indirect hours may be thought of as time you are investing in your practice while not face-to-face with a client. This can be understood in a number of ways. When you document your session, you are accumulating indirect hours. Time spent on a report or treatment summary, phone calls, as well as consultation are all indirect hours. Hours spent researching material on a certain diagnosis as well as ways to treat it, or discussing clients (i.e., case conference, individual and group supervision) are also indirect. The time you spend when you are new at your site and review charts and files of existing or previous clients all count as indirect hours. Time spent preparing case presentations or weekly narrative logs for your distance supervision is indirect. These hours accumulated during your internship or practicum experience sharpening your clinical skill to assist future clients count as indirect hours.

Professionalism to Represent Your Program and the Counseling Profession

A main component of being in a professional training program is learning the appropriate behaviors for a professional counselor. This is learned through course work in helping relationships, ethics, and field placement. These classes and your experiences influence professionalism, articulate your role within a professional community, define your function, and signify the importance of your professional relationships (Milson & Akos, 2005). As you progress in your program, you begin to act and think more independently as you apply your theoretical perspective to case analyses, demonstrate a command of counseling techniques, and create treatment and guide treatment interventions. Your field placement solidifies your training of how to demonstrate professional behavior. Going through the supervisory process allows you to define your professional competence and create your professional identity (Perry, 2012). Your faculty supervisor will model for you how to interact with clients, your placement supervisors, and colleagues.

Your faculty supervisor will aid in your professional development by helping you understand how to interact with placement supervisors. At the cornerstone of the supervisory relationship is feedback. As a counseling professional, you will have several supervisors with whom you will interact throughout the course of your career. Whether they are field placement supervisors, clinical supervisors, or licensing supervisors, a significant portion of your professional behavior will be comprised of interaction with a supervisor. Your interaction with these supervisors will help to create your professional representation and begin to define who you are professionally. You will learn through the relationship with your faculty supervisor how to respond to the feedback given by placement supervisors. Learning how to receive feedback and implement it into your practice will further your ability to represent your profession appropriately.

Another component of professional behavior is how you interact with your colleagues. Throughout your clinical training program, you will learn what it is to be professional and how to act professionally. Your field placement experience will give you the opportunity to interact with individuals outside your program. These individuals will come from the other branches of the helping profession such as social work, psychology, criminal justice, psychiatry, case management, and school counseling. How you manage those relationships will also inform professional identity and help to establish your professional reputation. Any relationship with which you are having difficulty can be addressed with both your faculty supervisor and site supervisor. The supervisory relationship is designed to help the counselor-in-training learn behavior and interaction patterns that are befitting of professional counseling. A strained professional relationship with a school counselor, psychiatrist, or case manager can negatively impact the quality of care being given to a client. Your supervisor is there to help you problem solve professional relationship difficulties to ensure you are maintaining a high level of professionalism.

The important thing to remember as you are progressing from a counselor-in-training into a professional counselor is the behaviors you demonstrate are a direct reflection of your profession, your faculty supervisor, and your site supervisor (Bogo, Regehr, Power, & Regehr, 2007). At all times you must be ethical and professional as you interact with clients, supervisors, and colleagues. This is the beginning of your professional career. The behaviors displayed at this point in your career will lay the groundwork for how you are perceived throughout the rest of your career. It is imperative you work with your supervisor to identify the behaviors that are becoming of a professional counselor.

Advocating for Yourself in a Field Experience

Being in a field placement allows you the opportunity to learn how to advocate for yourself and your profession by learning the attitude and skills you need to be a professional counselor (Reiner et al., 2013). In a field placement experience, learning takes place in the feedback a supervisor gives to the supervisee. As mentioned earlier, feedback is the cornerstone of field placement. Within the supervisory process, feedback is stressed in order to increase competency and self-efficacy (Aper, Reniers, Koole, Valcke, & Derese, 2012). Since field placement is centered on direct and indirect services, it is the role of the supervisor to ensure quality care is being given and professional behavior is being demonstrated. How you as the supervisee advocate for yourself lies within how you receive the feedback being given.

In order to receive feedback positively, the counselor-in-training must be an open and active learner, integrate feedback in a positive way, and work toward having a strong skill level (Bogo et al., 2007). The counselor-in-training must be ready to learn. You cannot go into the field placement experience unwilling to advance yourself and find resources to help in the process. Feedback should not be viewed as a personal attack. Your supervisor is not attacking your value system, your core beliefs, or who you are as a person. Instead, your supervisor is highlighting ways to enhance your growth and things you might need to do in order to become a more competent professional. The main goal of supervision is to increase your skill set. In order to advocate for the best placements and the best supervision, you must view the field placement experience as an exercise in advancing your skills.

Just as there are ways to receive feedback positively, there are things that might negatively impact the way in which you view supervision. If a counselor-in-training has difficulty understand his or her role in the supervisory relationship, has had previous work in the field of mental health, is not open to raising competency level, or has a personality style that conflicts with the supervisor, feedback may be viewed as negative and will not be assimilated into practice (Bogo et al., 2007). It is imperative for you to identify what your role in the supervisory relationship will be. Knowing your role will give you direction and a sense of concreteness when fulfilling your field placement responsibilities. Some students who enter into a professional counseling program have worked either as a mental health technician or as a case manager before deciding to advance their career. Although this experience is a great way to begin your field placement, you supervisor will demand a higher level of professional care and development. You must be willing to expand your definition of professional care and work toward gaining new competencies that will aid you in the completion of your graduate degree. There are times when a student's personality conflicts with that of his or her supervisor. This can cause a disruption in the way feedback is pursued and received. If you feel this is the case within your supervisory relationship, you need to address it with your supervisor so that you can continue to work on increasing your professional development.

In order for the counselor-in-training to have a positive experience, he or she must ensure that all behavior is goal oriented (Spieker & Hinsz, 2004). The supervisee and supervisor can take steps together to create a goal-oriented environment. Kirke, Layton, and Sim (2007) identified three ways to facilitate an optimum growing experience for the counselor-in-training. Within the supervisory relationship, there must be an opportunity to connect theoretical education with clinical practice. This can be done through direct service hours, case conceptualizations, and reviewing sessions. The supervisor must have a high level of competency, show enthusiasm for the profession, and communicate this to the supervisee. If the counselor-in-training does not feel his or her field placement supervisor is working toward the agreed-upon goals, he or she should consult with the faculty supervisor to seek a remediation to the problem. The counselor-in-training should also feel comfortable enough with the faculty supervisor to communicate any issues he or she has in that supervisory relationship. The supervisor should display effective teaching strategies that enhance the growth of the counselor-in-training. Again, if you do not feel as if you are growing, communicate this with the faculty supervisor.

Communication with your on-site and faculty supervisors is essential to a successful field placement experience. Counselors-in-training who interact frequently with their professors earn higher grades, are more satisfied, and are more likely to complete their program (Wasley, 2006). Supervision is a two-way process. It is not just a supervisor giving the supervisee feedback; it is also how the supervisee responds to the feedback and interacts with the supervisor (see Table 12.3). Field placement is a time of tremendous growth. You enter this portion of your counseling training with very little experience engaging clients and applying your theoretical orientation. This growth may challenge your self-confidence and create insecurities and fears. The only way to address them is to communicate them with your supervisor. Not identifying your need areas and creating goals to strengthen your skills may result in a stunting of your potential.

Table 12.3 Guide to Success Receiving and Responding to Feedback

Advocating for Yourself	Tips for Success
Positively Receive Feedback	
<ul><li>Be ready to learn.</li><li>Be an open and active learner.</li><li>Integrate feedback.</li><li>Work toward developing a strong skill set.</li></ul>	
Demonstrate Goal-Oriented Behavior	
<ul><li>Connect theory with practice.</li><li>Select a site supervisor with a high level of competency and willingness to help you learn.</li><li>Have open communication with site supervisor.</li><li>Speak with both your site supervisor and faculty supervisor about any problems you are having at your site.</li></ul>	

Working Within the Appropriate Scope of Practice

Completing a field placement experience means that you have had experience working directly with clients, become more grounded in your theoretical approach, and identified your scope of practice. Your scope of practice is a document that lists your competencies. These can include which populations you plan to work with, what diagnostic categories you will work with, and what assessments you plan to give. In the state of Arkansas, this must be submitted to the licensure board before you are given your license.

Determining your scope of practice will largely be impacted by your supervisory process. Supervision is a vital way to increase your effective practice of counseling skills (Taylor, Gordon, Grist, & Olding, 2012). Through this practice, you will work with your supervisor to identify your strengths and area for growth as well as ways to work inside your competencies. Supervision will give you the ability to stretch your clinical skills while being anchored to a supervisor who will ensure you are committed to ethical practice. Internship experiences will provide you with learning opportunities that will help you to develop and increase competencies in practicing counseling (Tony et al., 2004).

In order to understand what you are able and competent to do, you as a counselor-in-training must first believe in your ability to perform counseling duties. Self-efficacy is an important factor in predicting your ability to perform your role as a professional (Tony et al., 2004). A student must believe he or she can competently perform counseling skills in order to produce outcomes that are required (Bandura, Barbaranelli, Caprara, & Pastorelli, 1996). If a student completes field placement and meets all hour requirements but does not feel an increased sense of confidence in his or her ability to perform counseling skills, there will be a negative impact on quality of care. In order for the counselor-in-training to be a competent practitioner, there needs to be a high sense of self-efficacy. This is where the supervision process comes into play. Supervision is an integral component of increasing self-efficacy (Cashwell & Dooley, 2001). A supervisor will work with the counselor-in-training as he or she completes the requirements for field placement. Through face-to-face feedback and evaluation of skills, the supervisor will work with the student to understand his or her own personal competencies and limitations to those competencies.

Moss, Gibson, and Dollarhide (2014) identified developmental steps that mold how a counselor-in-training perceives his or her ability. The first step is adjustment. A student will begin field placement with a certain expectation of how the coursework will be accomplished. As the semester progresses, those expectations tend to change. How a counselor-in-training manages those expectations impacts competencies. The more flexible a student is, the more readily he or she will be able to adjust. The next step is autonomy. The field placement process begins with the counselor-in-training receiving multiple hours of supervision each week from the faculty supervisor and the site supervisor. It is designed this way to ensure the supervisee is working under intense supervision with all decisions and interactions being monitored by the supervisor. As field placement evolves from practicum to internship, the student is not required to attend so many supervision meetings. The intentions are that counselors-in-training will begin to feel more confidence in their decision-making and counseling abilities and have the freedom to make some decisions on their own. The third step is integration. At the beginning of field placement, students are focused on logging hours and meeting requirements. They will soon learn in order to be a grounded practitioner there has to be an integration of the personal self and the professional self. This will take the form of the counselor-in-training being more genuine in session and balancing work and life roles with more ease. The fourth step is connection. Throughout the field placement experience, the counselor-in-training should make strong connections with professional peers, mentors, and supervisors. Having these relationships will equip the student with a stronger command over his decision-making skills. The relationship provides a good venue to discuss the client issues and concerns. The last step is a commitment to continued education. A byproduct of field placement is the awareness that in order to be an effective clinician, you can never stop the learning process. Being aware of and embracing this knowledge will continue to increase self-efficacy and competency throughout your professional career. This takes place as you sign up for professional development units, attend agency staffing, and work through your licensure supervision. It also takes place as you work with your clients and identify the resources they need and ways in which you can become more knowledgeable of those resources.

Competency is important to client care. You will become more aware of this in field placement than in any other course you take throughout your program. You will use your supervisors' knowledge and skills as a way of shaping your practice, and through consultation with your supervisors, you learn the best ways to provide quality care. Field placement gives you the opportunity to understand your scope of practice and function within it by building relationships with peers and mentors and by doing professional things that will mirror what you will do as a licensed counselor (Perry, 2012).

Field placement demands you learn in a way that will sharpen your competency. This learning is an interaction of your educational setting, your behavior within the learning process, and personal factors such as self-esteem, dependency, and self-efficacy (Bandura, 1997). Field placement is a crossroad in which your textbook learning, your behavior, and personality characteristics meet. How you connect these three things will be how you define your competency and work within it. Fieldwork is designed to highlight your strength while you work on addressing your growth areas.

Summary

Investigating, selecting, and performing successfully in your field experience is one of the defining elements of your graduate counseling program. This chapter has outlined specific tasks that you can do early in your program all the way through the field experience to make this a substantive learning opportunity as you build toward your future as a professional counselor. By doing your due diligence in advance and remaining teachable throughout the process, most students will find field experiences to be some of the most meaningful training opportunities in their career.

About the Authors

Debra G. Leggett, PhD, is the program chair of the College of Behavioral Sciences at Argosy University—Sarasota. She received her PhD in Counselor Education from Mississippi State University where she began her study of clinical supervision, exploring beginning counselors' expectations and needs. She has taught courses in supervision for both master and doctoral students where she continued to conduct action research on current practices. She currently conducts distance supervision for doctoral Counselor Education and Supervision students via video conferencing. She has served as Chair of AMHCA's Professional Issues Committee and as the President of the Indiana Counseling Association. Dr. Leggett is a Certified Sex Offender Treatment Professional, Certified Expert Trauma Professional, National Board Certified Counselor (NCC), and a Licensed Mental Health Counselor. This summer, she had a study published in the *International Journal of Trauma Research and Practice* regarding therapist burnout when working with domestic violence.

Josh H. Strickland, MS, EdS, is an assistant professor for Harding University's Professional Counseling: Clinical and School Counseling program. He is a Licensed Professional Counselor (LPC) in the state of Arkansas, a National Board Certified Counselor (NCC), and currently a doctoral student in Counselor Education and Supervision at Argosy University. He has had extensive work supervising practicum and internship students who are completing coursework in clinical counseling and school counseling and is completing the requirements to receive his supervision specialty license in Arkansas. Mr. Strickland has worked in child advocacy centers, school-based mental health centers, and private practice. He has served as the president elect for Arkansas's chapter of the Association for Counselor Education and Supervision (ArACES) and is now serving as the president.

Elizabeth Krzewski, MA, is a doctoral candidate in the Counselor Education and Supervision program at Argosy University—Sarasota (November, 2014). As an adjunct professor, she has taught supervision/field placement. Her dissertation is focused on sexual abuse issues, specifically treatment protocols for juvenile sexual offenders. Elizabeth is a Licensed Mental Health Counselor, a Certified Addictions Professional in both Florida and New York State, Certified Clinical Trauma Professional, National Board Certified Counselor (NCC), and a Florida State DUI Instructor. Elizabeth has worked as an assistant to the Director of Clinical Training at Argosy University, assisting with CACREP auditing/accreditation and assisting students needing guidance with field placement.

References

Aper, L., Reniers, J., Koole, S., Valcke, M., & Derese, A. (2012). Impact of three alternative consultation training formats on self-efficacy and consultation skills of medical students. *Medical Teacher, 34*(7), e500–e507. doi:10.3109/0142159X.2012.668627

Bandura, A. (1997). *Self-efficacy: The exercise of control.* New York, NY: Freeman & Company.

Bandura, A., Barbaranelli, C., Caprara, G. V., & Pastorelli, C. (1996). Multifaceted impact of self-efficacy beliefs on academic functioning. *Child Development, 67,* 1206–1222.

Bogo, M., Regehr, C., Power, R., & Regehr, G. (2007). When values collide: Field instructors' experiences of providing feedback and evaluating competence. *The Clinical Supervisor, 26*(1–2), 99–117. doi:10.1300/J001v26n01_08

Cashwell, T. H., & Dooley, K. (2001). The impact of supervision on counselor self-efficacy. *Clinical Supervision, 20,* 39–47.

Council for Accreditation of Counseling and Related Educational Programs. (2009). *2009 standards for accreditation.* Alexandria: VA: Author.

Kirke, P., Layton, N., & Sim, J. (2007). Informing fieldwork design: Key elements to quality in fieldwork education for undergraduate occupational therapy students. *Australian Occupational Therapy, 54,* 13–22.

Milson, A., & Akos, P. (2005). CACREP's relevance to professionalism for school counselor educators. *Counselor Education & Supervision, 45*(2), 147–158. doi:101002/j.1556-6978.2005.tb00137.x

Moss, J. M., Gibson, D. M., & Dollarhide, C. T. (2014). Professional identity development: A grounded theory of transformational tasks of counselors. *Journal of Counseling & Development, 92*(1), 3–12. doi:10.1002/j.1556-6676.2014.00124.x

Myers, J. E., Sweeney, T. J., & White, V. E. (2002). Advocacy for counseling and counselors: A professional imperative. *Journal of Counseling & Development, 80,* 394–402.

Perry, C. (2012). Constructing professional identity in an online clinical training program: Possibilities for online supervision. *Journal of Systemic Therapies, 31*(3), 53–67. doi:10.1521/jsyt.2012.31.3.53

Reiner, S. M., Dobmeier, R. A., & Hernandez, T. J. (2013). Perceived impact of professional counselor identity: An exploratory study. *Journal of Counseling & Development, 9*(12), 174–183. doi:10.1002/j.1556-6676.2013.00084.x

Spieker, C. J., & Hinsz, V. B. (2004). Repeated success and failure influences on self-efficacy and personal goals. *Social Behavior and Personality, 32*(2), 191–198.

Taylor, K., Gordon, K., Grist, S., & Olding, C. (2012). Developing supervisory competence: Preliminary data on the impact of CBT supervision training. *The Cognitive Behaviour Therapist, 5*(4), 83–92.

Tony, M., Addison, K. D., LaSure-Bryant, D., Norman, R., O'Connell, W., & Stewart-Sicking, J. A. (2004). Factors that influence self-efficacy of counseling students: An exploratory study. *Counselor Education & Supervision, 44*(1), 70–80. doi:10.1002/j.1556-6978.2004.tb01861.x

Wasley, P. (2006). Underrepresented students benefit most from 'engagement'. *Chronicle of Higher Education, 53,* 195–197.

PART III

Completing Your Degree

13

Preparing for Employment

R. J. Davis

Chapter Overview

This chapter will provide you with some strategies to prepare for that ultimate goal of employment. Whether you are just beginning a counseling program or are ready to go out into the real world, this chapter will provide you with the tools and wisdom to successfully navigate moving toward employment. The importance of developing a resume, gathering references, and showcasing your skills is addressed. In addition, tips and strategies for interviewing are offered.

Learning Outcomes

Upon completion of this chapter, students will

- Prepare for employment
- Develop a job search strategy
- Create professional documents
- Build an electronic portfolio

- Understand the process of certification and licensure
- Identify a variety of professional examinations
- Select professional attire
- Engage in the process of interviewing

Introduction

The title of this chapter, "Preparing for Employment," is both an indication of what the chapter contains and an instruction. Seeking and securing a desired position requires careful preparation much like your course of study to become a counselor. From one perspective, you begin preparing yourself for employment in your first course, and from another, it is a continuous process. The chapter is about more than preparation or creating evidence of your graduate degree, however. It is also about your continued development as a professional. Part of that development should be about personal style and knowing how to handle yourself in a variety of situations. Personal style in this context involves more than a winning resume. It involves making decisions with specific intent regarding appearance, behavior, and attitude.

The next steps you take, or do not take, related to preparing for employment will have significant impact on your future success. Preparing for employment can be viewed as a process much like counseling is a process. Understanding the process is important and it is never too soon to begin your preparations. Being prepared will increase your self-confidence and your potential for success. The information in this chapter is provided to guide you through the process.

Developing Your Job Search Strategy

How do you go about developing a job search strategy? What can you do during your degree program to help get prepared? Like several aspects of preparing for employment, job search strategies have changed over time. Developing a successful strategy is essential and involves utilizing the resources available to you.

Modern jobseekers rely less on newspapers and employment offices than in the past. The Internet has changed everything in this regard. Searching for employment has never been more efficient or convenient. Visiting targeted company or agency websites allows jobseekers to learn about opportunities available and to engage in the application process with ease. Schools, agencies, and other organizations often have human resources sites with job postings and application procedures. While still in your degree program, you can spend time thinking about the type of environment in which you wish to work. Think of the different settings in which counseling services are offered. Do you prefer to work in group settings or more on your own? Consider the type of services and activities that you would like to offer or engage in on a regular basis. Then, visit websites of schools, agencies, or organizations that are of interest. As you learn more about job opportunities in the field, you will begin to hone a job search strategy for internship and subsequent employment.

Common Professional Documents

An essential component of your preparations involves creating or developing professional documents that represent you. Some counseling programs will require that you create an electronic portfolio which begin to organize many of these documents. Consider the type of impression you wish to make. When it comes to job seeking, a clean, conservative style that communicates professionalism, capability, and skill is the best approach. Just as you will become known by your professional affiliations, so too will you be known to some extent by the quality of your professional documents.

A number of documents such as resumes, curriculum vitae, and letters of interest are considered common or necessary within most professions. It is important that you have these components in an electronic and hard copy. Many examples or templates are available online at no cost. Be cautious when choosing a resume template as some of those posted will be dated or too trendy for the counseling profession. You need to create documents that look current, conservative, and professional in appearance and that showcase your skills and training. There are also services and professional resumes writers that will gladly help you create your documents for a fee but beware. The fees can range from reasonable to ridiculous and most will use a template to create your documents.

It is important to view these documents as "living documents." In other words, these documents are made to be updated over time or tailored to a specific position when needed. Employers and hiring managers are looking for employees that bring value to their agencies or organizations as well as specific skills to assist their clients. Applicants can make a mistake by adopting a one-size-fits-all approach. When you adjust or tailor a document to a specific position by using the employer's name in your cover letter or tweak the objective stated on your resume by using the company's name, you communicate care and focused interest. Career counselors often encourage job-seekers to keep a file of these documents at hand and update them periodically, especially resumes and curriculum vitae. By doing so, you will be less likely to forget or overlook your activities and accomplishments. As you progress through your program, continue to add to this document to cover all of your training and clinical experiences as well as honors and achievements.

All of your documents should be printed on good quality paper, sometimes referred to as resume bond paper. This type of paper is heavier, feels different in the hands, and adds some style that run-of-the-mill copy machine paper does not. The color of choice is white or cream and bright or strong paper colors should be avoided. Another good suggestion is to create a business card. As with the other documents listed, the card style should be conservative and include your name and contact information, typically telephone and e-mail, along with any credential you possess. There are low cost options for business cards available online. Remember the image you want to project: professional and prepared to be hired. Many counseling students prepare business cards before attending conferences so that they can network with potential employers or doctoral institutions.

Letters of Interest or Cover Letters

When you get to the application stage, a letter of interest or cover letter is often required as part of the process. Cover letters are typically the first contact with your potential employer. The letter is an opportunity to capture their attention and create interest in you as a candidate as you express interest in being one of their newest employees. In today's job market, these letters are often submitted through an online portal. However, paper copies are sometimes requested, and it is always a good idea to have one with you when interviewing. Files can be lost and printers can run out of ink or break down. Being prepared to deal with this possibility gives you the opportunity to save the day.

A well-written letter says more about you then you may think. First, it tells the potential employer that you are aware of the requirements for professional communication and that you are capable and competent in that area. Second, it informs the employer that you have taken some time to research the company and the position for which you are applying. Third, it communicates interest and respect for the process. Employment opportunities can be lost because of poor written communication skills. Employers may think, "Well, if the counselor can't write a cover letter, how can I trust him to write a case note or treat a client?"

In general, a letter of interest or cover letter is brief, to the point, and contains enough information and details to encourage further interest in you as an applicant. Long letters containing lists of accomplishments, explanations, or inappropriate personal information can block you before you get your foot in the door. In addition, they communicate disrespect for the reader's time. Most will be discarded without being read completely.

It is important that your letter contain the basic components of professional communication. These basic components include the date of the correspondence, a greeting, the reasons for the letter being sent and the position in which you are interested, your availability for interviews or questions, your name and contact information, and appropriate closure (University of Washington, 2015). In addition, you should observe common standards of spelling, grammar, and punctuation. Letters with mistakes of this nature can be distracting and communicate negative messages about you. These are professional documents containing formal communication and should not be written carelessly. Proofread your work and avoid using slang or contractions. Reading the letter out loud may help you create a letter that flows well and clearly communicates your intentions.

Understanding how to format the mechanics of your letter is important but so is the content. A number of strategies can be employed as you begin writing your letter. First, consider your greeting. One problem you may encounter is not knowing who will receive the letter. Sometimes, you will be instructed to send the letter to a specific individual and in others you may only know where to send or upload your letter. If that is the case, consider beginning your letter with a greeting such as Good Morning, Good Afternoon, or simply the word Greetings. The best of all possible circumstances is to know the name and title of the individual who will receive the letter. You may be able to obtain this information through your research. Calling to politely inquire to whom the letter of interest should be addressed is considered acceptable but not always possible.

Some consideration should be given to your contact information as well. Typically this information includes your name, your address, telephone number, and an e-mail address. Nicknames should be avoided. Your first and last name is usually your best choice. Some applicants may be more comfortable with providing their city and state rather than their street address. Applications will require this information, but there is some flexibility with letters of interest or cover letters. Supplying the potential employer with a telephone number remains a common practice although contact through e-mail should be expected as well. With regard to telephone contact, it is important that your recorded message is professional and courteous. Recordings of your favorite song or funny messages are not appropriate and may not communicate a message you wish to convey.

Your e-mail address should be professional as well. Unfortunately, many individuals still use the first e-mail address they ever created and are often not very professional. Personalized mail addresses such as surferdude89@gmail.com or pinkprincess1@hotmail.com or needlessly complicated addresses may not create a favorable impression of you. The best e-mail address will be brief and as close to your name as possible such as jlopez@yahoo.com. Some of these considerations may seem trivial but are important nonetheless. You are introducing yourself to the professional world and trying to create a positive impression. Remember that time is typically in short supply for hiring managers or supervisors, and they may have a lot of applicants to process. You increase your odds of making it past the first round of screening by having a professional cover letter.

Resumes

Preparing for employment typically includes creating a professional resume. Creating a professional resume is not difficult, but it should be done with care and with specific focus or intent. Like letters of interest or cover letters, resumes can be the first point of contact with a potential employer. Again, it is important that the documents be professional in appearance. As discussed, a quick Internet search for resume styles will yield hundreds of examples. The problem quickly becomes which format to select and perhaps more importantly which formats to avoid. Many such formats are outdated and no longer considered preferable. Modern resumes are brief, concise, snapshots of an individual's contact information, qualifications, and experience.

The focus should be on your skills that bring value to the employer, your education, and your experience.

As we have discussed, current trends in hiring practices often require electronic submission of your professional documents. It is important to pay close attention to submission guidelines including format (e.g., pdf, Word document). From one perspective, being able to correctly follow the application process is the first test of your ability. Applicants who are not able to follow directions are usually ignored. If you do not upload the proper format, the recipient may be unable to read the document in the system.

Another common practice in work environments and human resource departments is to utilize software programs to conduct word searches on electronically submitted documents such as resumes. Keywords are drawn from posted job descriptions. The number of keywords found or "hits" may determine whether or not your resume is reviewed at a higher level. A good strategy is to incorporate words or phrases from the job description into your cover letter or resume. For example, the job description may call for the ability to use common software such as excel to track client data. In some situations, the keywords are quite specific and include product names like Microsoft. Including keywords drawn from job descriptions can communicate important information about you as applicant.

Making your professional documents easy to read, understand, and hopefully remember (for all the right reasons) is the primary goal. The information on your resume should be arranged logically with headings to separate the various components. As mentioned earlier, hard copies of your resume should be printed on a high-quality bond paper in white or cream avoiding other paper colors as they can sometimes be difficult to read. The same is true of small or unusual fonts. While it is the wish of many to be creative and try to stand out, resumes are not the best way to accomplish that goal. The length of your resume is important as well. Years ago, applicants struggled to make the resume as long as possible including everything from skills to hobbies. Lengthy resumes are often viewed as less desirable these days. Much of the information that was once captured on a resume is now reserved for the application. Be brief and to the point. A general rule to follow is one page per 10 years of relevant experience. Your resume should include the following information or components:

- Your name and contact information
- Your objective

- Your education
- The skills you possess relevant to the position
- Your experience

Contact information can be formatted in a number of ways and positioned at the top of the document. The basic idea is for it to be easy to find and read. Consider utilizing one of the following formats.

Example 1

John Q. Student

123 Fair Street
Sunnyside, TX 70001
111-222-3333
john.student@email.com

In Example 1, note that the name is centered and bolded. The idea is to make the name stand out on the page. To that end, a 14- to 24-point, conservative, font such as Times New Roman in black ink is employed. The same font at 12 point in black ink is used for the rest of the document with single spacing.

Example 2

Jane Q. Student

123 Fair Street   111-222-333
Sunnyside, TX 70001   jane.student@email.com

Example 2 contains the same information but is arranged differently as you can see. This format saves at least one line of type that may be needed elsewhere in the document. In this example, note that the name is centered and bolded. Again, the idea is to make the name stand out on the page. To that end, a 14- to 24-point, conservative, font such as Times New Roman in black ink is employed. The same font at 12 point in black ink is used for the rest of the document with single spacing.

Both examples are considered to be appropriate and professional. The information is clear and easy to read and understand. You may choose to arrange this important information in a different way such as a right or left-hand alignment. That is about as creative as you need to get for the header. Mixing fonts and ink colors in the body of the document should be avoided. Remember, professional documents are conservative with regard to style and format.

Many professional resume writers suggest creating or including an objective immediately following your contact information. An objective serves to focus the document. An appropriate objective is more than expressing the desire to "secure employment" or "utilize skills and education." One approach is to include the name of the position for which you are applying along with the company or organization's name. Objectives should be succinct and may be written as a clause or phrase as shown in the following example.

Example 1

Objective: To secure a position as a Mental Health Facilitator with National Care America

In this example, it is clear to anyone reading the document why the document was received and what the applicant is wishing to accomplish. It indicates to the reader that the applicant has read the job description posted by the company. Formatting the objective in this manner indicates that the resume has been created with intent for a specific company or organization.

Example 2

Objective: To secure a position in which I can apply my skills and education

The objective in Example 2 is vague and generic. Formatting your objective in this manner misses the opportunity to individualize your document and communicates less focus. Objectives of this type are often utilized by individuals who use the one-size-fits-all approach that should be avoided as mentioned. Individualizing or tailoring your resume for each employer is encouraged. Why not take the opportunity to let a potential employer know, even in a small way, that they are special and were selected by the applicant on purpose?

Another common practice in resume development is to include a brief summary of yourself as a professional. This is sometimes referred to and labeled as an Executive Summary or Professional Profile. If you decide to create one place it immediately following the objective. Two examples are provided of this component for your consideration.

Example 1

Executive Summary: Highly trained and licensed counseling professional with experience working in agency settings with individuals struggling with substance abuse issues

Example 2

Professional Profile: Certified Global Career Facilitator–Licensed Professional Counselor–Member, National Career Development Association

As you can see, an Executive Summary or Professional Profile is another opportunity to communicate information about yourself as an applicant. The information included could reflect requirements for the position that were included in the job posting or are qualities that the applicant wishes to highlight.

Education is often the next category of information you will share with the person(s) reading your resume. Many positions that counselors will seek require an advanced degree or license. Sorting applicants based on requirements of this type is common. Being able to note this information at a glance is usually desired and appreciated. Depending on your situation, you may be reporting a degree that is in progress or one that is completed. Either is appropriate with some minor adjustments for degrees in progress. For counselors, the same is true for reporting a credential or license. The information included on the resume is generally the full name of the degree, the name and location of the institution, and the year it was completed or the planned completion date. The same guideline generally applies for a credential with some possible differences such as whether or not it is current or active. Typically, you will include the name of the credential and the state or body that issued it. The following examples are provided for you.

Example 1

Education: Master of Education in School Counseling
Lamar University   2012 Beaumont, TX

Example 2

Education: Master of Education in School Counseling   Lamar University
Expected Completion: May 2012   Beaumont, TX

Example 1

Credentials: Licensed Professional Counselor, Texas 2012 to Current

The next category of information you will share is Skills. As you might expect, this category is viewed as very important in the field of professional counseling. You may choose to list your skills in bullets, lists, or short phrases. It is a good idea to construct the skills component with an eye to the job description. Include any skills you possess that are mentioned in the job description. Individuals that review resumes often create a sort of checklist in their minds or focus on a specific group of skills they consider or identify as essential to qualify for the position. In some cases, the same individual may have written the job description. Think about the skills you possess that directly relate to the position and be specific as possible. Two examples are provided for you.

Example 1

Skills:

Interviewing   Case Management   Individual/Group Counseling
Assessment   Microsoft Office   Electronic Medical Records

Example 2

Skills

- Experienced Interviewer
- Trained in CBT/REBT
- Assessment for alcohol/substance abuse

The last category of information is Experience. The information in this category may be directly related to the position or it may not. This category may present a challenge to some for reasons including limited, irrelevant experience, or nonexistent work experience. There are ways to address these situations. Limited experience may be expected or understood for beginning counselors. Irrelevant experience can still provide evidence of work ethic or employability. For example, employers may be faced with resumes from two equally well-trained new counselors. However, one may have worked in retail for several years, while the other has no other work experience. This seemingly irrelevant retail experience may demonstrate work ethic and employability and is worth including. In the case of nonexistent work experience, projects done while in school or during training can be presented as work-related experience. The goal is to communicate awareness of what is required to perform the job or position being sought. Some additional information can be provided in this area such as specifics about the previous position or tasks that were performed by you. Experiences that occurred in the distant past or within the last 10 years may not be as relevant as you might imagine and should be included only on a limited basis, with preference given to more current experience or activities. Consider the example that follows and think about how you can best present the information in a clear, organized manner. Common practice is to include the position title, the company or organization, the time spent in the position, and some information about the tasks related to the position.

Example 1

Experience: Intake Specialist National Care America

2012 to Current
Beaumont TX

- Intake interviews, creating client files, general reception
- Preparing written communication and directing incoming calls
- Use of Microsoft Office and electronic medical records system

The goal of the Experience section is to provide sufficient information to understand the nature of the position and some general tasks that were performed. This section helps to create a picture of you as an employee. Provide enough information to cover important details and to capture interest in your application. Be prepared to discuss the work you performed and think about how you can relate it to the position you are seeking. You will have that opportunity in the interview.

As mentioned earlier, resumes have changed over the years. Professional resumes are straightforward documents, conservative in appearance, streamlined for quick reading, and provide verifiable information about the applicant. They are not a life story. Additional categories of information can be included such as Awards or Service to share your accomplishments or your activities but should be related to the position you are seeking. The document should conclude with the phrase *References provided upon request* that is centered at the bottom of the page and generally italicized and bolded. In the past, professional references were often included on the resume. Current practice is to create a separate document with this information that may be uploaded or shared when requested. Professional references are discussed in a later section of this chapter.

Creating an organized, well-written resume is an important step in preparing for employment. A professional resume will serve as your introduction. An example of a complete resume containing the information discussed is included at the end of the chapter for your convenience.

Curriculum Vita

Curriculum vitae, CVs, or vitas may be viewed as an extended form of a resume and are typically found or required in higher education. A loose translation of the term curriculum vitae is life study. Doctoral graduates and others seeking a position as a faculty member are expected to provide a curriculum vitae. As with resumes, styles vary but most contain similar information. Unlike resumes, however, there is no guideline or recommendation regarding length. Remember, unlike a resume, a CV is a life study. Information found on most curriculum vitaes include your contact information, your education and credentials, professional affiliations, teaching experience, awards or related accomplishments, publications, presentations, grants received, and other scholarly activities, especially those related to the position you're seeking. The information should be factual and arranged in a logical manner. The document should be conservative in appearance, free of any errors, and neatly printed on good quality paper when hardcopies are required. It is a good idea to create a PDF of the document if allowed for electronic submission as the PDF will preserve formatting. Like resumes, this document should be consistently updated. Unlike resumes, this document should be titled Curriculum Vitae and centered at the top of the first page. Information about publications and presentations should be formatted in APA style beginning with the most current activity. Examples and templates can be found online, and many colleges or universities post the curriculum vitae of faculty members.

Since this type of document is typically many pages long, an example is not provided in this handbook. However, many of the same guidelines used in creating a professional resume apply to creating a vita. For example, the document should begin with your contact information as indicated in the outline provided. Some categories are considered optional. Information contained in the document should be organized and clearly labeled for easy reading.

Sample Outline:

Curriculum Vitae

Contact Information (aligned left or right; opposite name of institution if currently employed)

Education (include all degrees with terminal degree listed first with dates and granting institutions)

Credentials (licenses, certifications, and dates received)

Experience (relevant positions/institutions)

Professional Affiliations/Leadership

Awards (optional)

Teaching Experience

Publications

Presentations

Grants

Other Scholarly Activity (optional)

As you can see from this outline, a curriculum vitae is an expanded form of resume and the two have much in common. Additional categories of information should be created as needed. For example, you may wish to create a category such as Community Engagement or Collaboration. If you are a newly minted Counselor Educator, your vita may not be as full as you would like, but do not despair. You will have the opportunity to add to it. To maintain your position and seek tenure, you will be expected to do so on an annual basis.

Letters of Reference

Providing letters of reference is a common practice in many employment environments and application procedures. Like your other professional documents, you may be asked to submit them electronically. Alternately, some organizations prefer to send a link to the reference so that they can complete the reference form electronically. If providing hardcopies, follow the same guidelines discussed earlier with regard to paper quality and color.

One common error people make is to assume that someone is willing to give you a reference. Many times students will list the names of faculty members or former supervisors but did not ask that person first. It can be quite a shock to receive a reference call about someone who did not first speak with you about providing one. Therefore, it is recommended that you discuss the need of a letter of reference well in advance. Asking for a letter of reference on short notice, or after the fact, is not professional and is disrespectful of the individual's time. Naturally, you will want to ask for letters of reference from individuals who regard you in a positive light. It is important to be referred or endorsed by individuals who can speak to your abilities in relation to the position you are seeking. As you might imagine, these individuals are typically former employers, supervisors, teachers, or individuals who have known you for a period of time and can speak to your work ethic, skills, or character.

When possible, a letter of reference should be created on letterhead and signed by the individual providing the reference. Like letters of interest, the reference should include the title of the position for which you are applying along with the company or organization. Providing this information along with the position description or job posting to the person providing the reference is helpful. It may also be helpful to provide some sample text to the person completing the letter that they can customize. In that sample text, be specific about how your skills and abilities are a good fit for the position. In general, it is a good idea to collect three letters of reference. These letters are an additional opportunity to provide the potential employer with information about you as a potential employee.

Electronic Portfolios

Creating an electronic portfolio is another option you may consider. As previously mentioned, some counselor education programs will ask that you develop a portfolio along the way. Generally, these portfolios are an opportunity to showcase examples of your best work or range of experience. Professional portfolios have been utilized in education settings for some time. Another option at your disposal is creating a professional website. Although portfolios and websites may not be created with the same conservative approach as your professional documents, the style and format should be appropriate for professional work environments or settings.

If you choose to create an electronic portfolio, there is a variety of presentation software available for your use. Like resumes, companies or individuals can be hired to help you construct them. If your college or university has such systems in place, you will have access to them for a specific amount of time, typically 1 to 7 years.

The information you include in your electronic portfolio can range from the general to the specific. For example, an individual applying for a position as a school counselor may include examples of guidance lessons or character education presentations. An individual applying for a position as a clinical mental health counselor may include a presentation or research paper on therapeutic techniques as related to specific issues faced by specific client populations. Other types of information you may wish to consider including are certificates you have earned through additional training, awards presented to you, or published works.

The pervasiveness of computer technology may cause electronic portfolios to become a required component for job seekers like the common professional documents discussed in this chapter. Ease of access and portability is one benefit of electronic portfolios. In addition, being able to provide one to a potential employer may set you apart from other applicants.

Licensure and Certification

There is often some confusion surrounding the process of licensure and certification. The two are quite different although related. Both are important to counselors for a number of reasons including the shaping of your professional identity and employment options. Obtaining credentials beyond your degree is recommended.

Licensure within the profession of counseling is typically controlled by states and maintained through the rule of law. The primary purpose of these laws is to protect the public. Universities and colleges do not grant licenses but they do prepare you to meet most licensure requirements. States vary in their requirements although many are similar. Most states require you to possess a graduate level degree and pass an examination to obtain a license to legally provide counseling services (Sheperis & Sheperis, 2014). Details about the process of licensure within your state can usually be found online at state board websites. The American Counseling Association (ACA) is another excellent source for this type of information, and state-by-state requirements can be found on the ACA website at counseling.org. Part of your preparation for employment should include understanding the requirements of the state in which you intend to work.

Portability is another concern and should also be considered. According to Wheeler, Bertram, and Anderson (2008), momentum is building in the drive for portability of licensure and reciprocity. Current state laws require counselors to complete a licensure process or reapply in each state in which they wish to work often with additional requirements that must be met. Unfortunately, no nationally recognized license exists at this time for counselors. State law governs the type or title of the license as well. The most common professional designations are Licensed Professional Counselor (LPC), Licensed Mental Health Counselor (LMHC), and Licensed Clinical Mental Health Counselor (LCMHC).

Both licensure and certification can impact your prospects for future employment as stated earlier. Being licensed or certified in a specific area or specialty is not always a requirement for some jobs you might pursue. However, having both will increase your options and make you more valuable as a potential employee. Preparing to become certification and license eligible while in your training program is one way to prepare for future employment. Because licensure and certification increases your credibility and informs the public that you have met additional standards and specialized training beyond your academic preparation, successfully navigating these processes is one way that you can advocate for yourself and for the profession of counseling.

Professional examinations. Passing professional examinations is a common component of the credentialing process. Although state licensure requirements may vary, many states utilize the same professional examinations. Successfully preparing for and passing a professional examination is another way that you can prepare in advance for future employment. The most widely used professional examinations for counselors are the National Counselor Examination (NCE), the National Clinical Mental Health Counseling Examination (NCMHCE), and the National Certified School Counselor Examination (NCSCE). While these examinations share some content areas, they differ in design and format.

The NCE tests general content knowledge of the eight content domains and five related work behaviors (see Table 13.1) developed by the Council for Accreditation of Counseling and Related Educational Programs (CACREP). The examination consists of 200 multiple-choice questions assessing areas directly related to the practice of counseling and is available in paper and pencil format as well as computer-based administration. Examinees have 4 hours to complete the NCE.

Table 13.1   CACREP Content Domains and Work Behaviors

Content Domains	Work Behaviors
Professional Orientation and Ethical Practice	Fundamentals of Counseling
Social and Cultural Foundations	Assessment and Career Counseling
Human Growth and Development	Group Counseling
Career and Lifestyle Development	Programmatic and Clinical Intervention
Helping Relationships	Professional Practice Issues
Group work	
Appraisal	
Research and Program Development	

The NCMHCE differs markedly from the NCE. The examination is designed around clinical scenarios and requires the examinee to engage in decision-making processes and is based on three general domains (see Table 13.2). The NCMHCE consists of 10 clinical scenarios, and examinees are given 4 hours in which to complete the examination.

The NCSCE combines the style and format of the NCE and the NCMHCE. The examination consists of seven scenarios or cases designed to address five specific areas of school counselor knowledge related to the practice of school counseling (See Table 13.3), requiring the examinee to gather information and make decisions. In addition to the case scenarios, the examination contains 40 multiple-choice questions drawn from the NCE. This approach yields information about the examinee's content knowledge and decision-making abilities. Like the NCE and NCMHCE, individuals taking the NCSCE are given 4 hours in which to complete the examination.

Many graduate-level counseling students are eligible to take the NCE after completing approximately 85% of their master's program through the National Board of Certified Counselors (NBCC). Information about taking the NCE before graduation can be found at the NBCC website, nbcc.org. Individuals applying to take the NCMHCE or the NCSCE

Table 13.2 NCMHCE Content Areas

Assessment and Diagnosis
Counseling and Psychotherapy
Administration, Consultation, and Supervision

Table 13.3 School Counseling Knowledge Areas

School Counseling Program Delivery
Assessment and Career Development
Program Administration and Professional Development
Counseling Process, Concepts, and Applications
Family-School Involvements

must complete a master's degree before taking these examinations. A wide range of popular study materials for these examinations are available for purchase online, however, free study guides and sample questions are available as well. Successful completion of your counseling program will help prepare you for these examinations. Additional study or review is always encouraged and some graduate programs offer prep courses that help students prepare for these exams. Conduct some preliminary research of these examinations and the study materials available to you and develop a study strategy. Consider incorporating these suggestions from Erford, Hays, Crockett, and Miller (2011) into your strategy:

1. Do not leave any items unanswered. There are no penalties for using your best judgment if you are unsure of the correct answer.

2. Read each item and the possible responses completely before making your selection.

3. Answer the items you know first and then return to those items you need to think about before making your selection.

4. Keep track of your time and stay on task.

5. Stay cool and remind yourself that the goal is a passing score not a perfect one. You can afford to miss some items and still pass the exam.

Engage in self-care and get some rest before the exam. It is important to stay hydrated so that you can think clearly and to eat something so that your energy level remains constant over the 4 hours you are given.

Professional attire. Years ago, the staff writers of a popular television sitcom created an episode in which one of the characters accidentally received an expensive designer suit that did not belong to the character. Through one comic circumstance after another, the character who was previously unemployed was hired to fill a high-level position based on the impression made by wearing the expensive suit. Hilarity aside, important messages were conveyed. One underlying message in the farce was that individuals can be influenced by appearances. Another underlying message is that one's appearance, in this case one's clothing, can make a favorable or unfavorable impression. One by one, the other characters in the comedy formed impressions, made assumptions, and attributed certain desirable qualities to the individual once he was professionally attired.

Conventional wisdom informs us that one aspect of impressions, especially first impressions, is that you only get one chance to make them. In addition, there is evidence that an individual's clothing or attire can have an effect on the wearer in a number of ways including performance and level of perceived competence (Adam & Galinsky, 2012). What should that tell you? Dressing appropriately and professionally, whether you are already employed or seeking employment, is important and it matters.

What constitutes professional attire? The answer to this question may depend on a number of factors including your work setting, your position and responsibilities, and the image you wish to project. In many circles, professional attire for both men and women can be captured in one word, suits. Styles change over the years, but suits remain the preferred and expected choice of professionals. You may already have an idea of how individuals employed in a specific agency or area dress for work. Keep in mind that you are an applicant and not one of the team—yet.

Generally speaking, trends should be avoided and a conservative business-like approach adopted. If you would wear the outfit on a date, it is probably not appropriate for an interview. Color selection is important and may be slightly modified according to seasonal changes. Colors such as navy, black, charcoal gray, and shades of brown and olive are considered conservative and appropriate for professional attire. Women may choose either slacks or skirts. Shirts and blouses should also be confined to conservative colors with white or cream being the most common choice. Trendy collars and plunging necklines are not appropriate for interviews. Consider where you want the focus to be. Ties and scarves should be conservative as well, avoiding bright colors, themes, or distracting patterns. To some, this may seem drab or boring. Conservative looks rely on cut and fit to communicate style. It is important that your suit fit you well and not be too tight or too short. It should be modern and project an air of competence and forward thinking. With regard to shoes, they should be clean or polished and in good condition. Black or brown is typically the best choice for men. For women, close-toed shoes and lower heels are recommended. Good hygiene, including clean nails, hair, and teeth should also be addressed.

The overall look you want to communicate is one of professional competence, appropriateness, and confidence. The clothes you select should be comfortable but not casual; conservative but not flashy or trendy. As mentioned earlier, your attire can affect the way you feel and influence the impression others form of you as a potential employee.

As you might imagine, much has been written on the subject of professional attire in popular literature including magazines and books. A colleague once stated that she paid attention to lists of do's and don'ts in these publications to ensure that she was not on the don't list! As a way to summarize this section, a list of suggested do's and don'ts for professional attire is included in Table 13.4.

Interviewing

The interview is really where the rubber meets the road. Interviewing can make even the best of us a little anxious! It would be great if potential employers could see that you were the perfect candidate without having to go through the interview process but that rarely, if ever, happens. It may help to keep in mind that interviews can be viewed as a two-way street. As you are being interviewed, assessed, and evaluated, so is the potential employer. Careful research, planning, and preparation are terrific ways to lessen anxiety and ensure that you put your best foot forward. Some believe that interviewing is an art form and others believe that it is all about strategy. The devil is definitely in the details.

Consider purchasing a small portfolio or briefcase to carry your documents in when interviewing. Large purses, backpacks, binders, and large key rings et cetera should be left behind if at all possible. Cell phones

Table 13.4 Do's and Don'ts of Professional Attire

Do	Don't
Prepare and plan your attire in advance	Leave clothing selection until the last minute
Choose conservative colors	Choose trendy outfits in bold colors
Pay attention to fit and cut	Wear tight or revealing clothing or clothing more suited to an evening out
Dress appropriately for weather or season	
Select shoes in dark or neutral tones with closed toes and lower heels	Wear strong perfume/cologne, excessive or distracting jewelry, complicated hairstyles, or overly dramatic makeup

could be included on the list but opinions vary on this point. At the very least, it is recommended to turn them off before you arrive for the interview. Include a good quality ink pen or two as well as some additional paper or notepad should you need them.

Researching your potential employer and learning all you can about the position you are after is an important component of any successful employment strategy. Most of us have heard the expression "knowledge is power." The expression is especially true with regard to interviewing. Information gained in your research can help you answer questions that may be asked in the interview and will give you an advantage over other less informed applicants.

Conducting research and utilizing what you learned to help shape your answers to the interview questions is an excellent way to communicate interest in the position. Websites are a great place to start. It is safe to say that most agencies and organizations will have an online presence. On the websites, you can typically find information about the company or organization's goals, missions, services, and client populations. Think about the skills you possess and how you would apply them on the job.

Any realistic strategy for seeking employment would include plans for what to wear to that all important interview. Naturally, you want to make a positive first impression. It is also important that you are comfortable and able to perform at your best. Selecting the right clothes to wear will allow you to stress less, be more effective, and make it to the finish line.

Sufficient forethought and planning is required to be as successful as possible. While practicing your skills will not make you perfect, it can make you better. It is a good idea to practice such things as introducing yourself, a presentation you may make, or answers to potential questions out loud. Saying these things out loud can make them more familiar to you. In doing so, you may catch mistakes or decide to phrase something differently.

Additional resources on interviewing and preparing for employment can be found on a number of professional websites. Many of the websites also include information on conducting job searches and creating your professional documents. It is important to do your research and utilize your resources. Guides to success (see Table 13.5) and primary challenges (see Table 13.6) are provided for your use. Finally, a list of suggested websites is included at the end of the chapter for your convenience.

Table 13.5 Guides to Success

Develop a Job Search Strategy	It is never too early to consider the type of career that interests you and to look into schools, agencies, and organizations that fit the bill.
Cover Letters	Tailor your cover letter to the specific job requirements listed by the potential employer.
Resumes	Keep resumes brief, to the point, and conservatively styled.
Letters of Reference	Ask if someone will serve as a reference well in advance of needing a letter from them.
Licensures and Certification	Prepare now for the types of licensure and certifications that will benefit your future career path.
Professional Exams	Plan to take all professional exams that may impact you even if they are not required for state licensure.
Professional Attire	Be conservative, neutral, and modest in your dress for interviews.
Interviewing	Come prepared with evidence of your work and questions for your potential employer that show you understand the position.

Table 13.6 Primary Challenges

Develop a Job Search Strategy	Don't wait until the last minute to research various career options.	
Cover Letters	Avoid boilerplate language or lengthy letters.	
Resumes	Don't forget to add work experience that demonstrates work ethic.	
Letters of Reference	Be careful not to assume that someone will give you a glowing reference.	

Table 13.6

Licensures and Certification	If you are not licensed, make it clear that you are on the path to licensure.	
Professional Exams	Be sure to study for these exams. Even the best students struggle with professional exams.	
Professional Attire	Don't assume you can dress like the employees when you go for an interview. Dress up, rather than down.	
Interviewing	You will need to be comfortable selling yourself. Do your research and practice.	

Summary

Becoming gainfully employed in a satisfying counseling position takes more than good luck and timing. Developing a strategy toward ultimate employment is critical. Beginning graduate students can start the process now by developing a vision for future employment, a resume, and a portfolio. Advanced students ready for permanent positions can develop their reference sources and prepare for interviews. The steps provided in this chapter will help students at all developmental levels prepare to reach the ultimate goal of successful employment in a position they desire.

References

Adam, H., & Galinsky, A. D. (2012). Enclothed cognition. *Journal of Experimental Social Psychology, 48*(4), 918–925.

Erford, B. T., Hays, D. G., Crockett, S., & Miller, E. M. (2011). *Mastering the national counselor examination and the counselor preparation comprehensive examination.* Upper Saddle River, NJ: Pearson Education.

Sheperis, D. S., & Sheperis, C. J. (2014). *Clinical mental health counseling: Fundamentals of applied practice.* Upper Saddle River, NJ: Pearson.

University of Washington. (2015). *Disabilities, opportunities, internetworking, and technology: Key elements of a cover letter*. Retrieved from https://www.washington.edu/doit/key-elements-cover-letter

Wheeler, A. M., Bertram, B., & Anderson, B. S. (2008). *The counselor and the law: A guide to legal and ethical practice*. Arlington, VA: American Counseling Association.

14

The Evolution of Counselor Training and Future of the Counseling Profession

Carl J. Sheperis

Chapter Overview

This chapter provides the culmination of your work preparing to be an online counseling student. In this chapter, we will move beyond the practicalities of being an online student and look specifically at how the future of the counseling profession fits with your decision to pursue an online degree. We will cover the development of online education; the growth of these programs; and the biases against online program graduates. To that end, we will help prepare you for addressing these biases with friends, families, and most importantly, employers. Finally, we discuss the future of online education and trends to come.

Learning Outcomes

After reading this chapter, you will be able to

- Understand the advancement of online learning
- Examine myths and facts related to online learning
- Analyze trends in professional counseling
- Evaluate market demands for professional counselors
- Identify changes in regulation that impact counselors

Introduction

You have made the choice to join an online education opportunity—congratulations! You are willing to put in the necessary sweat-equity in order to become a counselor. That wording is intentional—you may get degrees in other programs, but in this program you do more than just get a degree in counseling, you truly become! This program will be life changing for you, and because of it, you will go on to facilitate life changes for others.

Higher education is changing. What was typical even 5 or 10 years ago has changed dramatically today. As students in the most rapidly changing model of higher education, fully online education, you are on the cutting edge of this change. Because of this, you will need to be aware of the evolution of online learning and what is projected in the coming years. This knowledge will help you educate those who are less enlightened than you and may not value the opportunities offered by an online program.

Online Education

Opportunities for online education have exploded over the years as more and more programs have moved into the distance education model. Your experience in online education will be substantially different from when the concept first emerged. Originally, distance learning was conducted using a correspondence model. At that time, students would receive a packet of information and complete the packet, mail it back, and get another packet. Wow, we have come a long way!

Part of the change has come in the global advent of the use of Internet. In 2005, there were approximately 1 billion Internet users (Maples and Han, 2008). In 2015, that number has almost tripled to 2.92 billion

(Statistica, 2014). Chances are, you are a US-based student reading this text. You might assume that the United States has the most Internet users out of that number. However, the highest Internet use is actually in China, with almost 3 times the users of the United States (Statistica, 2013). However, current projections are that online education programs will soon outnumber traditional education models in the United States (Keeton, 2004; Tallent-Runnels et al., 2006).

Online Counselor Education

In counselor education, the trend has moved a bit more slowly. Many programs began as traditional brick-and-mortar programs and dipped their toes into the online world slowly. In our experience, taking a program from brick and mortar to fully online is a challenging process. Many programs offer hybrid or blended courses where at least a portion of the content is delivered in an online format. Others offer some classes fully online. When a program makes a commitment to deliver the entire curriculum fully online, the program is joining the ranks of technological innovation. In addition, faculty in those programs report an increase in program quality by making the shift to online provision (Watson, 2014). You have chosen an innovative program—again, congratulations!

The fully online model is appealing to students who desire the flexibility and portability of the old correspondence model but also want the technological advancement that has occurred since the development of that model. As an example, students who may need to move during their program or who live far from a traditional campus can still participate in a graduate education program. Students who live near a campus but are working and raising families are also finding the online program as a desirable option. As you can see, your online cohort or class will be made up of a lot of different types of students who are choosing this option for various reasons.

As unique and wonderful as online counseling programs are, online education has received its fair share of criticism over the years. Twenty years ago, the counseling profession believed that online graduate training was impossible (and it may have been at that time) for producing competent professional counselors. Counseling students had to sell themselves to practicum and internship sites that may never have heard of or didn't trust the online model. Today, thousands of counselors graduate from online programs. Even though online programs have become part of the mainstream for graduate education, there are still individuals who have biases against this model. These personal and institutional biases impact graduates of online programs seeking employment and licensure. This chapter will help you to address the biases with confidence.

Biases Against Online Education

Online programs have taken a hit in the public eye in recent years. Largely due to unscrupulous, undergraduate or certificate diploma mills, the public perception of online programs has not always been positive. You have probably heard these stories yourself and may even have had to overcome your own doubt about online learning. Many students tell us that they find themselves defending their online degree choice with family and friends, not just potential employers. The perception is slowly shifting, however, with employers now acknowledging that when students are equally prepared, having an online degree is not viewed as a deficit (Society for Human Resource Management, 2010). Let's take a look at some of the myths and facts about online education listed in Table 14.1.

As a graduate of an online program, you will have to be well versed in the benefits and drawbacks to your model of preparation and will also have to be able to discuss how online preparation is the cutting edge model. You may even need to be able to project the evolution of counselor preparation in order to legitimize the format to those who continue to be naysayers. Our goal in this chapter is to provide you with a conversation that can help educate others about the quality of your online degree and to help others to understand the ongoing evolution of higher education. Let's take a look at the rationale for training as many counselors as possible.

Changes in Higher Education and Need for More Health-Related Professionals

As graduate students entering a master's in counseling program, it is essential that you not only understand the climate of online education but that you also understand the climate of health care. Regardless of initial specialization area, many counselors eventually seek additional credentials to practice independently. Because of this phenomenon, all counselors should be familiar with the overall professional marketplace. Counselors are part of a larger group of helping professionals that includes

Table 14.1   Myths and Facts of Online Education

Myth	Fact
Online education is in the future.	Online education is right now!
"Real" schools don't offer online degrees!	Even the dean of Harvard Business School had to retract his assertion that they would never go online; Harvard now offers a host of fully online programs (Byrne, 2014).
Students in online programs don't build networks and connections like those in traditional programs.	Students in online programs often develop national networks that far exceed the professional reach of traditional programs.
Online students don't learn the same content as students in traditional classrooms.	There is no difference in online students learning outcomes and traditional classroom student learning outcomes (Redpath, 2012).
Online degrees are only for people of privilege.	The majority of online degree holders are minorities (University of Phoenix, 2011).
Faculty who teach online are less qualified.	Faculty in accredited online programs have the same qualifications and credentials as traditional program faculty. In fact, many of them are *more* qualified having the time to operate private practices in addition to teaching.

social workers, psychologists, case managers, and others. Despite the number of subgroups that make up helping professionals, there is still a shortage of health care workers. Let's take a look at why that is.

Increasing Demand for Health Care

Several changes to health care coverage in recent years have impacted the demand and opportunities for residents of the United States to receive health care. The Mental Health Parity Act of 2008 required mental health needs to be covered at the same level as physical health needs by insurance providers (Civic Impulse, 2015). This equity bill increased client access to mental health and substance abuse treatment by making them eligible under insurance. Consequently, client numbers accessing these services increased.

Adding to these numbers is the impact of the Affordable Care Act. The Affordable Care Act increased opportunities for adults and children to be served by Medicaid and lifted barriers to access for others (Patient Protection and Affordable Care Act, 2010). Like the Mental Health Parity Act, these legislative changes allowed access to health care that previously was not possible, thus increasing the demand for services. In fact, the number of individuals eligible for mental health services increased by 20% in January 2015.

Inadequate Numbers of Health Related Professionals

As the number of clients and patients grows, and the demand for trained professionals increases, the actual number of trained professionals is not keeping up with the demand. Here are some statistics that will help you see the problem. In 1980, the United States had about 220 health care workers per every 100,000 people. By the year 2000, that ratio had dropped to 158 health care workers for every 100,000 people. According to the Paraprofessional Healthcare Institute, by 2020 the nation will need 220 health care workers per 100,000 people, which means 1.1 million additional direct-care workers, including counselors (Association of Schools of Public Health, 2008). These numbers impact school counselors, clinical mental health counselors, rehabilitation counselors, and other specialty areas of training. We know that the counseling profession is poised to help address these shortages in health care. In fact, the Bureau of Labor Statistics predicts a 30% growth in mental health counselors between 2006 and 2016 (Institute of Medicine, 2008).

Increasing Demand for School Counselors

Mental health counselors aren't the only area where increased service providers are needed. The American School Counselor Association (ASCA) recommends a 250 student per 1 counselor ratio as the ideal for the school counseling model to be effective (ASCA, 2012). However, the most recent numbers for a national average show that the actual ratio is closer to 470 students per counselor with some states coming in at 700, 800, or over 1,000 students per counselor (ASCA, 2011). You can see how out of line the actual ratios are with the best practice ratios. Finally, the Bureau of Labor Statistics (2015) projects a 12% growth or higher in school counseling jobs in the coming years but cautions that the actual placement of school counselors will likely be far lower than the need due to budget cuts in school funding.

So what do all of these numbers mean? Essentially, you want to be a counselor, and there simply aren't enough of them. As a result, you have broad opportunities in the world of practice. Second, you chose an online education program, which is an innovative approach to meeting the health care shortage outlined in these numbers. Finally, you may be in a position to educate seasoned health care professionals and entities as to the incredible merits of an online education to meet this national shortage.

Increase in CACREP Accreditation of Online Programs

Students in traditional or online counseling programs should be familiar with the Council for Accreditation of Counseling and Related Educational Programs (CACREP), which accredits counseling master's and doctoral degree programs offered by colleges and universities in the United States and around the world (CACREP, 2014a). Many of those accredited programs are land based, but more and more frequently the programs CACREP accredits are fully online counselor education degree programs. Researchers have studied the relationship between accreditation and success on a licensure and credentialing exam (National Counseling Exam) and found that graduates of CACREP programs perform better than graduates of non-CACREP programs (CACREP, 2014b). When a program seeks accreditation, the program is showing a commitment to the highest academic standards in the profession. CACREP standards are reflected in many state licensure laws, and graduates of CACREP programs can work within the Veteran's Administration. As such, it is a show of quality when a program applies for and receives this designation.

As of this writing, CACREP accredits hundreds of programs in hundreds of universities but only accredits 24 fully online programs in 12 universities (CACREP, 2015). Many of these online programs are housed within traditional land-based universities but some are in fully online university settings. Some online programs are for profit, while others are part of the state university system. Some online programs are faith based, while others are secular. As you can see, although there are fewer online programs than there are land-based programs, there are a lot of options when selecting an accredited online counseling program. Even if your program is not currently accredited, chances are that it is seeking accreditation or planning to do so.

Growth in Traditional Institutions Offering Online Formats

The face of higher education is changing. Long gone are the days of the new graduate student who goes to school full time, lives in the university town, and holds an assistantship or part-time job. Most of the graduate students we have worked with have probably been a lot like you, working, with a family or other commitments, and perhaps far from a university setting.

Students enrolled in online programs are growing. The number of students taking at least one online course rose from 1.6 million in Fall 2002 to 7.1 million in Fall 2012 (DiRienzo & Lilly, 2014). In a College Board study, 65% of all colleges and universities reported incorporating online learning as a primary component in their strategic plan. The next increase is in fully online programs. In April 2013, Penn State announced a $20 million investment into its online operation to support their plan to grow online enrollment from 12,000 to 45,000 students by 2023 (American Distance Education Consortium, 2014).

Employer Stigma

What is likely to raise questions from employers about your online degree program when you go for an interview? First of all, you may attend a fully online program that began as a land based program. If that land based program is more than 300 miles from your home, your prospective employer may wonder how you were able to attend! This is an easy explanation of the role of online learning to clarify how you could matriculate from a program so far away. Conversely, if you attended a program that does not have a land-based campus, your employer may ask where the university is located. Because online-only schools can have the false perception of being less rigorous (Phillips, 2013), you will need to be able to speak to that. Finally, if your program is not accredited, you may encounter questions. Find out why the program is not accredited. It may be that the program is pursuing CACREP accreditation but is simply still in the process.

Preparing Yourself for an Interview

As graduate students, you will engage in interviews for your practicum and internship experiences as well as for employment opportunities. In an online program, you may be the only student from your university or program in the area. Given this reality, how will you prepare yourself for these interviews? The following are some preparation guidelines to help get you started.

1. Do your homework in advance. Know the agency, its mission and philosophy, and how you can be an asset to the site.

2. Know your university and program. Read the mission and philosophy of your program. Know how it matches the site you are applying to.

3. Know if your program is accredited and if so, by whom.

4. If a local counseling program exists in your area, do a coursework comparison. Have you been trained at a similar or higher level than your competitors?

5. If you are a mental health counselor, look up regional data related to health care provision and, more importantly, health care shortages.

6. If you are a school counselor, know the counselor: student ratios for the school you are applying to and know how you can impact that ratio.

7. Bring your talking points. Be prepared to discuss your training, experience, and how that compares to land-based programs.

8. If your program requires residencies and/or taped sessions for supervision, be ready to talk about those realities. Employers like to know that you have been observed in your clinical work.

9. Be open and nondefensive. Not everyone is as enlightened as you are about online learning. You may be the only face of online learning these employers see!

Sample Interview

Now that you are well versed on the history of online education in general, and of online counselor education specifically, let's take a look at how an interview might proceed. We are going to offer you two examples. The first will be a less-than-desirable approach to interviewing. You might call this one what NOT to do!

Interviewer: Hi Joe, thanks for coming in. I understand you are looking for an internship placement?

Joe Student: Yes, sir. Thanks for having me in. I am finishing up my degree program to be a counselor and need to get some hours so I can graduate.

Interviewer: OK, so you are looking for an internship?

Joe Student: Yeah, I guess so. They just told me I need hours.

Interviewer: Hmmm, well I see you are enrolled at Avatar State University. I'm not familiar with them. What can you tell me about the program?

Joe Student: Well, not much. I just knew I wanted to be a counselor and saw their ad, so I've been taking classes and went to some residencies.

Interviewer: They have a campus several hours away from here. How do you manage that program?

Joe Student: I am an online student. We don't have to go to campus.

Interviewer: Is the program accredited?

Joe Student: I'm not sure.

Interviewer: How are your skills assessed?

Joe Student: Well I sent some tapes in so I guess I'm ok.

Interviewer: I graduated some years ago myself and am not very familiar with online programs in counseling. Can you tell me about your preparation? How do I know you get the same type of training as the students from State U that intern here all the time?

Joe Student: Oh, I am trained well. Just put me to work and you'll see!

Interviewer: Hmmmm . . . maybe I could talk to your internship or field experience coordinator. Who would that be?

Joe Student: I don't really know, but my last teacher was Dr. Awesome. I'm sure she'd talk to you.

Interviewer: Great! Can I have her contact information?

Joe Student: I don't have it. I'll have to get it for you.

Interviewer: I don't know, Joe. I just don't trust online programs.

Joe Student: OK, sir. I understand. Let me know if anything does come open.

Joe Student leaves the interview determined to call his advisor and let her know that he can't get an internship anywhere! Clearly, Joe could have benefited by taking some of the suggestions we discussed earlier in the chapter. Let's see how our next student fares:

Star Student: Hi, I'm Star. I'm a master's student at Asynchronous University. Thank you for taking the time to meet with me!

Interviewer: Nice to meet you, Star! Tell me about the program at Asynchronous University.

Star Student: I am in a 60-hour Clinical Mental Health Counseling program. We just received CACREP accreditation. I have taken all of my content courses and am now ready for my internship. All of my coursework is online, but I have completed two academic residencies in person so that I could build my skills and be assessed by faculty. Because of my performance at residency and in the courses, I have been moved onto Field Experiences. I am a member of our chapter of Chi Sigma Iota, which is the Counseling International Honor Society and am looking to specialize in child and adolescent counseling.

Interviewer: Great, Star. I have never had an intern from an online university. We usually take interns from State University here in town.

Star Student: I looked at State when I first started my master's, and they have a great program, but I was interested in continuing to work full time. An online degree that was accredited was a better fit for me. One of the reasons I picked your agency is because of your social justice philosophy. I am passionate about child and adolescent care and really appreciate how your program mission targets this underserved population in our area. Can you tell me about a typical workday for your interns?

Interviewer: You sound like a great fit, Star. Let me tell you how our internship program works . . .

Star Student leaves the interview and calls her advisor to say that the preparation for finding a placement worked. She feels like she could get an internship anywhere!

So, what is the difference? Star Student knew how her program compared to others, had a career plan, and knew her site. This preparation served her well! We hope you will take the approach that Star

Student took and do your homework about your program, your training, and your site before any interview.

Changes in Practice of Professional Counseling

Once you complete your interview process, you will have to be prepared for upcoming changes in the counseling profession. Since counseling began as a profession, the counseling process has been somewhat static. In most cases, the process has involved a counselor sitting in a chair and talking with a client sitting in a chair across from them. Of course, there have been some variations such as in-home counseling or adventure counseling, but these have been alternative formats rather than common practice. For the first time in history, the counseling process is evolving across the board and your world of practice will look quite different from what it looks like even today. In just the last few years, innovations like telehealth have become widely adopted in counseling and behavioral health care; more counselor education programs are using distance supervision models; and credentials have been developed for counselors who provide online services. We will review each of these innovations and how they impact the future of the counseling profession.

Telehealth. Over the last decade, the medical profession has increasingly used telehealth to provide clinical health care from a distance. In general, telehealth involves the use of electronic information and telecommunications technologies for any health-related service provision. Telehealth services have been used primarily for health-related education but in recent years advancements in technology have allowed for more physician–patient interaction via technology with the result being additional medical services being provided at a distance. Along with the increase in medical services, counseling has begun to offer a wider variety of telehealth behavioral health care or telemental health services. A number of behavioral health care service provider networks have emerged and licensed counselors can now join a large practice group that provides telemental health services at a distance. In just the last few years, a number of telemental health organizations have emerged and there are innumerable continuing education training options now available that can add to your current training pursuit. Some organizations are also offering credentials or certificates in telemental health. Clearly, the telemental health field continues to evolve and the process should be even more widespread by the time you complete your graduate degree and the manner in which it is delivered will continue to evolve.

Distance Supervision. Counseling programs began to explore options for providing distance supervision over 20 years ago. While telephone supervision has been a practice for many years, the evolution of computers has moved distance supervision from the telephone to computer-based technologies. In the early days of Internet technology, distance supervision involved online chat functions only. Today, there are numerous video options that allow for a highly functional and interactive process in real time. As technology continues to evolve, the opportunities for supervision at a distance will continue to increase. Of course, your ability to participate in these innovations will depend on your Internet capabilities. The more complex these distance supervision processes become, the more Internet bandwidth they will require. We suggest that you already begin to plan for the distance supervision at the end of your program. Technology innovations occur so rapidly that we can predict with full confidence that there will be completely new innovations by the time you reach that point and that the process will be even more involved than it is today. It is interesting to consider how distance supervision will continue to evolve over the next 5 years. The possibilities are endless.

Distance Credentialed Counselor (DCC)

The counseling profession has recognized that technology is now a reality within counseling practice. As a professional counselor, you will be able to pursue recognition as a Distance Credentialed Counselor (DCC) through the National Board for Certified Counselors. This credential can provide you with a means for demonstrating to the public that you have advanced training in providing counseling services through electronic or technology-assisted means (e.g., telecounseling, videoconferencing, or other technology-assisted approaches). The ways in which you can use distance counseling methods in your counseling practice will continue to evolve, and we will discover new and innovative ways to help clients through technology.

Imagining the Counseling Profession in 20 Years

As we stated earlier in the chapter, the process of counseling hasn't changed much since the profession began. The development of distance counseling procedures such as telemental health are revolutionary compared to the traditional face-to-face process that has been in place for decades. The manner in which counseling services are delivered will continue to evolve as the need for counseling services continues to outpace the number of providers available. Because the demand for services will continue to grow, so will the need for new and innovative delivery methods. While it may be hard to imagine, consider the possibility that technology will evolve to a degree where virtual reality becomes as vivid and real as typical reality. You might be conducting counseling sessions in a virtual reality room that has your degrees and credentials on the walls. The experiences in that office look and feel like they would if you were in an actual office. You and your clients are even able to have emotional responses based on the experiences that occur in real time. You might be able to tap into numerous senses during your virtual work and also be able to track the emotional and physiological reactions of your clients. You might even have a virtual waiting room outside of your office that helps your clients to enter a relaxing state through virtual bio/neuro-feedback while preparing for their therapy sessions. That is one way that we see the future of counseling . . . how do you see it?

Summary

Counseling is an evolving profession. The fact that you are pursuing this portion of your professional preparation via an online process is evidence that we are on the cusp of new methods of professional counseling. No doubt, you will participate in the developments as you enter into professional practice. In order to be successful, you should be willing to adapt and to innovate with the profession. We hope that you will not just be a part of the changes but that you will be the next generation of leaders in counseling. As a graduate student, it was hard to imagine past the idea of having a job as a professional counselor. However, my professors encouraged me to look beyond the role that was in front of me and to take an active role in counseling organizations, advocacy, and to pursue leadership opportunities. I encourage you to do the same. As Ghandi said, "Be the change you want to see in the world." You have already taken the first steps.

References

American Distance Education Consortium. (2014). Quality framework for online education. Retrieved from www.adec.edu/earmyu/SLOANC~41.html

American School Counselor Association. (2011). *Student to school counselor ratio 2010–2011*. Retrieved from http://www.civicenterprises.net/MediaLibrary/Docs/counseling_at_a_crossroads.pdf

American School Counselor Association. (2012). *The ASCA national model: A framework for school counseling programs* (3rd ed.). Alexandria, VA: Author.

Association of Schools of Public Health. (2008). *ASPH policy brief: Confronting the public health workforce crisis*. Retrieved from http://www.healthpolicyfellows.org/pdfs/ConfrontingthePublicHealthWorkforceCrisisbyASPH.pdf

Bureau of Labor Statistics. (2015). U.S. Department of Labor, *Occupational Outlook Handbook, 2014–15 Edition*, School and Career Counselors. Retrieved from http://www.bls.gov/ooh/community-and-social-service/school-and-career-counselors.htm

Byrne, J. A. (2014). Why Harvard Business School's dean says he was proven wrong about online ed. Retrieved from https://www.linkedin.com/pulse/20141104175437-17970806-why-harvard-business-school-s-dean-says-he-was-proven-wrong-on-online-ed

CACREP. (2015). Directory [Data file]. Retrieved from http://www.cacrep.org/directory/

Civic Impulse. (2015). H.R. 6983—110th Congress: Paul Wellstone and Pete Domenici Mental Health Parity and Addiction Equity Act of 2008. Retrieved from https://www.govtrack.us/congress/bills/110/hr6983

Council for Accreditation of Counseling and Related Educational Programs (2014a). What is CACREP? Retrieved from http://www.cacrep.org/

Council for Accreditation of Counseling and Related Educational Programs (2014b). Directory. Retrieved from http://www.cacrep.org/directory/page/2/

DiRienzo, C., & Lilly, G. (2014). Online versus face-to-face: Does delivery method matter for undergraduate business school learning? *Business Education & Accreditation, 6*(1), 1–11.

Institute of Medicine. (2008). *Retooling for an aging America*. Washington, DC: The National Academies Press.

Keeton, M. T. (2004). Best online instructional practices: Report of Phase I of an ongoing study. *Journal of Asynchronous Learning Networks, 8*, 75–100.

Maples, M. F., & Han, S. (2008). Cybercounseling in the United States and South Korea: Implications for counseling college students of the millennial generation and the networked generation. *Journal of Counseling & Development, 86*, 178–183.

Patient Protection and Affordable Care Act, 42 U.S.C. § 18001 (2010).

Phillips, V. (2013). *Are online degrees respected?* Retrieved from http://www.getedu cated.com/careers/318-should-i-tell-employers-i-earned-my-degree-online

Redpath, L. (2012). Confronting the bias against on-line learning in management education. *Academy of Management Learning & Education, 11*(1), 125–140. doi:10.5465/amle.2010.0044

Society for Human Resource Management. (2010). *Hiring practices and attitudes: Traditional vs. online degree credentials SHRM poll.* Retrieved from http://www.shrm.org/research/surveyfindings/articles/pages/hiringpracticesandatti tudes.aspx

Statistica. (2013). Countries with the highest number of Internet users 2013. Retrieved from http://www.statista.com/statistics/262966/number-of-internet-users-in-selected-countries/

Statistica. (2014). Global number of worldwide Internet users 2000–2014. Retrieved from http://www.statista.com/statistics/273018/number-of-internet-users-worldwide/

Tallent-Runnels, M. K., Thomas, J. A., Lan, W. Y., Cooper, S., Ahern, T. C., Shaw, S. M., & Liu, X. (2006). Teaching courses online: A review of the research. *Review of Educational Research, 76,* 93–135. doi:10.3102/00346543076001093

University of Phoenix. (2011). Academic annual report 2011. Retrieved from http://cdn.assets-phoenix.net/content/dam/altcloud/doc/about_uopx/academic-annual-report-2011.pdf

Watson, J. C. (2014). Online learning and the development of counseling self-efficacy beliefs. *The Professional Counselor.* Retrieved from http://tpcjournal.nbcc.org/online-learning-and-the-development-of-counseling-self-efficacy-beliefs/

Additional Resources

American Counseling Association. (2010). *Mental health parity FAQs.* Retrieved from http://www.counseling.org/docs/public-policy-resources-reports/mental-health-parity-faqs.pdf?sfvrsn=0

American Counseling Association. (2011a). *2011 Statistics on mental health professions.* Retrieved from http://www.counseling.org/docs/public-policy-resources-reports/mental_health_professions-_statistics_2011.pdf?sfvrsn=2

American Counseling Association. (2011b). *The effectiveness and need for professional counseling services.* Retrieved from http://www.counseling.org/docs/public-policy-resources-reports/effectiveness_of_and_need_for_counseling_2011.pdf?sfvrsn=2

Index

Practicum. *See also* Field experience
   hours required, 249
   student experiences in, 253–254
Preparation for employment. *See*
   Employment, preparing for
Presentations
   online, 22
   software for, 22, 24, 25
   video clips and photographs in,
     27–28
Presentation software, 22, 24, 25
   electronic portfolios and, 286
Preventative approach to invalidation,
   162–163
Prezi presentation, 22, 25
Pride in becoming professional
   counselor, 8–9
Primary sources, 205
Priority One Worldwide, 8
Privacy, lack of anonymity in online
   environment, 135–136
Privilege, 166
Process notes, 254
Professional affiliations, 92–98
Professional attire, 96, 290–292, 293
   do's and don'ts of, 292
Professional behavior and disposition,
   residency and, 237
Professional communication, 96.
   See also Communication
Professional conduct, 98–104
   appealing grades and other
     decisions, 101–102, 142
   building professional online profile,
     103–104
   ethical functioning in online
     environment, 100
   patience in online environment, 100
   professional contact
     information, 104
   professional dispositions and
     rubrics, 99
   protecting the public, 98–99
   social media and online presence,
     102–104
   student evaluation process, 100–101

Professional conferences
   ACA, 74, 95
   professional growth, 91, 94–95
   research topic inspiration and, 197
   residency and preparing to attend,
     238–239
Professional contact information, 104,
   145–146
Professional counseling
   changes in practice of, 308–309
   future of, 309–310
   online graduate programs in (*See*
     Online counselor education)
The Professional Counselor, 213
Professional databases, 201–203
Professional development, 226
Professional documents, 273–274
Professional examinations, 288–290
Professional growth conferences, 91,
   94–95
Professional identity and professional
   engagement, 89–106. *See also*
   Professional conduct
   building a professional identity,
     90–92
   collaborating with other
     professionals, 97–98
   continuing education and
     professional growth
     conferences, 94–95
   professional affiliations, 92–98
   thinking like a professional, 95–97
Professional image
   attire and, 290–292, 293
   professional documents and, 274
Professionalism, representing
   program and counseling
   profession with, 258–259
Professional online profile, building,
   103–104, 144–145
Professional organizations, 75
   affiliation with, 92–98
   national-level, 94
   professional identity and, 91
   research topic inspiration and,
     197–198